An Introduction to AutoCAD AutoSurf

An Introduction to AutoCAD AutoSurf

A. Yarwood

Addison Wesley Longman Limited
Edinburgh Gate, Harlow
Essex CM20 2JE, England
and Associated Companies throughout the world

First published 1996

British Library Cataloguing in Publication Data
A catalogue entry for this title is available from the British Library

ISBN 0-582-29820-2

Set by 24 in 10/13pt Melior
Produced by Longman Singapore Publishers (Pte) Ltd
Printed in Singapore

Contents

List of plates

Colour plates are between pages 82 and 83.

Preface

AutoCAD AutoSurf is a Computer Aided Design (CAD) 3D modelling software package, which works within AutoCAD. The version of the software with which this book is concerned – AutoCAD AutoSurf Release 2.1 – works within AutoCAD Release 13. In this book it is the Windows version of AutoCAD Release 13 within which all descriptions of constructing with the aid of AutoSurf are described.

AutoSurf is a software package designed for the construction of 3D surfaces. When using the software it is important to realise that the data developed by the models whose surfaces are being constructed can be transferred for use in CNC (Computer Numerical Control) machinery for the mechanical production of the models by machine. If this is borne in mind, the operator is less likely to make errors, such as leaving a tiny part of a surface unconstructed on the realisation that such an error would lead to an error in machining. However, despite the importance of this concept, no attempt is made in this book to describe how to make such transfers. The book has been written on the assumption that it is best to understand how to use the software for constructing accurate models before going on to its possible uses in CAM (Computer Aided Machining).

The computer mathematics involved in creating surfaces in 3D space is very complex. This means that when using AutoSurf, even with the fastest of computers, the constructions will take time to complete. In order to avoid wasting time, there is a temptation, if anything appears to be going wrong, to press the **Esc** key to cancel a command. I would advise operators using AutoSurf not to do this as it can cause the system to crash. It is better to wait for even the longest of processes to end and then to undo the action by pressing the **U** (abbreviation for Undo) key of the keyboard. If, however, the system does crash, it can usually be recovered by erasing the file *asrf.pwd* from the AutoSurf directory (usually *asrf*). When going back into AutoSurf, all that is then required is to re-enter the authorisation code for AutoSurf when requested to do so. The file *asrf.pwd* carries the authorisation code number.

Any model created with AutoSurf can be rendered in a variety of colours and materials and with any suitable lighting effects either with the set of AutoCAD Render commands (tools) or in Autodesk AutoVision. The files of AutoSurf models can also be loaded into Autodesk 3D Studio for rendering if required. A number of examples of rendered AutoSurf models, both in black and white and in colour, are given in this book.

The content of the book is designed for the beginner new to AutoSurf and is suitable for students in Further and Higher Education as well as those in industry who wish to learn how to use the software. A basic knowledge of how to use AutoCAD itself is assumed, because some of the methods of working – such as the use of the **Modify** tools Move, Copy, Mirror and constructing profiles from plines, lines and arcs – are carried out with AutoCAD tools when constructing AutoSurf models. It is also best if the reader understands 3D coordinate systems to some extent and is able to think in terms of 3D coordinate geometry – i.e. in terms of *x,y,z* when constructing models on screen.

It has been assumed that the computer and software packages in use have been correctly configured to run both AutoCAD Release 13 and AutoCAD AutoSurf Release 13 in Windows 3.X. No details are given in the book concerning such configuration. All the illustrations throughout the book were constructed in AutoCAD Release 13 for Windows.

As this book was about to be published, Autodesk released a new version of AutoSurf (Release 3) designed to work within AutoCAD Release 13 for Windows 95. Two of the colour plates show the results of using AutoSurf Release 3 within Windows 95. All the methods of working described in this book are as applicable to readers using Release 3 of AutoSurf as they are to readers using Release 2.1.

A. Yarwood
Salisbury 1996

Acknowledgements

The author wishes to acknowledge with grateful thanks the help given to him by members of the staff at Autodesk Ltd.

Registered trademarks

A. Yarwood is a Registered Developer with Autodesk Ltd.

CHAPTER 1

Introduction

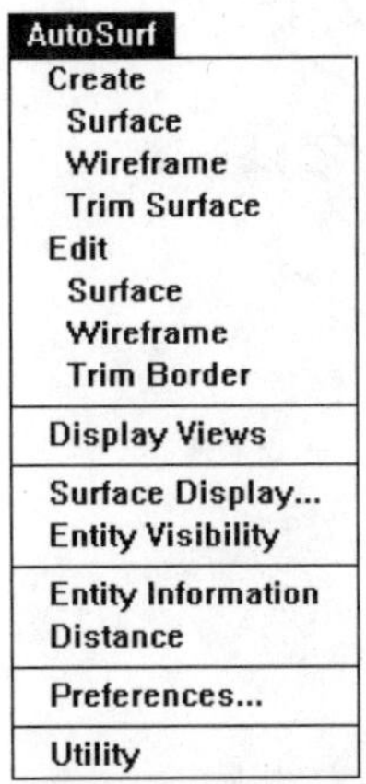

Fig. 1.1. The **AutoSurf** pull-down menu in Windows 3.1

AutoSurf is a 3D modelling package

AutoSurf Release 2.1 is a three-dimensional (3D) construction and surface-modelling software which works inside AutoCAD Release 13. As far as the contents of this book are concerned it is only the 3D modelling and surfacing properties of the software which will be described. The uses of AutoSurf files derived from 3D models produced with the aid of the software in connection with machining such as CNC (computer numerical control) are not included in this book.

Once AutoSurf is installed, the command systems of the software form an integral part of the AutoCAD command menu (*acad.mnu*). In addition to being able to construct complex 3D models with AutoSurf, AutoCAD commands (tools), such as the **Modify** tools, can be effectively employed on AutoSurf models.

Although AutoSurf Release 2.1 works just as well in the AutoCAD Release 13 MS-DOS version as in the Windows version of Release 13, it is only the Windows version of Release 13 which will be described here. However, all the examples included in this book can just as well be constructed in the MS-DOS version as in the Windows version. All illustrations have been taken from AutoCAD Release 13 working in Windows 3.1, but the software works in Windows 95. The only real difference between working in Windows 3.1 and in Windows 95 is in the appearance of the pull-down menus, as shown in Figs 1.1 and 1.2.

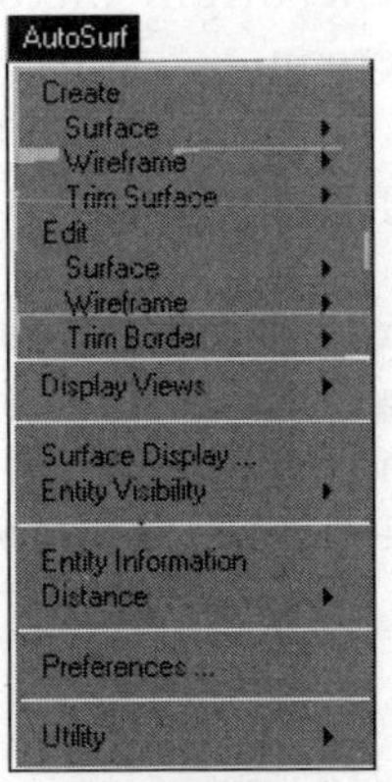

Fig. 1.2 The **AutoSurf** pull-down menu in Windows 95

When working in AutoSurf all constructions are based entirely in 3D, working to the 3D coordinate system of AutoCAD in which the ***x*** direction is horizontal on the screen, the ***y*** direction vertical on the screen and the ***z*** direction at right angles to the screen (Fig. 1.3)

3D coordinates *x,y,z*

The position of any point on the screen in an AutoCAD window can be determined in terms of the two coordinates *x* and *y*. For the

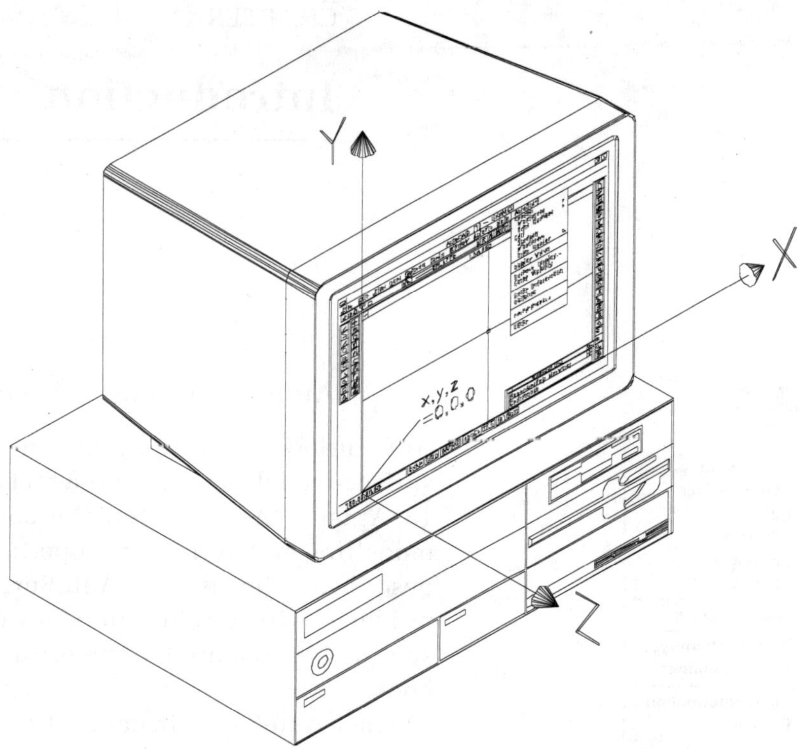

Fig. 1.3 The directions of the **x**, **y** and **z** axes in relation to the AutoCAD window

purposes of descriptions given in this book, the **Origin** of the *x,y* coordinate system is taken to be at the bottom left-hand corner of the AutoCAD window. When working in 3D, a third axis **z** is used which determines positions of points at right angles to the screen. Thus, in normal circumstances, the **z** coordinate direction is towards the operator from the screen (Fig. 1.3). This makes the origin 0,0,0 because the origin is at 0 distance in front of the screen.

The negative coordinate point **–x** is horizontally to the left of the AutoCAD window; **–y** is vertically below; **–z** is perpendicularly behind the face of the screen.

x,y,z points can either be set by *entering* all three coordinates from the Command Line or by using the *filter* **.xy**, followed by *entering* the **z** coordinate. For example, to draw a line from point *x,y* 100,100 to point *x,y,z* 200,100,100 can be carried out by two methods; either by:

Command: *enter* l (Line) *right-click*
Command: *enter* l (Line) *right-click*
From point: *enter* 100,100 *right-click*
To point: *enter* 200,100,100 *right-click*

To point: *right-click*
Command:

or by:

Command: *enter* l (Line) *right-click*
From point: *pick* 100,100
To point: *enter* .xy *right-click*
.xy of *pick* 200,100
(need Z): *enter* 100 *right-click*
Command:

Prototype drawing

Most of the drawings shown in illustrations in this book have been constructed in the AutoCAD prototype drawing *acadiso.dwg,* with the scroll bars of the AutoCAD window not showing. Scroll bars can be turned on or off in the AutoCAD **Preferences** dialogue box (Fig. 1.4). This means that the drawings have been constructed in a screen with **Limits** set to 420,300 (A3 sheet size). The following changes have also been made to the *acadiso.dwg* prototype drawing used here:

Units set to 0 figures after the decimal point
Text Style set to **Simplex.shx** of height 6

The reader, however, can equally well work in the original *acadiso* prototype drawing editor.

Commands (tools)

In AutoCAD 13 for Windows, commands are usually referred to as 'tools'. The AutoSurf commands can be selected from the **AutoSurf** pull-down menu or they can be *entered* at the Command Line. They can also be selected from toolbars (see page 5). Both selection from the **AutoSurf** pull-down menu and its sub-menus and *entering* command names at the command line will be shown in the following pages, but all descriptions of command line entries, prompts, options and responses will be shown as if commands are *entered* at the AutoCAD command line as shown in the following example:

Command: *enter* primsf *right-click*
To invoke advanced options enter '??'...
Primitive type COne/CYlinder/Torus/<Sphere>: *enter* co *right-click*
Center of base: *enter* 200,150 *right-click*

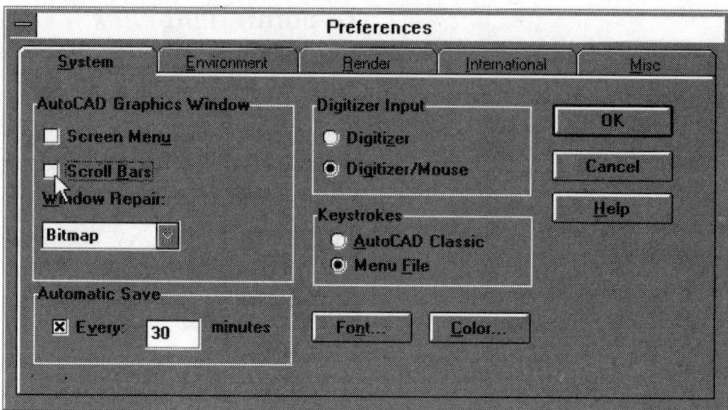

Fig. 1.4 Turning off **Scroll Bars** in the AutoCAD **Preferences** dialogue box

Diameter of base/<Radius of base><1.0>: *enter* 50 *right-click*
Diameter of top/<Radius of top><0.0>: *enter* 35 *right-click*
Height of cone: *enter* 75 *right-click*
Command:

The features in the above example show:

Command: always showing at the command line before a command is *entered*

Primitive type COne/CYlinder/Torus/<Sphere>: the options available in the primsf command system. The option in brackets **<Sphere>** is the default option. To use another option, *enter* the capital letters of the option name.

enter – type the letters or figures following *enter* at the keyboard.

co – the capital letters of the option (COne) *entered* at the keyboard.

right-click – press and release the right-hand button of the mouse. Pressing the *Return* key of the keyboard has the same effect.

Other terms used in this book

Return – press the keyboard key marked **Return**, **Enter** or showing an arrow.

left-click – press and release the left-hand button of the mouse.

double-click – press and release a button of the mouse twice in quick succession.

select – move the screen cursor under movement control of the mouse over the feature to be selected and *left-click*

pick – move the screen cursor under movement control of the mouse and *left-click*

The AutoSurf toolbars

At the command line:

Command: *enter* as toolbar *right-click*
Command:

and two toolbars with icons representing the AutoSurf tools (commands) appear on screen as shown in Fig. 1.6.

Associated with these toolbars are **tool tips** and **flyouts**. Every tool icon has its **tool tip** which, when the screen cursor is placed over the icon shows the name of the tool (command). The toolbars can be dragged into different shapes – vertical or horizontal lines of icons or rectangular sets of icons. Those tool icons which show a small arrow to the bottom right-hand corner of the icon, also show a **flyout** with further icons, each of which has its own **tool tip**. Figure 1.7 shows several forms of toolbar, together with tool tips and flyouts. To call a command (tool) from toolbars, select its icon by moving the cursor under mouse control, onto the icon, followed by a *left-click*.

Fig. 1.6 The two AutoSurf toolbars in AutoCAD Release 13 for Windows

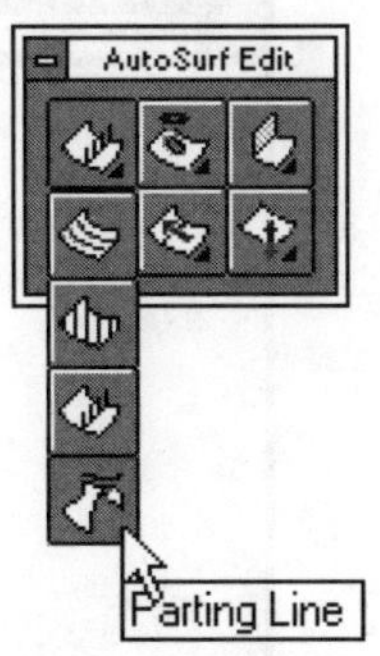

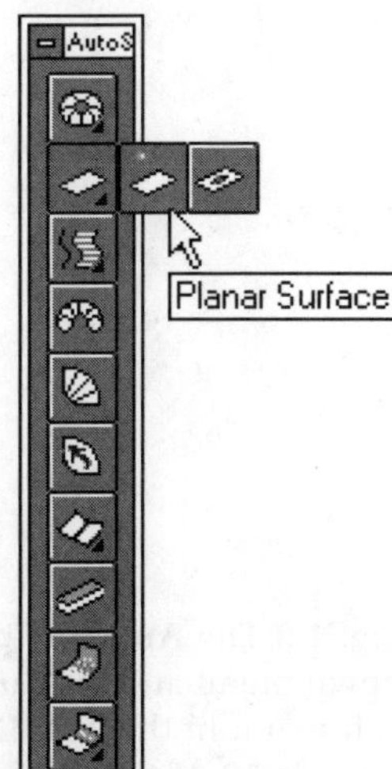

Fig. 1.7 Toolbars, tool tips and flyouts

The AutoSurf pull-down menu and its sub-menus

Figure 1.9 shows the AutoCAD Release 13 window with the **AutoSurf** pull-down menu. The **Surface** sub-menu has been selected and from this the **Cylinder** command. An arrow next to a command name in the main pull-down menu brings a sub-menu on screen. A command followed by three fullstops (**...**) brings a dialogue box on screen.

When a command has been selected from the **AutoSurf** pull-down menu the command name appears at the command line preceded with a bar (_) as in the example below (Fig. 1.8):

From this example, it will be seen that command names at the command line usually end with sf. When *entering* a command at the command line from the keyboard, most (not all) AutoSurf commands end with sf.

```
Command: _primsf
To invoke advanced options enter "??"...
Primitive type COne/CYlinder/Torus/<Sphere>: _cylinder
Center of base:
```

Fig. 1.8 **Primsf** and its options at the command line

AutoSurf primitives

The construction of AutoSurf 3D models commences with the building up of 3D wireframes. Among other methods of construction are the AutoSurf primitive commands which allow construction of cones, cylinders, toruses and spheres. In addition, although not an

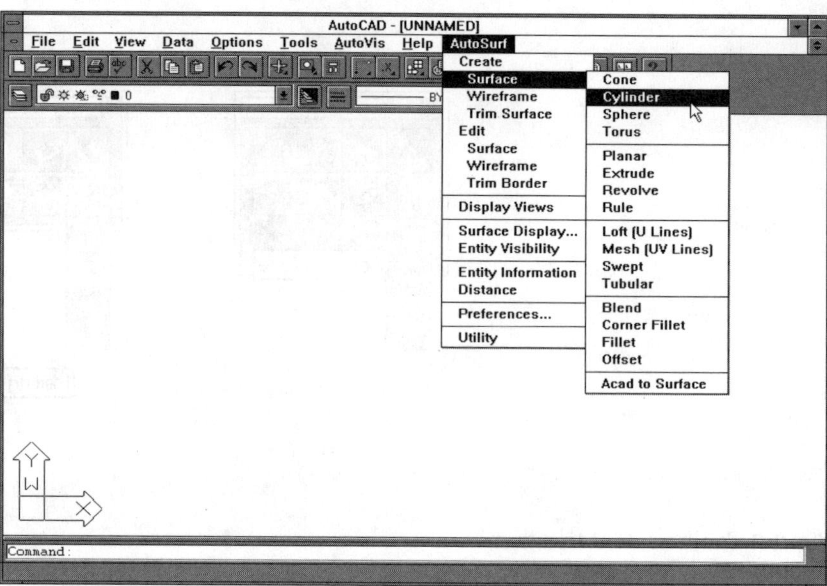

Fig. 1.9 The **AutoSurf** pull-down menu and the **Surface** sub-menu in the AutoCAD Release 13 window

AutoSurf primitive as such, I have included planar surfaces here because of their importance in 3D model construction.

Examples of these primitives are shown in Fig. 1.10. In this illustration there are two cones, because the options and prompts in the command system for primsf (COne) allows the apex of the cone to be either of radius 0 (i.e. coming to a point), or of a radius determined by the operator. Note the following in Fig. 1.10:

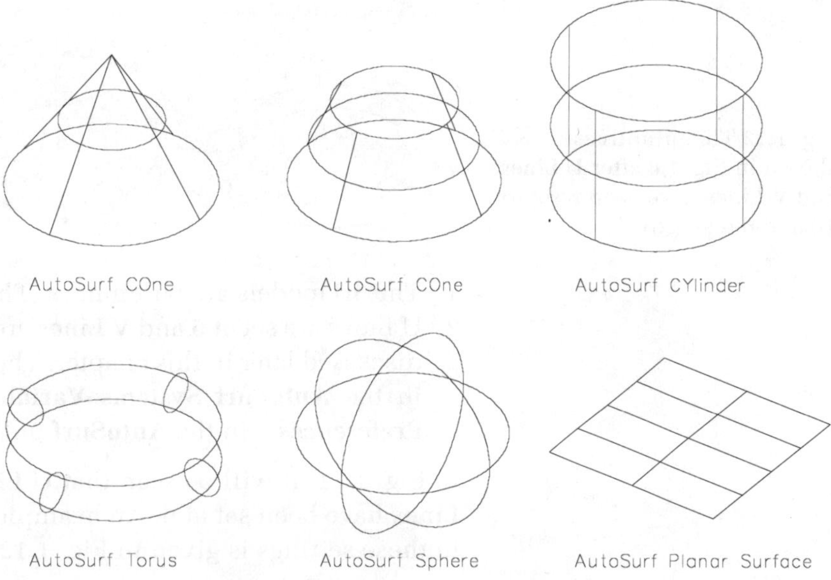

Fig. 1.10 Examples of AutoSurf primitives with **U Lines** set at 5 and **V Lines** set at 3

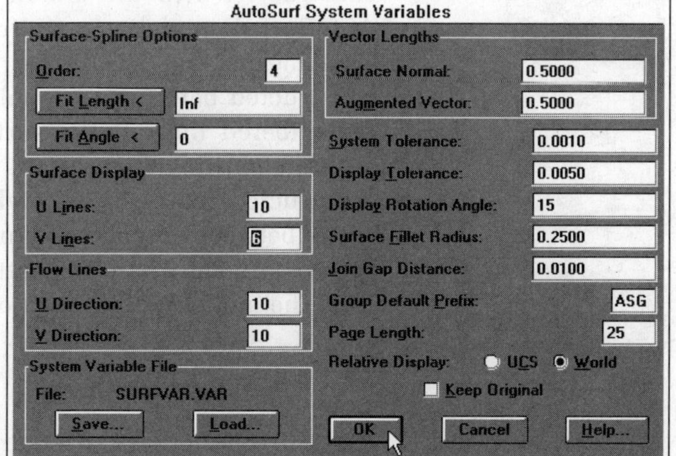

Fig. 1.11 **U Lines** and **V Lines** reset to 10 and 6 in the **AutoSurf System Variables** dialogue box

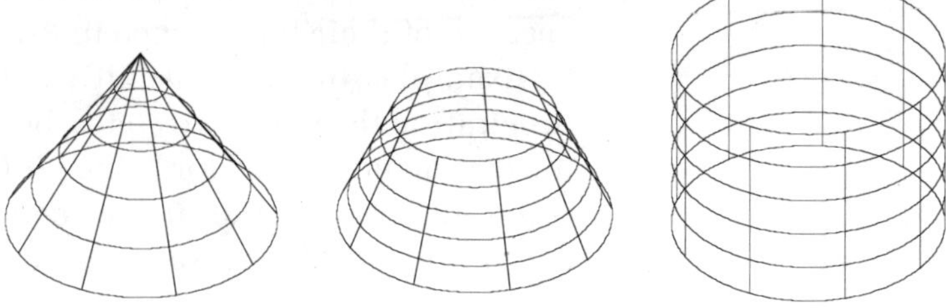

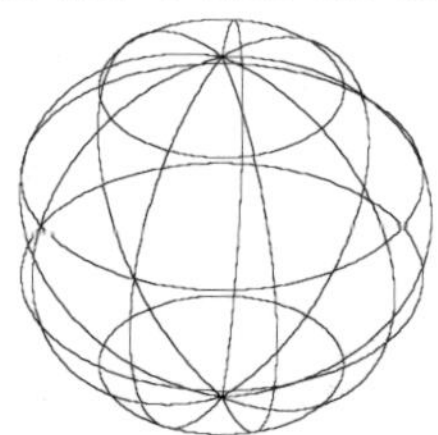

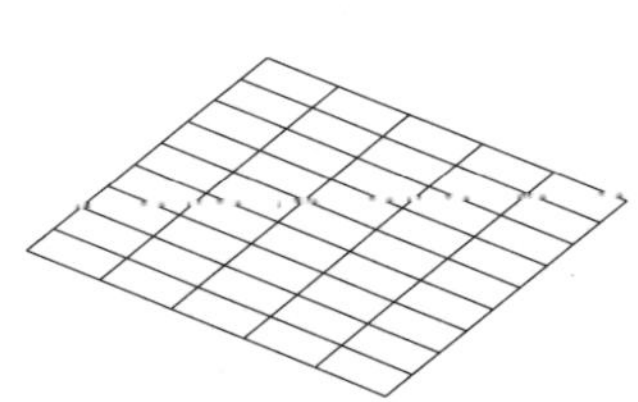

Fig. 1.12 The primitives shown in Fig. 1.8 after **U Lines** and **V Lines** have been reset to 10 and 6 respectively

1. The 3D models are wireframes. They do not have a surface mesh.
2. U Lines are set at 5 and V Lines are set at 3. U and V Lines will be discussed later in this chapter. These two settings can be changed in the **AutoSurf Systems Variables** dialogue box, called from **Preferences...** in the **AutoSurf** pull-down menu (Fig. 1.11).

In Fig. 1.11, it will be seen that **U Lines** have been set at 10 and **V Lines** have been set at 6. An example of the primitives constructed to these settings is given in Fig. 1.12.

All surfaces must be constructed

It is important for operators to understand that, unlike 3D models constructed with the aid of the **Solids** tools of AutoCAD R13, AutoSurf 3D models are wireframes until surface meshed (see later). This means that **ALL** outer surfaces of the wireframe must be constructed before the model is truly completed. It must also be remembered that all the surfaces of an AutoSurf 3D model are separate entities. Figure 1.14 shows a simple AutoSurf 3D model constructed mainly from **Cylinders**, with the addition of fillets added between the central cylinder and the top and bottom cylinders. Figure 1.15 shows the separate wireframes of each surface moved from the model with the aid of the AutoCAD tool **Move**.

Fig. 1.13 An example of a simple 3D model constructed in AutoSurf

Surface meshing

AutoSurf 3D models can be surface meshed by first selecting **Surface Display...** from the **AutoSurf** pull-down menu. After selecting the

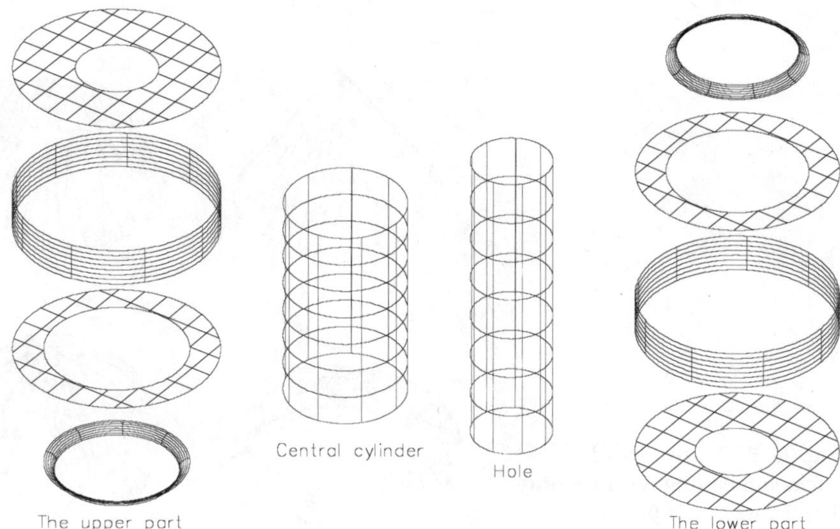

Fig. 1.14 The 10 separate surfaces of the 3D model shown in Fig. 1.13

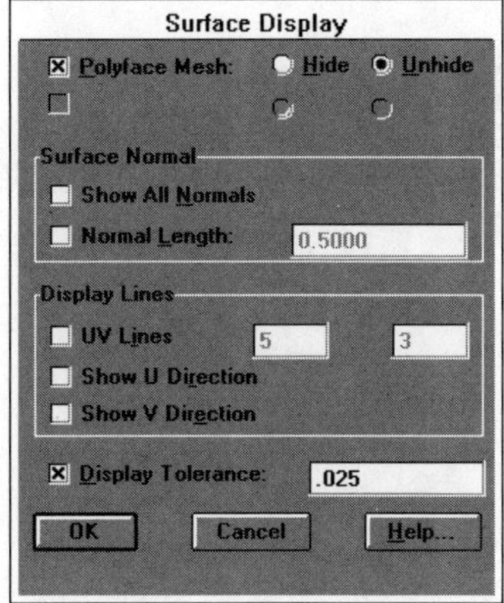

Fig. 1.15 The **Surface Display** dialogue box showing the settings for surface meshing the examples in Fig. 1.13

parts of the 3D model to be surface meshed, the **Surface Display** dialogue box appears (Fig. 1.15).

An example of the primitives shown in earlier illustrations after surface meshing is shown in Fig. 1.17. The settings in the **Surface Display** dialogue box for these examples are shown in Fig. 1.15 – the **Polyface Mesh** check box is set; the **Unhide** check box is set; **Display Tolerance** has been entered as **0.025**.

If the **Display Tolerance** is changed to **0.1** as shown in Fig. 1.16, then the surface meshing changes as shown in Fig. 1.18.

Notes

1. The AutoCAD tool **Hide** has been called to hide hidden lines in Figs 1.17 and 1.18.
2. The setting of **Display Tolerance** is partly dependent upon the **Limits** to which the AutoCAD window is set. It will be seen that when the **Surface Display** dialogue box first appears, the **Display Tolerance** will probably be set at **0.0001**. This setting is for the USA size screen set to **Limits** of 12,9. Our screens for this book are set to **Limits** of 420,300. Hence the need to change the original setting.

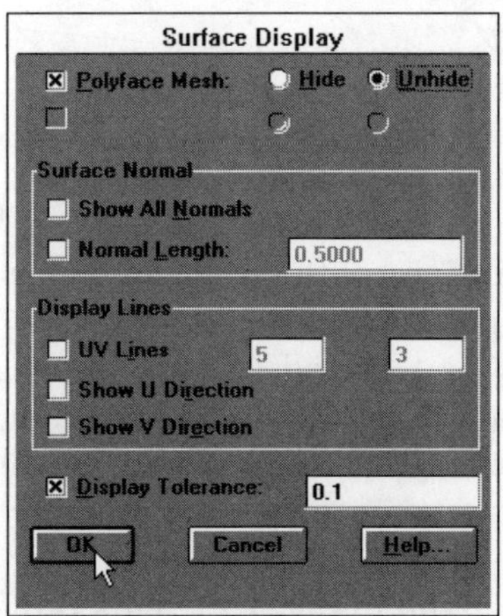

Fig. 1.16 The **Display Tolerance** changed to **0.1**

Rendering

Throughout this book, renderings of the AutoSurf 3D models used as example will be included. Once an AutoSurf 3D model has been constructed as a wireframe and then surface meshed, it can be rendered with the aid of either AutoCAD **Render** or the add-on

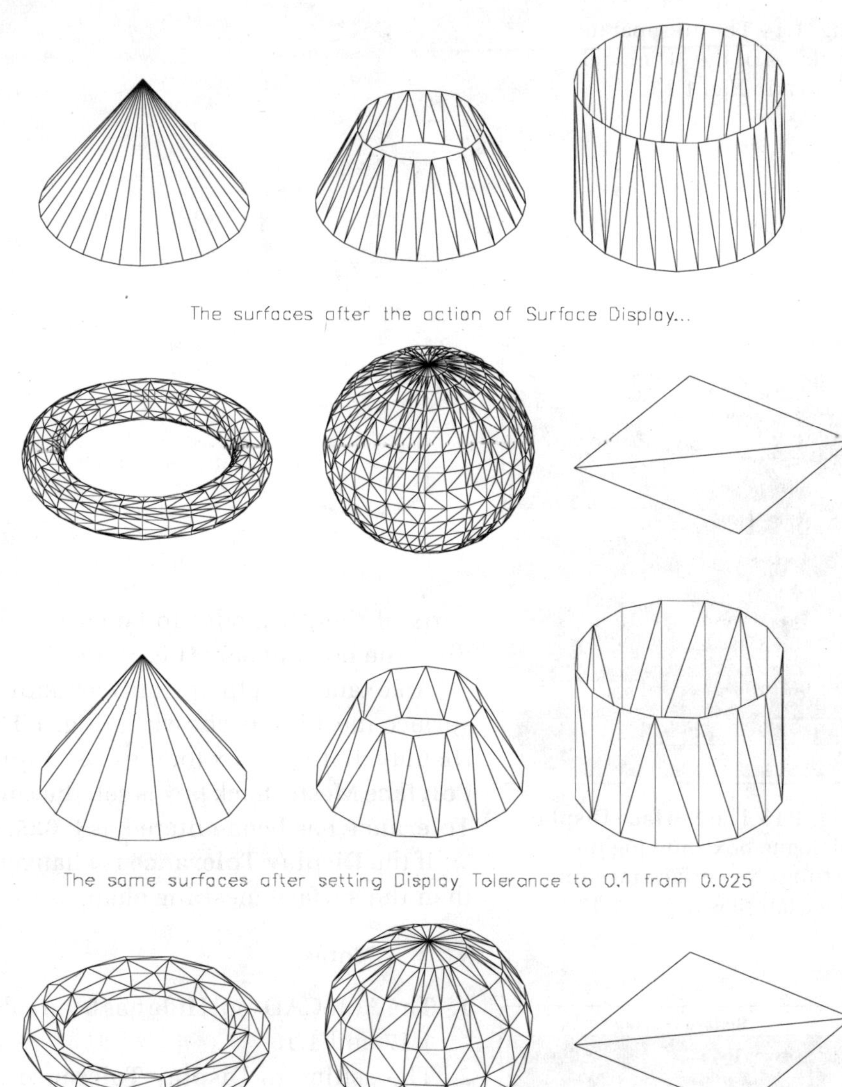

Fig. 1.17 The results of surface meshing with **Display Tolerance** set at **0.025**

Fig. 1.18 The primitives after surface meshing with **Display Tolerance** set at **0.1**

software **AutoCAD AutoVision**. Descriptions of the procedures for renderings will be given in a later chapter.

The surface-meshed 3D models of Figs 1.17 and 1.18 are shown rendered in various materials with the aid of **AutoVision** in Figs 1.19 and 1.20. Note the differences in the two illustrations. These two examples of rendering show the importance of setting **Display Tolerance** to obtain the best results.

A further example of a rendering is given in Fig. 1.21. This is of the 3D model shown in Fig. 1.13. Note that the model had to be surface meshed before rendering could take place.

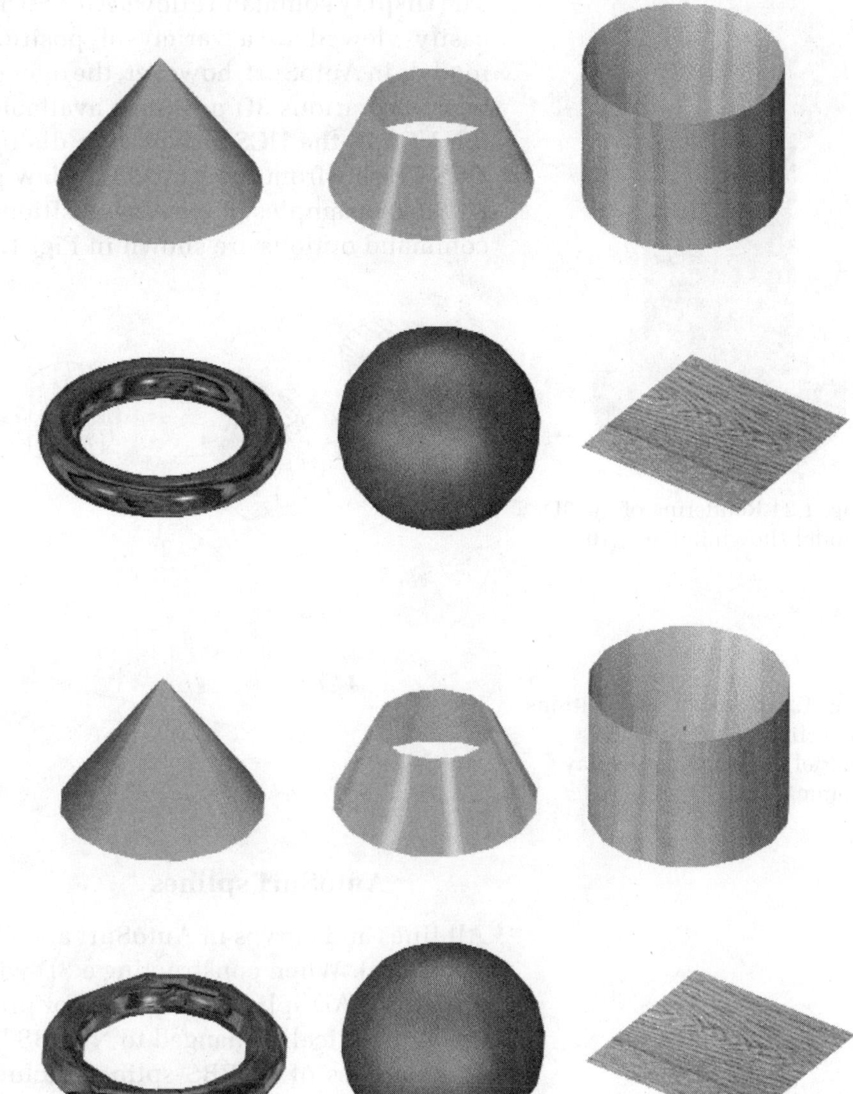

Fig. 1.19 Renderings with **Display Tolerance** set at **0.025**

Fig. 1.20 Renderings with **Display Tolerance** set at **0.1**

The AutoSurf command Display

When working in AutoSurf, the 3D model under construction can be placed in a variety of viewing positions with the aid of the command **Display**. Note this is an AutoSurf command and not an AutoCAD tool (command). To call **Display**, either select **Display Views** from the **AutoSurf** pull-down menu (see Fig. 1.1) or, at the command line:

Command: *enter* display *right-click*
FOld/Iso/Plane/Rotate/Xy/Yz/xZ/<Fit>:

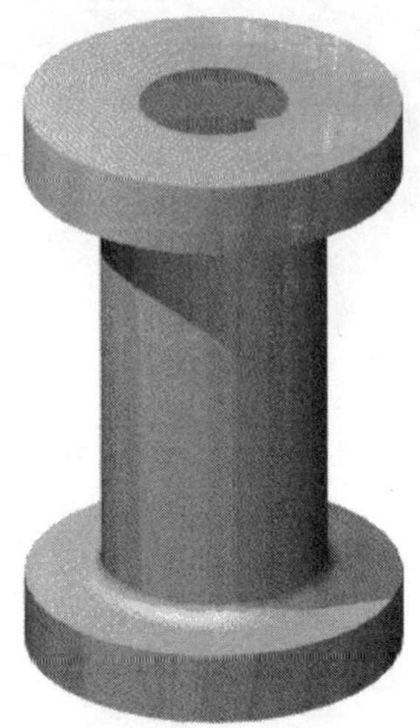

Fig. 1.21 Rendering of the 3D model shown in Fig. 1.10

The **Display** command allows AutoSurf 3D models to be quickly and easily viewed in a variety of positions. When constructing 3D models in AutoSurf, however, the operator may find it easier to work with the various 3D positions available by setting the positions of the **UCS in the UCS Orientation** dialogue box, called by selecting **UCS Presets** from the AutoCAD **View** pull-down menu.

Some examples of viewing positions resulting from the **Display** command options are shown in Fig. 1.22.

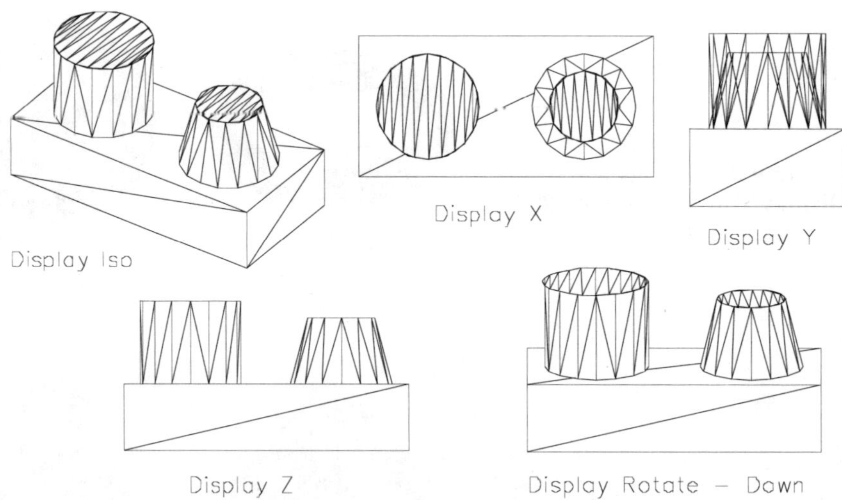

Fig. 1.22 Some of the positions of a simple AutoSurf 3D model by using the **Display** command

AutoSurf splines

All lines and curves in AutoSurf are NURBS (non-uniform rational B-splines). When constructing a 3D wireframe model in AutoSurf, any AutoCAD splines, lines, arcs or plines used in the construction are automatically changed to NURBS by AutoSurf.

Examples of NURBS splines including 'control points', which can be seen by using the advanced options of the AutoSurf command **spline3d** are shown in Fig. 1.23. When **spline 3d** is called, the command line shows:

Command: *enter* spline3d
To invoke advanced options enter '??'...
Create spline by Entities/<Locations>: *enter* ?? *right-click*
Spline by creation type COntrol points/Interpolate/<Optimize>: *enter* co (COntrol points) *right-click*
Order<4>: *right-click*
Create spline by Entities/<Locations>: *enter* e *right-click*
Select objects: *pick* the pline already drawn
Command:

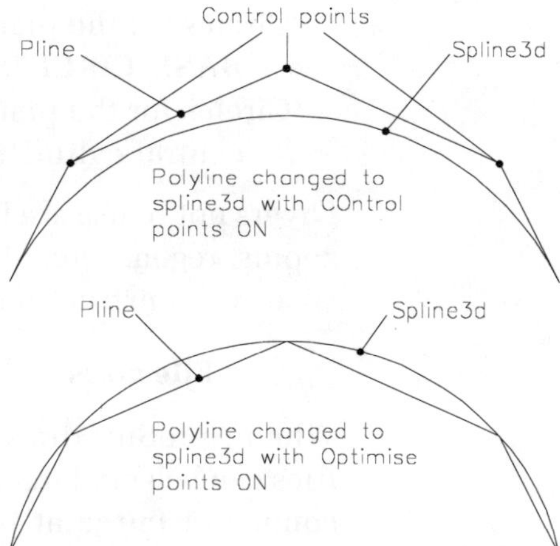

Fig. 1.23 Control points associated with NURBS splines used in AutoSurf

Some notes on using AutoSurf

Layers

In order to make the task of constructing the large number of surfaces which are common in AutoSurf 3D models easier, it is advisable to make a different layer for each part of the construction. Taking as an example the 3D model shown in Fig. 1.13 (page 8), the **Layer Control** dialogue box for the model is shown in Fig. 1.24. As the work proceeds layers can be frozen so that their contents do not appear when other parts of the model are being constructed. In this example (Fig. 1.13) the various parts of the model were constructed on the following layers:

The central cylinder and its hole – on layer **0**.
The top cylinder – on layer **TOP**.
The bottom cylinder – on layer **BOTTOM**.

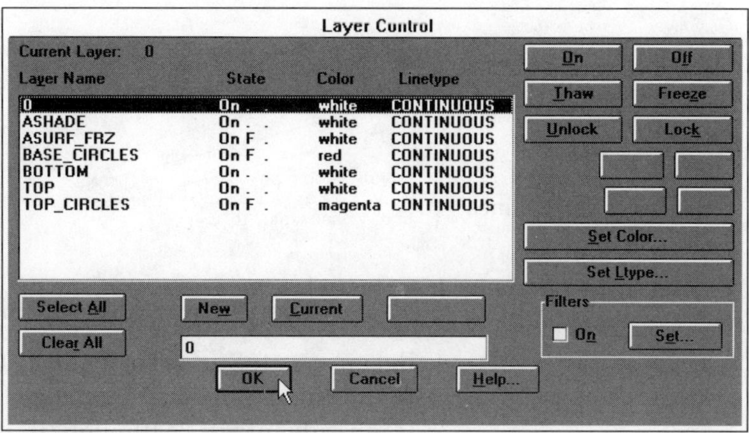

Fig. 1.24 The **Layer Control** dialogue box for the construction of Fig. 1.13

Circles for the planar surface at the base and top – on layer **BASE_CIRCLES**.

Circles for the planar surfaces between top and bottom and the central cylinder – on layer **TOP_CIRCLES**.

Layers not in use are frozen – preferable to being turned off because zooms, regens, etc., do not take notice of frozen layers, making for speedier constructions.

File sizes

When AutoSurf drawings are saved to file on disk, the sizes of the files can be very large. In order to save disk space, use the AutoCAD command **Purge** at intervals and purge all unnecessary material from memory before saving. When working in AutoCAD Release 13, **Purge** can be used at any time, either just after a file is loaded or during construction of a drawing. An example of calling the command is given in Fig. 1.25.

```
PURGE
Purge unused
Blocks/Dimstyles/LAyers/LTypes/SHapes/STyles/APpids/Mlinestyles/All: a
Purge block *U2? <N>
```

Fig. 1.25 The command line when **Purge** is called

U Lines and V Lines

Figure 1.26 shows the U and V Lines on two similar AutoSurf planar rectangles. From this illustration the reader should be able to see which are U Lines and which are V Lines.

It is not advisable to use too many U and V Lines because time and file size may be wasted, but in some circumstances the operator may find it better to work with higher figures than the default U as 5 and V as 3.

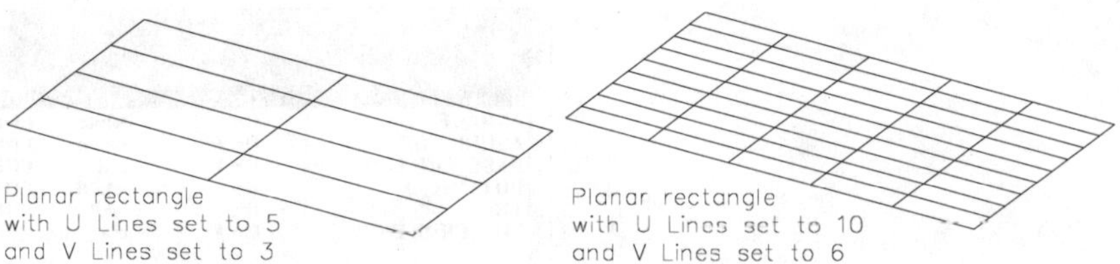

Fig. 1.26 U Lines and V Lines

The UCS variable UCSfollow

Because AutoSurf is basically a 3D constructional program it will be found that being able to change the positions of the UCS with ease is an advantage. Although it will be found that the AutoSurf command **Display** will place a model under construction in a variety of viewing positions, it is necessary to reset the UCS in order to add further constructions to a model. All drawings in this book have been produced with **UCSfollow** set to 1 (ON) in the prototype drawing used for constructions.

Filletsf and cornersf

Although these two commands will be dealt with in later chapters, a reference to them here is not amiss because it will be found that they will be frequently used when constructing 3D models for engineering purposes. Figure 1.27 shows a 3D model made up from planar surfaces with edges filleted externally with the aid of the command **filletsf** and corners rounded off with **cornersf**. We shall discuss these two commands further in later chapters.

Another example of internal filleting is shown in Fig. 1.28.

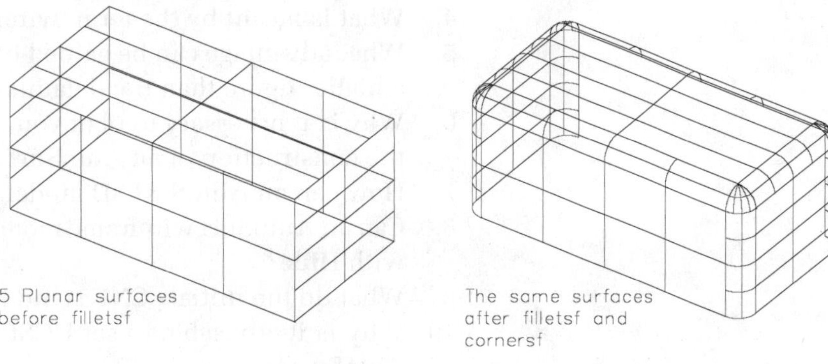

Fig. 1.27 An example of external fillets and corners constructed with the aid of **filletsf** and **cornersf**

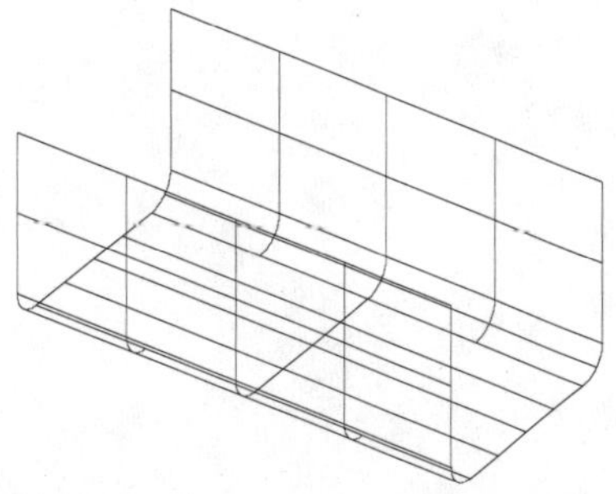

Fig. 1.28 An example of internal fillets constructed with the aid of **filletsf**

Speed of computer

Construction of 3D models in AutoSurf invariably takes time. The faster the computer the better. Although a PC fitted with a DX2 operating chip running at 66 MHz performs satisfactorily, a faster Pentium or equivalent operating chip will make for easier (faster) construction times.

Planning

AutoSurf constructions can be complicated, mainly because every surface of the model must be constructed. This makes it very necessary to think out the methods of construction before commencing the work. It may be desirable to make notes of the order in which the various surfaces are to be constructed before commencing. Failure to plan ahead when working in AutoSurf can result in considerable waste of time and energy.

Questions

1. Will AutoSurf Release 2.1 work in AutoCAD Release 12? In AutoCAD Release 13 for MS-DOS?
2. Can you name the primitive types of 3D model in AutoSurf?
3. How can toolbars be called on screen when working with AutoSurf in AutoCAD Release 13 for Windows?
4. What is meant by the term 'wireframe'?
5. What advantage can be gained by setting U Lines and V Lines to a higher figure than the defaults?
6. Why is it necessary to plan your procedures before commencing the construction of an AutoSurf 3D model?
7. How can an AutoSurf 3D model be surface meshed?
8. Can an AutoSurf wireframe model have its hidden lines removed with **Hide**?
9. What do the initials **CNC** stand for?
10. Why is it advisable to set **UCSfollow** ON when constructing in AutoSurf?

CHAPTER 2

Constructing AutoSurf 3D models

Introduction

The sequence of operations required to construct the 3D model shown by the rendering of the model in Fig. 2.1 will be described in detail in this chapter. The sequence starts with describing how the necessary 3D wire model is constructed. The 3D model is then surface meshed. Finally the surface-meshed 3D model is rendered with the aid of AutoVision.

Fig. 2.1 A surface rendering of the completed AutoSurf 3D model

In this chapter all AutoSurf commands will be shown as if they were *entered* at the command line from the keyboard and also as they can be selected from the **AutoSurf** pull-down menu and its sub-menus. Each stage of the sequence will be accompanied by illustrations of the **AutoSurf** pull-down menu or sub-menus and by line drawings of the constructions at each stage.

The construction of the wireframe model

Stage 1 – setting layers

In order to ensure that each part of the model can be constructed with ease, make layers as shown in Fig. 2.2. Note that some of the layers for this example show the following settings:

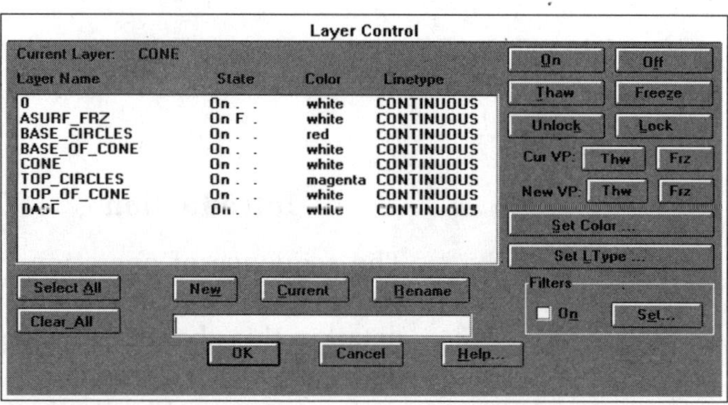

Fig. 2.2 The settings of layers for this example

Layer **ASURF_FRZ** must be frozen. Make no attempt to thaw or change the contents of this layer.

Layers **BASE_CIRCLES** and **TOP_CIRCLES** are coloured. This allows features on these layers to be easily seen and *picked* when necessary.

Layer **CONE** is the current layer.

Stage 2 – constructing the cone

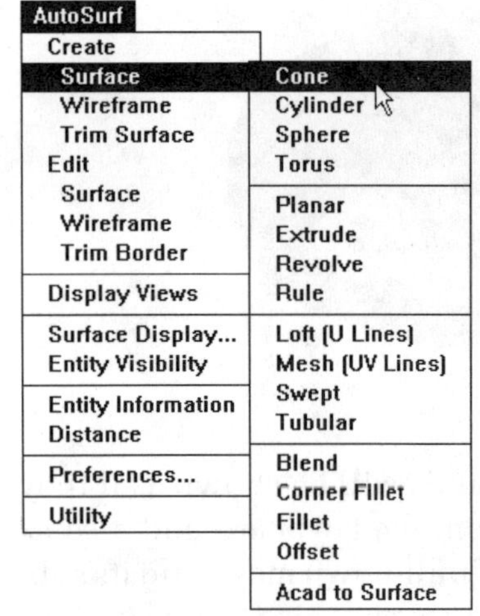

Fig. 2.3 Selecting **Cone** from the **Surface** sub-menu of the **AutoSurf** pull-down menu

1. Make layer **CONE** the current layer.
2. Either select **Cone** from the **AutoSurf** pull-down menu (Fig. 2.3) or, at the command line:

Command: *enter* primsf *right-click*
To invoke advanced options enter '??'...
Primitive type COne/CYlinder/Torus/<Sphere>: *enter* co (COne) *right-click*
Center of base: *enter* 200,150 *right-click*
Diameter of base/<Radius of base><1.0>: *enter* 50 *right-click*
Diameter of top/<Radius of top><0.0>: *enter* 35 *right-click*
Height of cone: *enter* 75 *right-click*
Command:

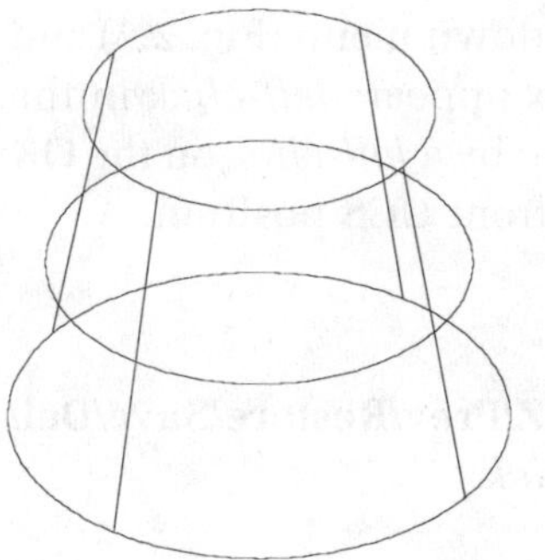

Fig. 2.4 The cone in a **Display** isometric view

3. At the command line:

Command: *enter* display *right-click*
FOld/Iso/Plane/Rotate/Xy/Yz/xZ/<Fit>: *enter* i (Iso) *right-click*
Command:

and the cone constructed with the **primsf** call is placed in an isometric viewing position (Fig. 2.4). Note that **Display** is an AutoSurf command – not an AutoCAD tool.

Stage 3 – constructing the hole through the model

Note that the hole will be constructed in two stages, although it could at this stage be constructed 95 high instead of 75 high, by setting its base centre at Z = –20 and its height at 95.

AutoSurf
Create
Surface
Wireframe
Trim Surface
Edit
Surface
Wireframe
Trim Border
Display Views
Surface Display...
Entity Visibility
Entity Information
Distance
Preferences...
Utility

Cone
Cylinder
Sphere
Torus
Planar
Extrude
Revolve
Rule
Loft (U Lines)
Mesh (UV Lines)
Swept
Tubular
Blend
Corner Fillet
Fillet
Offset
Acad to Surface

Fig. 2.5 Selecting **Cylinder** from the **Surface** sub-menu of the **AutoSurf** pull-down menu

1. At the command line:

Command: *enter* ucs *right-click*
Origin/ZAxis/3point/OBject/View/X/Y/Z/Prev/Restore/Save/Del/?/<World>: *right-click* (to accept the World UCS)
Command: *enter* z (for Zoom) *right-click*
All/Center/Dynamic/Extents/Left/Previous/Vmax/Window/<Scale (X/XP)>: *enter* 1 *right-click*
Command:

2. Either select **Cylinder** from the **Surface** sub-menu of the **AutoSurf** pull-down menu (Fig. 2.5) or, at the command line:

Command: *enter* primsf *right-click*
To invoke advanced options enter '??':
Primitive type COne/CYlinder/Torus/<Sphere>: *enter* cy (CYlinder) *right-click*
Center of base: *enter* 200,150 *right-click*
Diameter of base/<Radius of base><1.0>: *enter* 20 *right-click*
Height of cylinder: *enter* 75 *right-click*
Command: *enter* display *right-click*
FOld/Iso/Plane/Rotate/Xy/Yz/xZ/<Fit>: *enter* i (Iso) *right-click*
Command:

and the cylinder, constructed with the **primsf** call within the cone is placed in an isometric viewing position (Fig. 2.6).

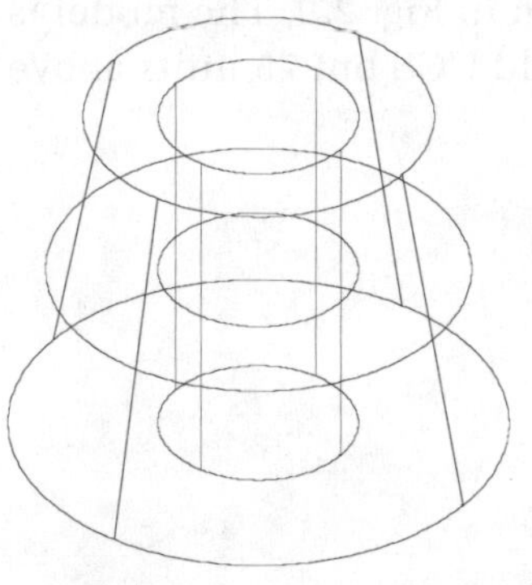

Fig. 2.6 The cone and cylinder in a **Display** isometric view

Stage 4 – constructing the top of the cone

In order to add a surface to the top of the cone and cylinder it is necessary to place the model so far constructed in a suitable **3point** UCS as follows:

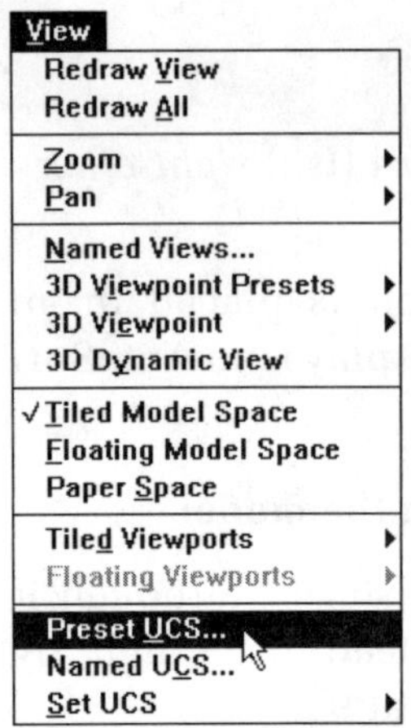

Fig. 2.7 Selecting **Preset UCS...** from the **View** pull-down menu

1. Select **Preset UCS...** from the **View** pull-down menu (Fig. 2.7) and when the **UCS Orientation** dialogue box appears *left-click* in the **FRONT** box of the dialogue box, followed by a *left-click* on the **OK** button (Fig. 2.8). The model assumes a front UCS position.
2. At the command line:

   Command: *enter* ucs *right-click*
   Origin/ZAxis/3point/OBject/View/X/Y/Z/Prev/Restore/Save/Del/?/<World>: *enter* 3 (3point) *right-click*
   Origin point: *enter* 150,75 *right-click*
   Point on positive portion of the X-axis <151,75,0>: *enter* 250,75 *right-click*
   Point on positive Y-portion of the UCS XY plane <150,76,0>: *enter* .xy *right-click*
   (need Z): *enter* 1 *right-click*
   Regenerating drawing.
   Command:

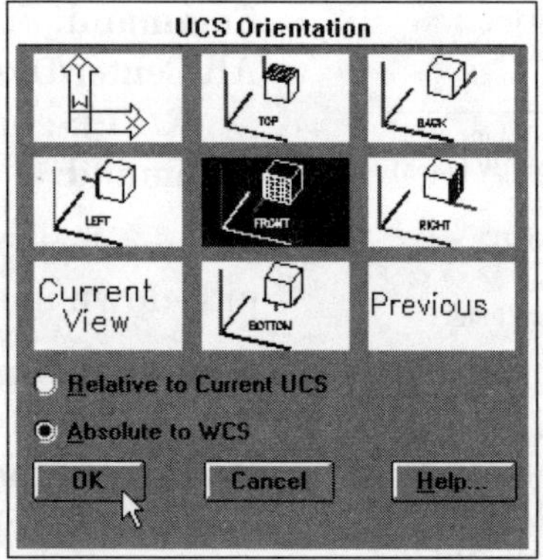

Fig. 2.8 Selecting **FRONT** from the **UCS Orientation** dialogue box

These **3point** coordinate points are shown in Fig. 2.9. The model is now set in a new UCS parallel to the World UCS but 75 units above it.

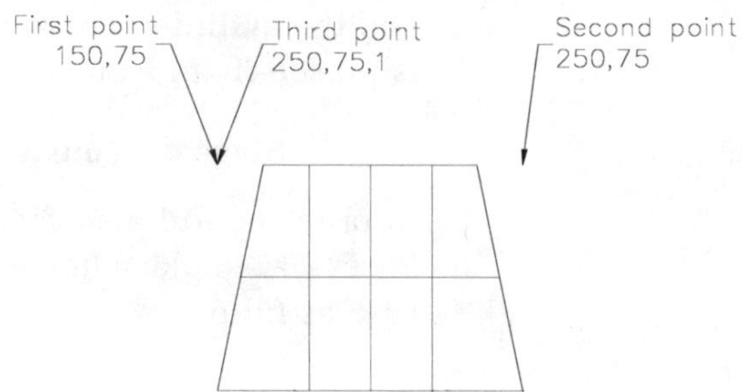

Fig. 2.9 The cone in the **FRONT UCS** showing the three coordinate points to give the next **UCS** plane

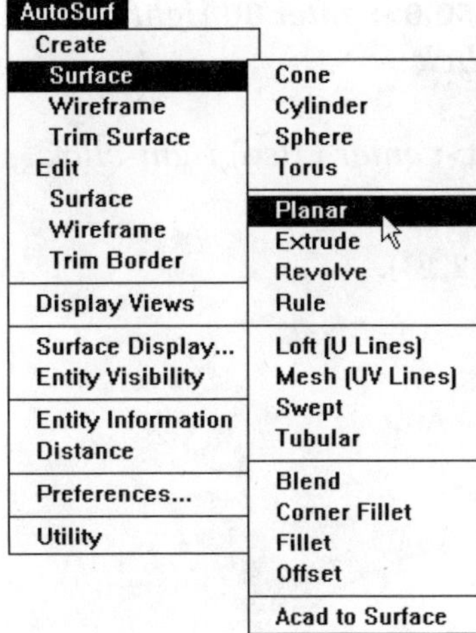

Fig. 2.10 Selecting **Planar** from the **Surface** sub-menu of the **AutoSurf** pull-down menu

3. Make the layer **TOP_CIRCLES** current.
4. Draw circles of centre 200,150 and radii 35 and 50 (radii of top and bottom of cone).
5. Freeze layer **CONE**.
6. Either select **Planar** from the **Surface** sub-menu of the **AutoSurf** pull-down menu (Fig. 2.10) or, at the command line:

   Command: *enter* planesf *right-click*
   Entities/<Rectangle>: *enter* e (Entities) *right-click*
   Select object: *pick* the outer circle (Fig. 2.11)
   Select object: *pick* the inner circle (Fig. 2.11)
   Select object: *right-click*
   Command:

   and the area of the top of the cone becomes a **planesf** surface.
7. Thaw the layer **CONE** and freeze the layer **TOP_CIRCLES**. The results so far are shown in **Display** (Iso) in Fig. 2.12.

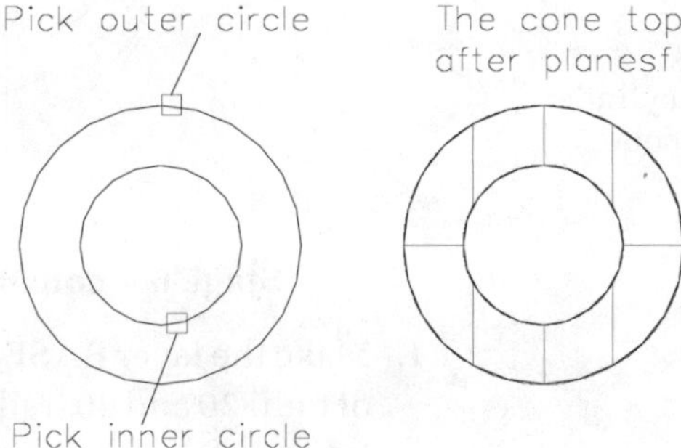

Fig. 2.11 Constructing the **planesf** surface of the top of the cone

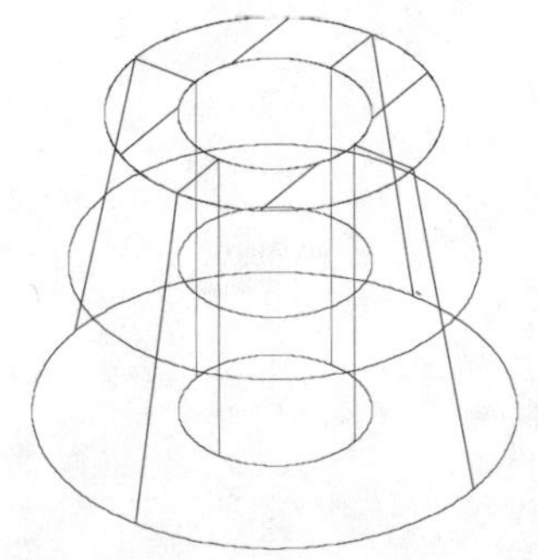

Fig. 2.12 The cone with its top surface

Stage 5 – constructing the base

1. Set the **UCS** back to the **WORLD UCS** by:

   Command: *enter* ucs *right-click*
   Origin/ZAxis/3point/OBject/View/X/Y/Z/Prev/Restore/Save/Del/?/<World>: *right-click*
   Command:

2. Make the layer **BASE** the current layer. Either select **Cylinder** from the **Surface** sub-menu of the **AutoSurf** pull-down menu or, at the command line:

   Command: *enter* primsf *right-click*
   To invoke advanced options enter '??'...
   Primitive type COne/CYlinder/Torus/<Sphere>: *enter* cy (CYlinder) *right-click*
   Center of base: *enter* 200,150 *right-click*

Diameter of base/<Radius of base><50.0>: *enter* 80 *right-click*
Height of cylinder: *enter* –20 *right-click*
Command: *enter* display *right-click*
FOld/Iso/Plane/Rotate/Xy/Yz/xZ/<Fit>: *enter* i (Iso) *right-click*
Command:

The cylinder for the base is formed (Fig. 2.13).

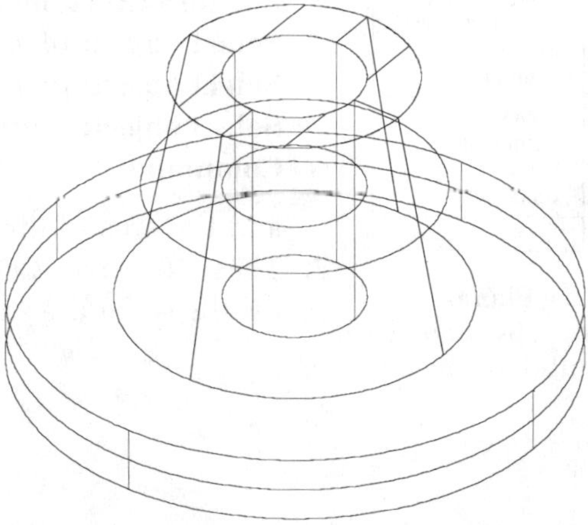

Fig. 2.13 The base cylinder included with the cone

Stage 6 – constructing the top of the base

1. Make the layer **BASE_CIRCLES** the current layer. Draw two circles of radii 20 and 80 (radii of hole in the cone and the base itself). Draw four circles of radius 5 for each of the holes to be constructed in the base. Freeze all layers other than the **BASE_CIRCLES** and the **BASE**

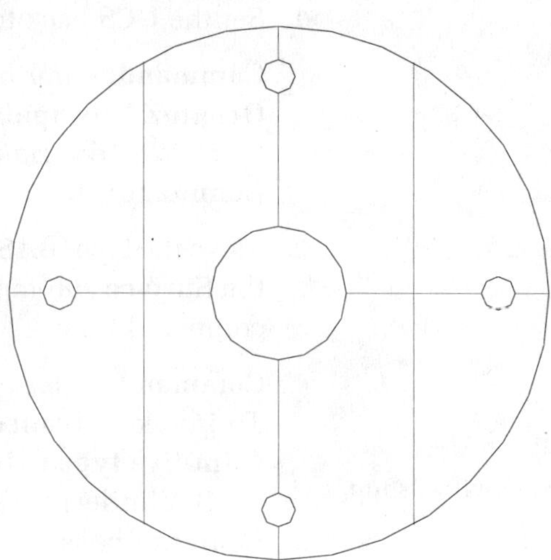

Fig. 2.14 The **planesf** surface of the base top

layers. **Planesf** the area between the two circles and the four holes in a similar manner as in item 6 of Stage 4 of this sequence. All six circles must be picked in this instance (Fig. 2.14).

2. Thaw layers **CONE** and **BASE**. Freeze layer **BASE_CIRCLES**. Call the **Iso** prompt of the **Display** command. The model now appears as in Fig. 2.15.

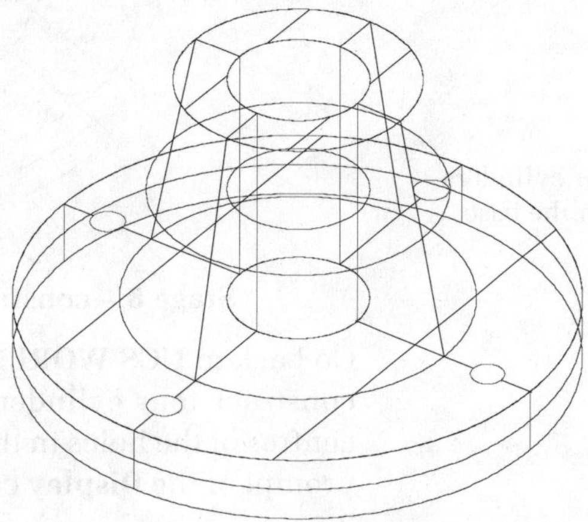

Fig. 2.15 The cone and base with their **planesf** top surfaces

Stage 7 – constructing the bottom of the base

Set the **UCS** to the **FRONT UCS** in the **UCS ORIENTATION** dialogue box by selecting **Preset UCS...** in the **View** pull-down menu. While in the **FRONT UCS** copy the base top surface to the bottom of the base. Call the **Iso** prompt of the **Display** command. The model now appears as in Fig. 2.16.

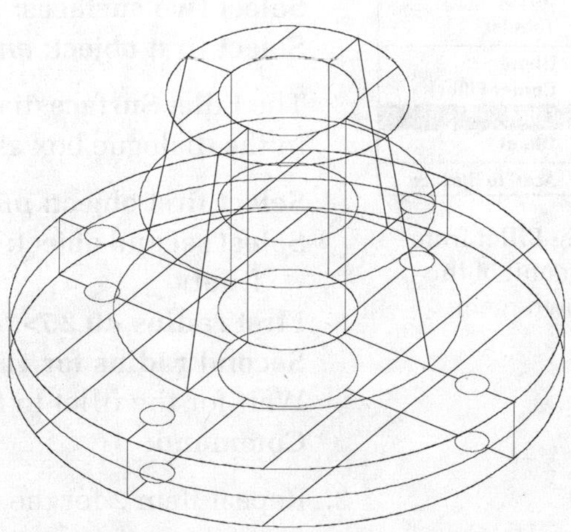

Fig. 2.16 The bottom surface of the base copied from the top surface of the base

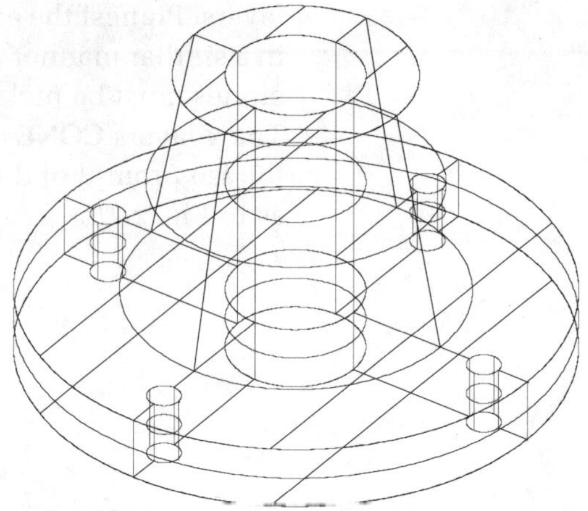

Fig. 2.17 The four cylinders added as holes in the base

Stage 8 – constructing the four holes in the base

Go back to **UCS WORLD** and with the aid of the command **primsf**, construct four cylinders, each of radius 5 and height –20 at the centres of the holes in the top and bottom base surfaces. Call the **Iso** prompt of the **Display** command. The model now appears as in Fig. 2.17.

AutoSurf
Create
Surface
Wireframe
Trim Surface
Edit
Surface
Wireframe
Trim Border
Display Views
Surface Display...
Entity Visibility
Entity Information
Distance
Preferences...
Utility

Cone
Cylinder
Sphere
Torus
Planar
Extrude
Revolve
Rule
Loft (U Lines)
Mesh (UV Lines)
Swept
Tubular
Blend
Corner Fillet
Fillet
Offset
Acad to Surface

Fig. 2.18 Selecting **Fillet** from the **Surface** sub-menu of the **AutoSurf** pull-down menu

Stage 9 – constructing fillets

1. Thaw all layers except **ASURF_FRZ**, **BASE_CIRCLES** and **TOP_CIRCLES**.
2. With the model still in the **Iso** viewing position, either select **Fillet** from the **Surface** sub-menu of the **AutoSurf** pull-down menu (Fig. 2.18) or, at the command line:

   Command: *enter* filletsf *right-click*
   To invoke advanced options enter '??'...
   Select two surfaces:
   Select first object: *enter* ?? *right-click*

   The **Fillet Surface** dialogue box (Fig. 2.19) appears. Make settings in the dialogue box as shown.

   Select first object: *pick* one of the surfaces between the fillet
   Select second object: *pick* the second of the surfaces between the fillet
   First radius <0.25>: *enter* 5 *right-click*
   Second radius for variable fillet <5>: *right-click*
   Wait for the fillet to form.
   Command:

3. Repeat item 2 for the other two filleted edges, until the top of the cone, the surfaces between the cone and the top of the base and the

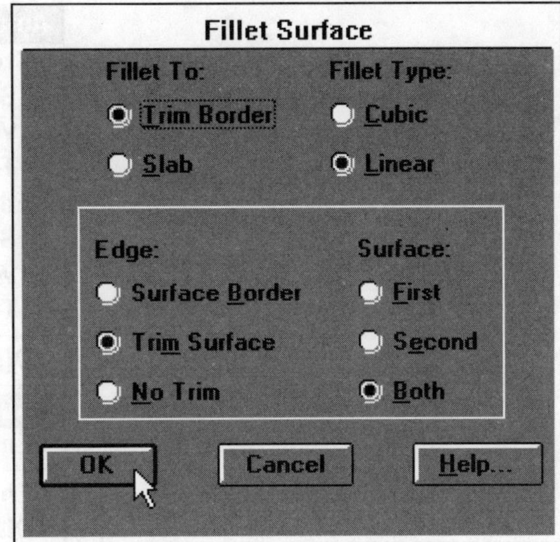

Fig. 2.19 The settings in the **Fillet Surface** dialogue box

circular edge of the base are all filleted to 5 units. Call the **Iso** option of the **Display** command and the model now appears as in Fig. 2.20. The construction of the model is now completed.

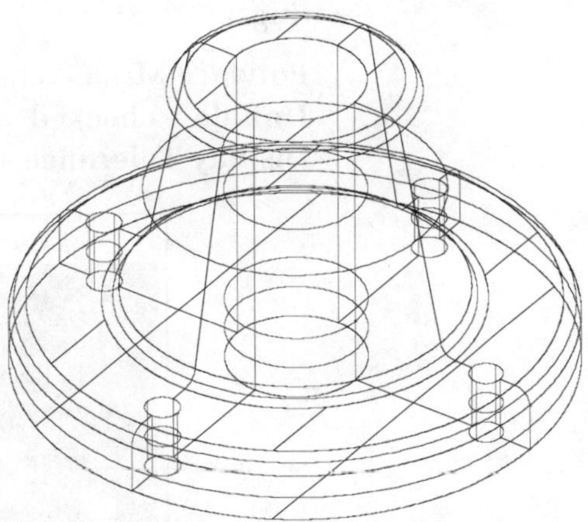

Fig. 2.20 The completed AutoSurf model

Stage 10 – surface meshing the model

Either select **Surface Display...** from the **AutoSurf** pull-down menu (Fig. 2.21) or, at the command line:

Command: *enter* dispsf *right-click*
Select surfaces: *enter* w (for Window) *right-click*
First corner: *pick* **Other corner:** *pick* (window the whole model)
15 found.
Select surfaces: *right-click*

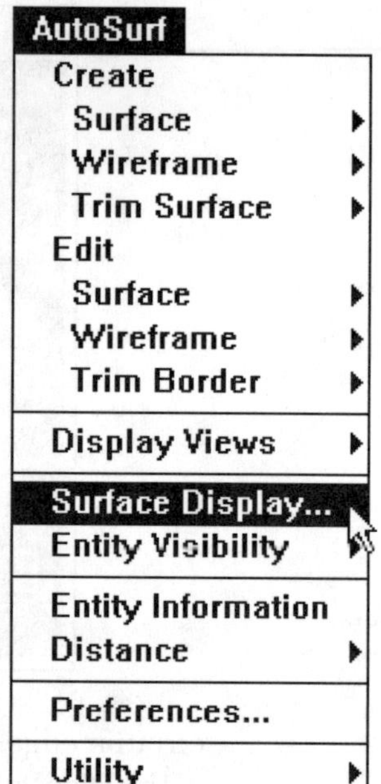

Fig. 2.21 Selecting **Surface Display...** from the **AutoSurf** pull-down menu

In the **Surface Display** dialogue box (Fig 2.22) make the following settings:

Polyface Mesh – checked
Unhide – checked
Display Tolerance – set at 0.25.

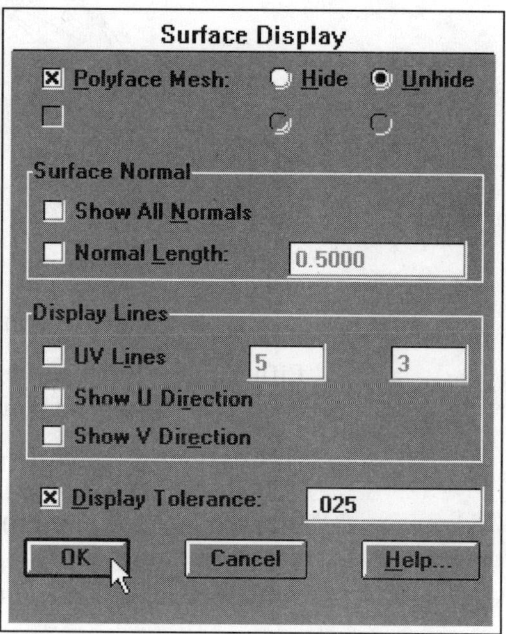

Fig. 2.22 The settings to be made in the **Surface Display** dialogue box

After some time has elapsed, the model becomes completely surface meshed and **Command:** once again appears at the Command Line. Figure 2.23 shows the resulting surface meshed model after **Hide**.

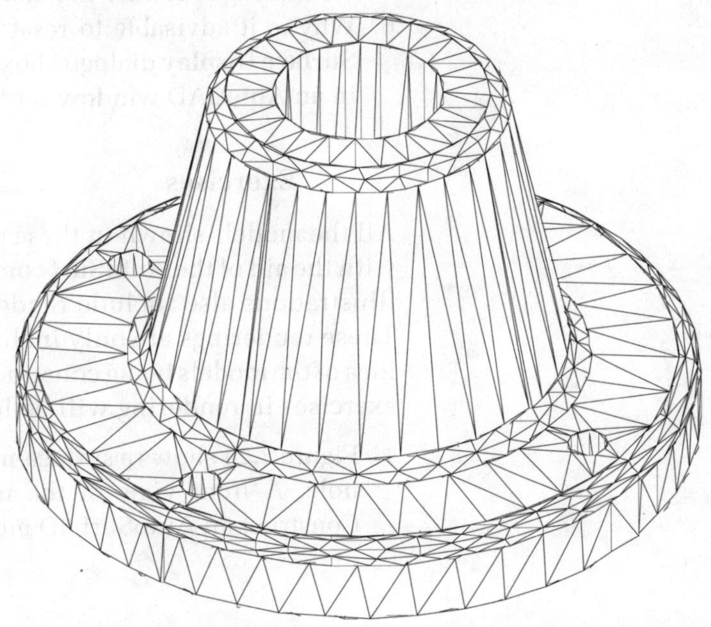

Fig. 2.23 The completed model after surface meshing. The command **Hide** has been called

Stage 11 – rendering

If necessary the model can now be rendered in AutoCAD Render or in AutoVision. Descriptions of the methods of rendering of AutoSurf Models in AutoVision are left until Chapter 9. If you go back to Fig. 2.1 on page 17, you can see a rendering of this model.

Questions

1. Can you write down a typical sequence of operations for constructing an AutoSurf 3D model? You could begin like this:

   (a) Make the necessary layers.

2. Why is it advisable to work on a number of different layers when constructing an AutoSurf 3D model?
3. What usually happens when **??** is *entered* at the command line in response to options from many of the AutoSurf commands?

4. Have you tried using the **Display** command to place your model in a suitable position for constructing a surface which is not parallel to the **WORLD UCS** surface? If you have done so, what happens?
5. Why is it necessary to surface mesh an AutoSurf 3D model before attempting to render the model?
6. Why is it advisable to reset the **Display Tolerance** figure in the **Surface Display** dialogue box from its default figure when working in an AutoCAD window set for **Limits** of 420,300?

Exercises

All the models shown in these exercises have been surface meshed with the aid of the AutoSurf command **Surface Display**. Some of the illustrations also include renderings of the completed 3D models. These renderings are only included here to give the reader a better idea of the models being constructed. As far as this book is concerned, exercises in rendering will be left for a later chapter.

1. Figure 2.24 shows a surface-meshed 3D model of a cylinder with a hole. A front view of the model showing sizes is also given. Construct an AutoSurf 3D model to the given dimensions.

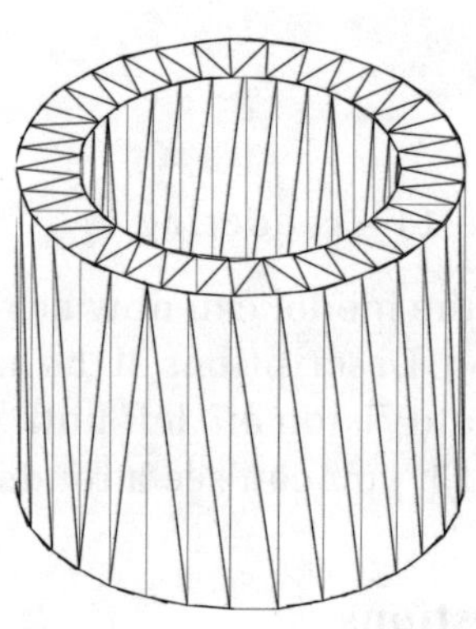

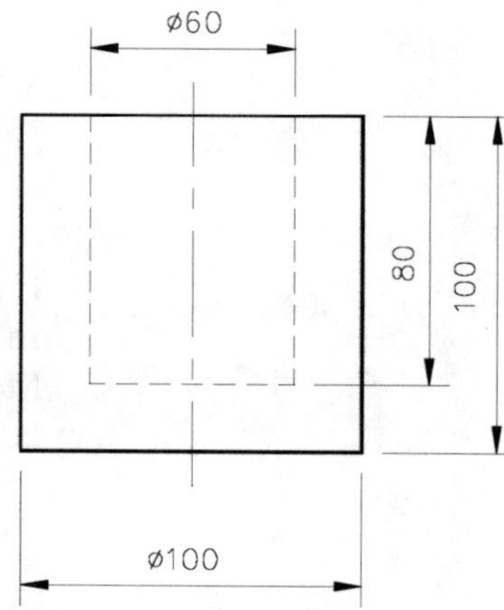

Fig. 2.24 Exercise 1

2. A rendering of an AutoSurf 3D model is shown in Fig. 2.25. The illustration also shows the surface-meshed model of the rendering, together with a front view and plan in first-angle orthographic projection.

   Construct an AutoSurf 3D model to the given dimensions.
3. A surface-meshed AutoSurf 3D model is shown, together with a dimensioned front view, in Fig. 2.26. Construct the model to the given dimensions.

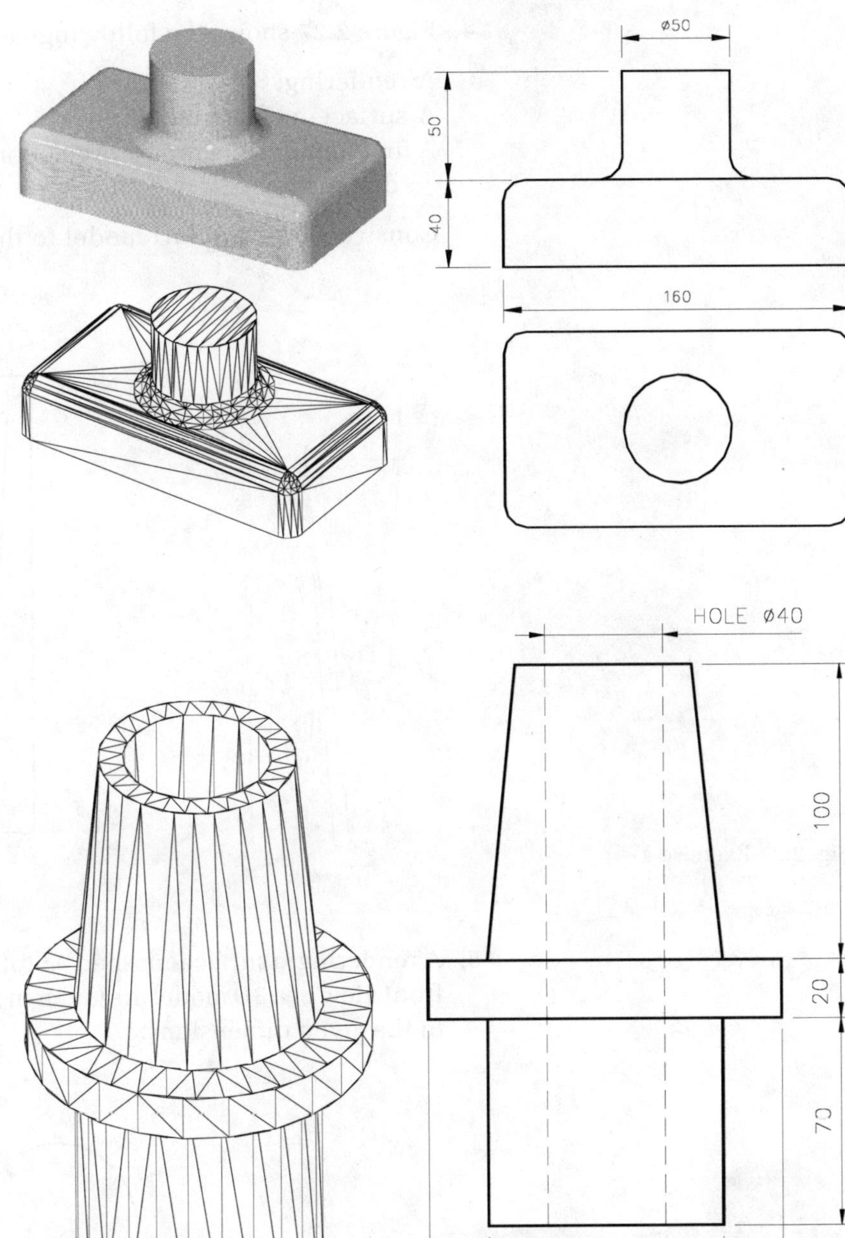

Fig. 2.25 Exercise 2

Fig. 2.26 Exercise 3

4. Figure 2.27 shows the following views of a door handle:

   A rendering;
   A surface-meshed model;
   A first-angle orthographic projection which includes the principal dimensions.

   Construct an AutoSurf model to the given sizes.

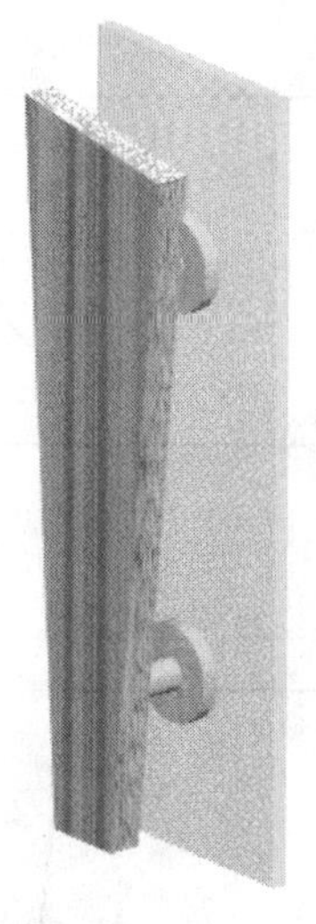

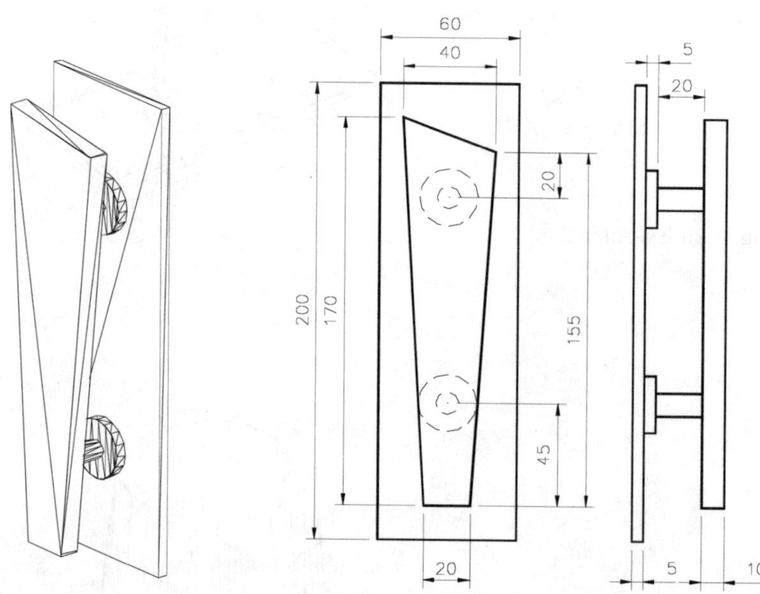

Fig. 2.27 Exercise 4

5. A rendering, a surface-meshed AutoSurf model and a dimensioned front view of a 3D model are given in Fig. 2.28. Construct the model to the given dimensions.

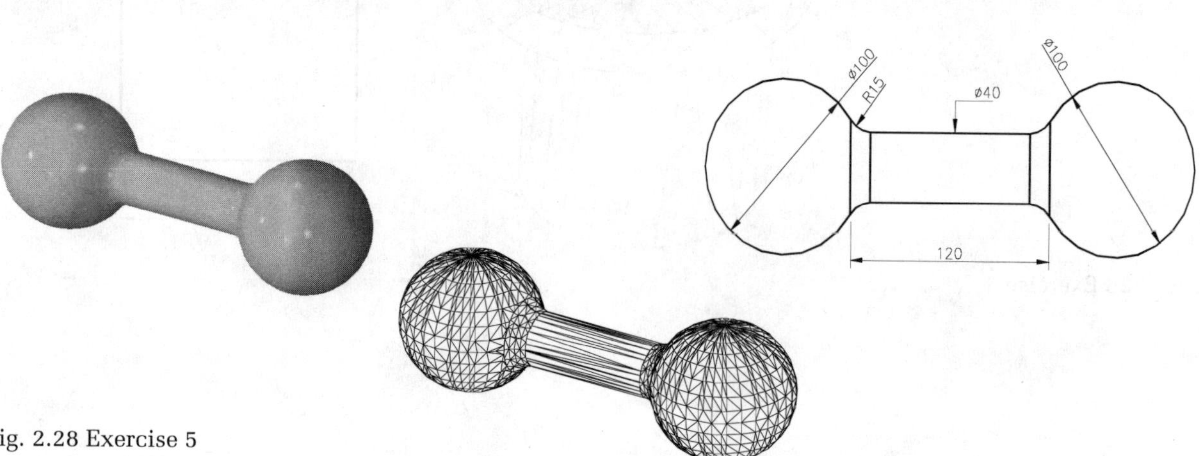

Fig. 2.28 Exercise 5

CHAPTER 3

Extruded and Revolved surfaces

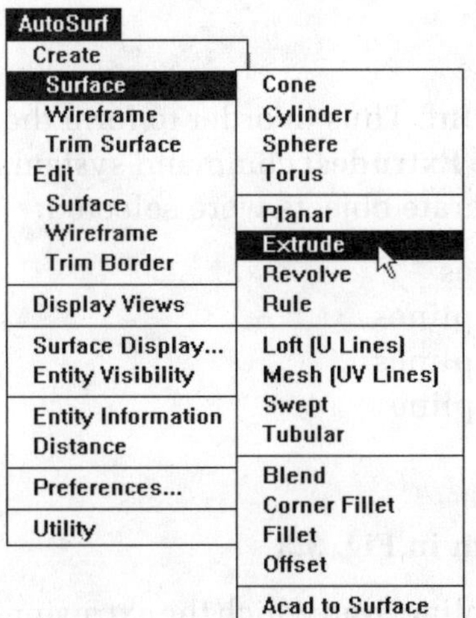

Fig. 3.1 Selecting **Extrude** from the **AutoSurf** pull-down menu

The AutoSurf Extrude command

The AutoSurf command **Extrude** is used for the construction of extrusions from AutoCAD plines, splines, arcs and circles. Examples of extrusions are given in Fig. 3.3. Further examples are shown in Fig. 3.5. These examples have been constructed with **U Lines** set to 5 and **V Lines** set to 3 in the AutoSurf **Preferences** dialogue box.

Associated with the command is the **Extrudesf** dialogue box, which appears when **??** is *entered* at the command line in response to the options appearing when the command is called.

To construct the left-hand drawing of Fig. 3.3, in which the **Fit Length** box in the **Extrudesf** dialogue box is the default **Inf**, either select **Extrude** from the **AutoSurf** pull-down menu (Fig. 3.1) or, at the command line:

Command: *enter* extrudesf *right-click*
To invoke advanced options enter '??'...
Select objects: *enter* ?? *right-click*
The **Extrudesf** dialogue box appears (Fig. 3.2). *Left-click* on the **OK** button.
Select objects: *pick* the pline outline
Select objects: *right-click*
Direction Entity/Viewdir/X/Y/Z/<Start point>: *enter* z *right-click*
Enter distance <1>: *enter* 50 *right-click*
Draft angle <0>: *right-click*
Warning – C0 surface created.
Command:

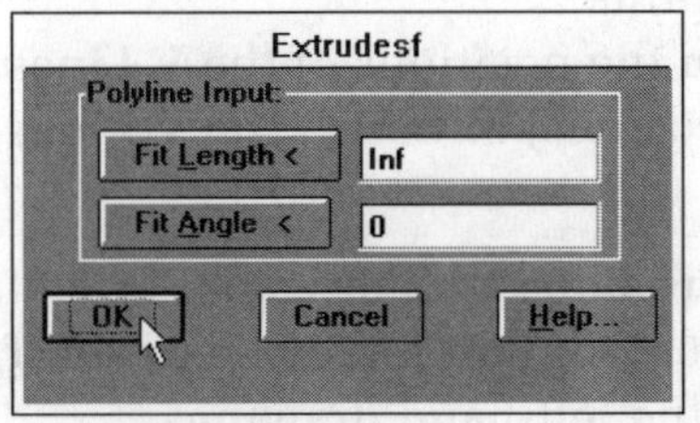

Fig. 3.2 The **Extrudesf** dialogue box

The right-hand drawing of Fig. 3.3 was constructed with the **Fit Length** set to 25 units (Fig. 3.4) – less in length than any of the sides of the pline outline (90 by 60) from which the extrusion was produced. The central drawing of Fig. 3.3 was constructed from four

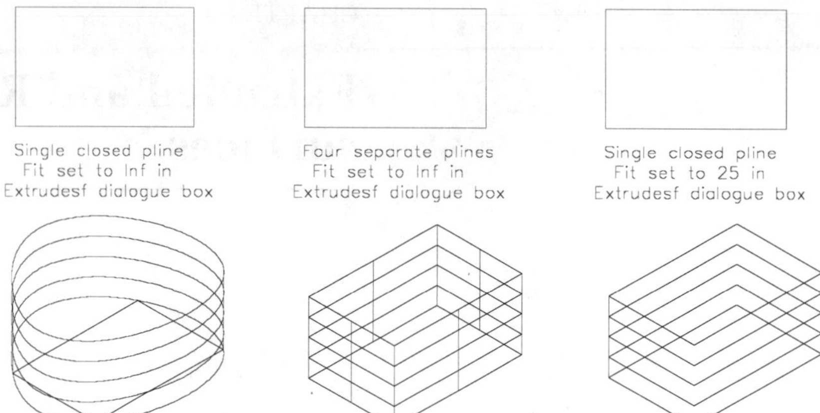

Fig. 3.3 Three examples of AutoSurf extrusions with **Draft angle** set at 0

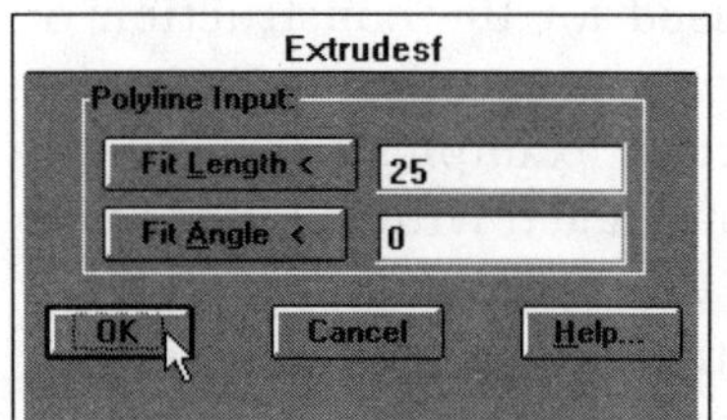

Fig. 3.4 *Enter* **25** in the **Fit Length** dialogue box

separate plines, with **Fit** remaining at **Inf**. Thus in order to form the central extrusion, in the options of the **Extrudesf** command system, at the **Select objects:** option, four separate objects were selected:

Select objects: *pick* one of the plines
Select objects: *pick* another of the plines
Select objects: *pick* another of the plines
Select objects: *pick* the remaining pline
Select objects: *right-click*

Notes on the extrusions shown in Fig. 3.3

Left-hand extrusion: the corners of the pline from which the extrusion was formed has been treated as if they were the control points of a NURBS spline – with resulting distortion of the extrusion. In this example, **Fit Length** was set at **Inf** (Infinity).

Central extrusion: each pline was extruded as a separate entity, thus the pline was treated as a straight NURBS spline. Again **Fit Length** was set at **Inf**.

Right-hand extrusion: in this example **Fit Length** was set to a figure less than the length of any side of the pline (25), thus each side was treated as a straight NURBS spline.

U and V Lines: note the differences in the positions of the **V Lines** (the upright lines of the three extrusions) although the **V Lines** setting was 3 for all examples.

Two further examples of AutoSurf extrusions are shown in Fig. 3.5. The response to the **Draft angle <0>:** option in the **extrudesf** command system was, in the case of the left-hand drawing:

Draft angle <0>: *enter* 30 *right-click*

and for the right-hand drawing:

Draft angle <0>: *enter* 330 *right-click*

In both the extrusions in Fig. 3.5, **Fit Length** in the **Extrudesf** dialogue box was set at 25.

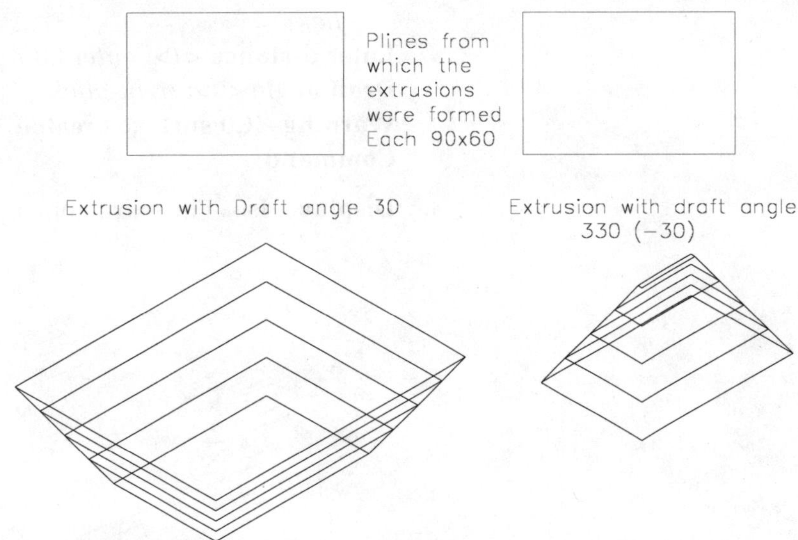

Fig. 3.5 Two further examples of AutoSurf extrusions with Draft angles set at 30 and 330

Two examples of extrusions

First example

1. Draw the pline outline shown in Fig. 3.6.

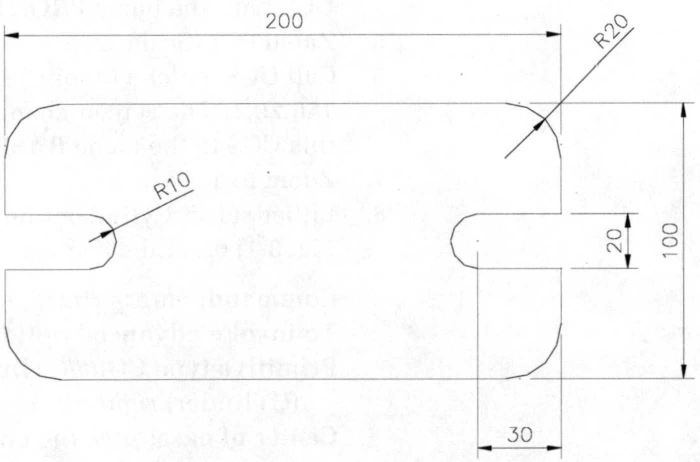

Fig 3.6 The pline outline for the first example

2. Either select **Extrude** from the **AutoSurf** pull-down menu or, at the command line:

   Command: *enter* extrudesf *right-click*
   To invoke advanced options enter '??'...
   Select objects: *pick* the pline outline (Fig. 3.6)
   Select objects: *right-click*
   Direction Entity/Viewdir/X/Y/Z/<Start point>: *enter* z *right-click*
   Enter distance <1>: *enter* 20 *right-click*
   Draft angle <0>: *right-click*
   Warning – C0 surface created.
   Command:

3. **Display** – Iso. The extrusion appears as in Fig. 3.7.

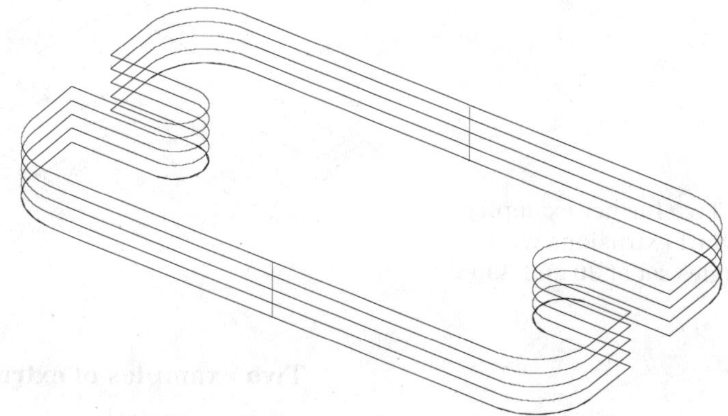

Fig. 3.7 The 20 units high extrusion formed from the pline Fig. 3.6

4. Select **Preset UCS...** from the **View** pull-down menu, and from the **UCS Orientation** dialogue box select the **FRONT UCS**. Save this UCS with the name **FRONT**.
5. **Zoom** to 1 (Scale 1:1).
6. Call **UCS**, *enter* 3 (3point) and *enter* the 3 points: 150,20; 350,20; 150,20,1. The screen changes to the required 3point UCS. Save this UCS to the name **BASE_TOP**.
7. **Zoom** to 1.
8. Either select **Cylinder** from the **AutoSurf** pull-down menu (see Fig. 3.1) or, at the command line:

   Command: *enter* primsf *right-click*
   To invoke advanced options enter '??'...
   Primitive type COne/CYlinder/Torus/<Sphere>: *enter* cy (CYlinder) *right-click*
   Center of base: *pick* the centre of the pline outline

Diameter of base/<Radius of base><1.0>: *enter* 40 *right-click*
Height of cylinder: *enter* 80 *right-click*
Command:

9. Call **UCS** followed by *right-click* to get into the **World UCS.**
10. Either select **Cylinder** from the **AutoSurf** pull-down menu or, at the command line:

Command: *enter* primsf *right-click*
To invoke advanced options enter '??'...
Primitive type COne/CYlinder/Torus/<Sphere>: *enter* cy (CYlinder) *right-click*
Center of base: *pick* the centre of the pline outline
Diameter of base/<Radius of base><1.0>: *enter* 30 *right-click*
Height of cylinder: *enter* 100 *right-click*
Command:

11. **Display** – Iso. The 3D model now appears as in Fig. 3.8.

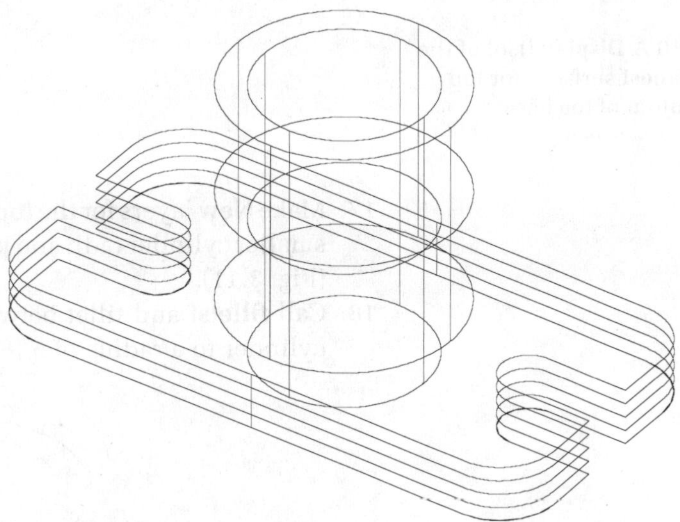

Fig. 3.8 The two cylinders formed with the extrusion

12. **UCS World.**
13. On **New** layers draw a pline outline for the base, include a circle of the smaller cylinder radius. Freeze layer **0** and **planesf** the resulting outlines (Fig. 3.9).
14. Recall the **UCS BASE_TOP** and construct a similar **planesf** but with the circle of radius of the larger cylinder. Figure 3.10 shows both of the **planesf** surfaces for top and bottom of the base.
15. Call **UCS** and Restore the **FRONT** UCS.
16. Set a new 3point **UCS** at the top of the two cylinders.

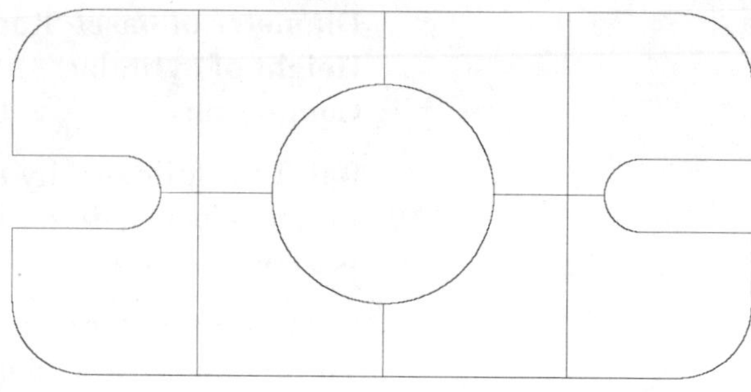

Fig. 3.9 The **planesf** base

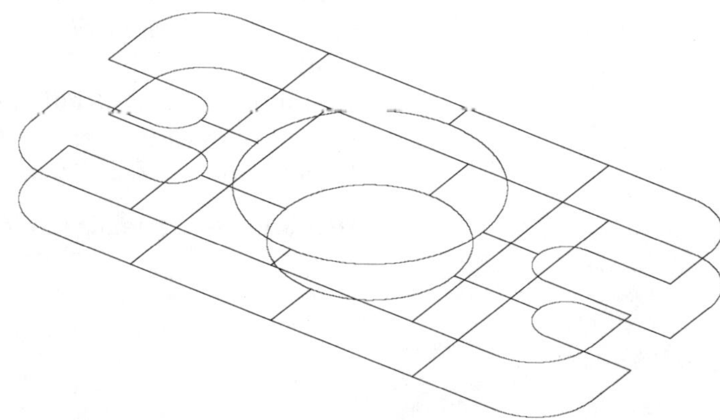

Fig. 3.10 A **Display** (Iso) of the two **planesf** surfaces for top and bottom of the base

17. Make **New** layers for the top surface, draw two circles of larger and smaller cylinder radii and **planesf** the area between the two circles (Fig. 3.11).
18. Call **filletsf** and fillet between the top of the base and the outer cylinder to a radius of 5 (Fig. 3.12).

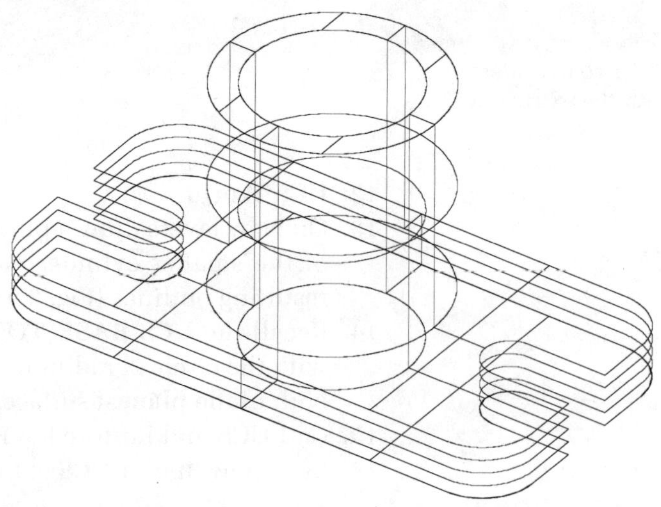

Fig. 3.11 The top surface between two cylinders with a **planesf** surface

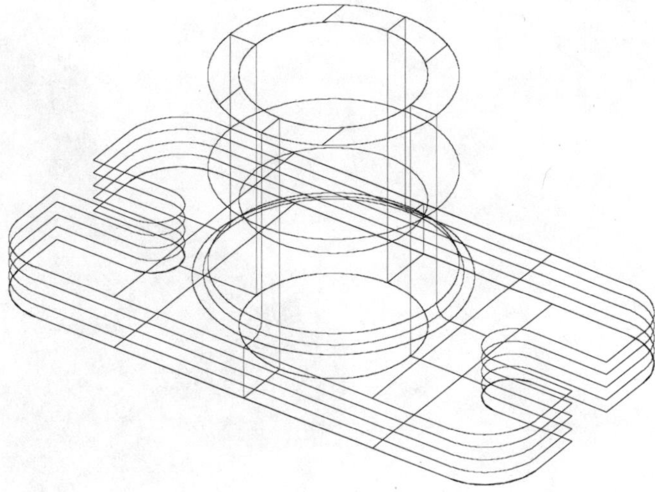

Fig. 3.12 The radius 5 fillet added to the 3D model wireframe

Note: The 3D model wireframe is now complete. If desired the operator could now go on the surface meshing the model as shown in Fig. 3.13, followed by rendering as shown in Fig. 3.14.

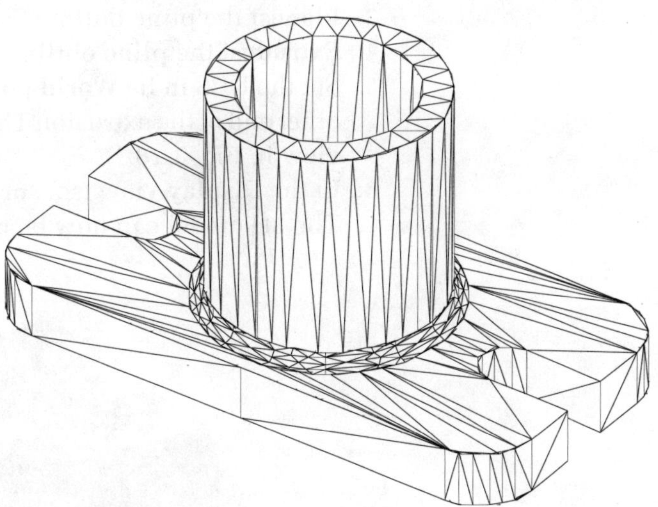

Fig. 3.13 The 3D model after surface meshing

Second example

This example is an extrusion of a simple V-block. A rendering of the surface-meshed model is given in Fig. 3.15.

1. Call **UCS** and set a suitable 3point vertically on which to commence drawing the pline outline on which the **extrudesf** is based.

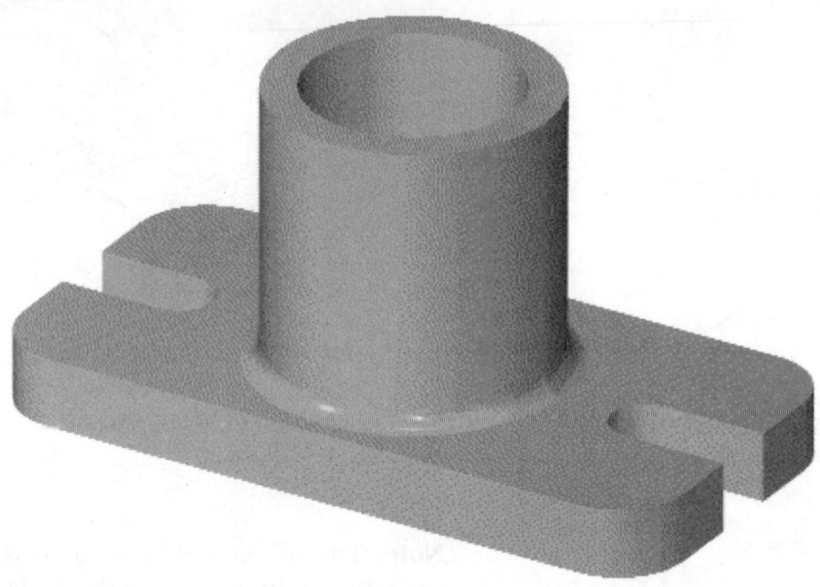

Fig. 3.14 The 3D model after surface meshing, followed by rendering in AutoVision

2. Draw the pline outline on this 3point UCS (Fig. 3.16).
3. **Planesf** the pline outline (Fig. 3.17).
4. **Extrudesf** the pline outline 200 units high in the **Z** direction.
5. Set the UCS in its **World** position and copy the end **planesf** to the other end of the extrusion The results are shown in the **Display** (Iso) view in Fig. 3.18.
6. In the **Display** view Iso, surface mesh the 3D model (Fig. 3.19).
7. The 3D model can now be rendered if required (Fig. 3.15).

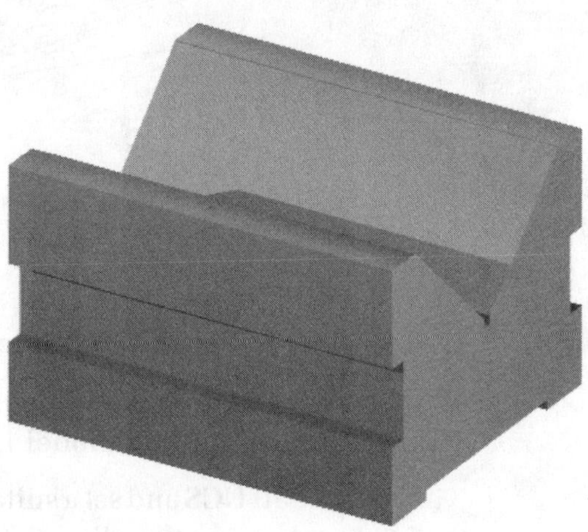

Fig. 3.15 A rendering of the surface-meshed 3D model of the second example

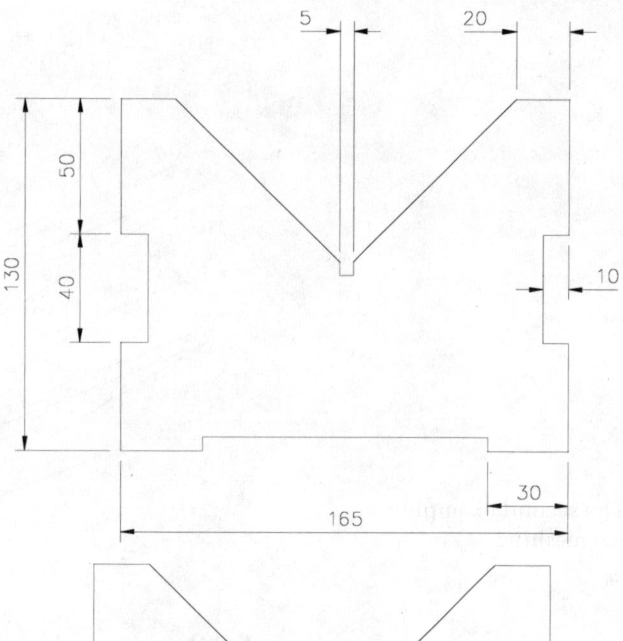

Fig. 3.16 The pline outline for the second example

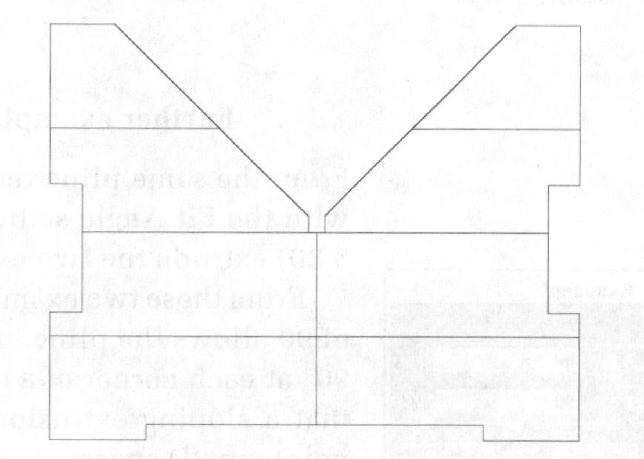

Fig. 3.17 The pline outline after **planesf**

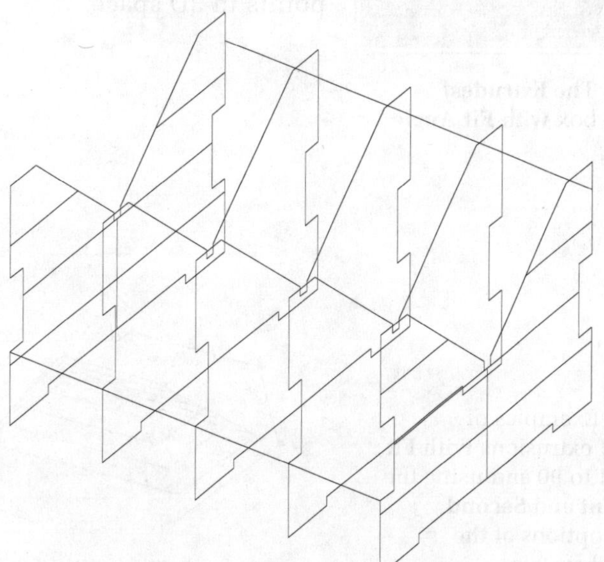

Fig. 3.18 The extrusion with both ends with their **planesf** surfaces

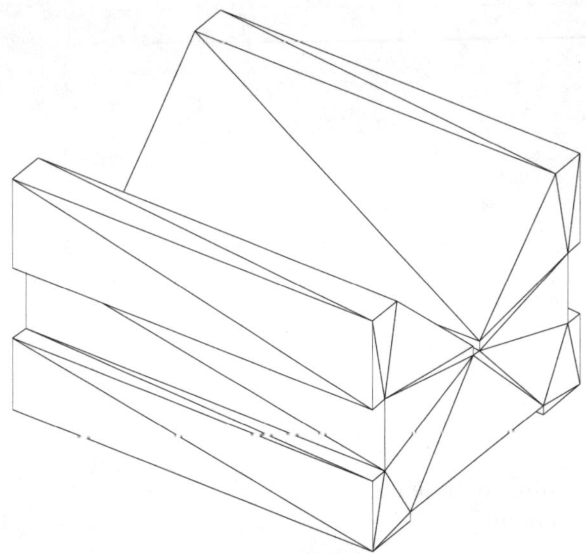

Fig. 3.19 The second example after surface meshing

Further examples of AutoSurf extrusions

From the same pline rectangles as in the examples of Fig. 3.3 and with the **Fit Angle** setting in the **Extrudesf** box *entered* as 90 (Fig. 3.20) extrude the two examples given in Fig. 3.21.

From these two examples it will be seen that the **Fit Angle** setting of 90 allows the pline to be used as a NURBS spline with angles of 90° at each corner of a continuous pline. The examples also show that a sloping extrusion can be constructed from the use of two points in 3D space.

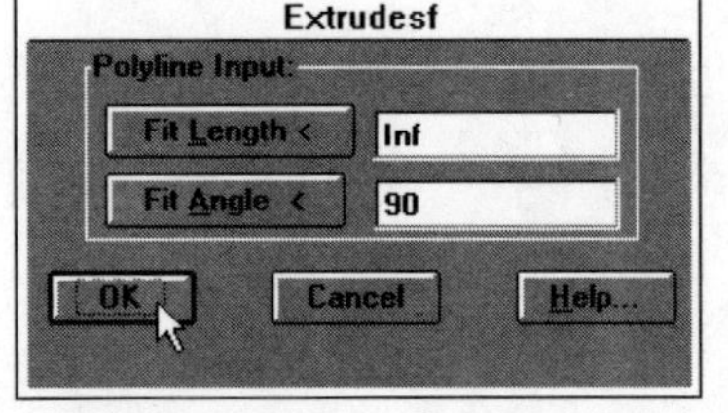

Fig. 3.20 The **Extrudesf** dialogue box with **Fit Angle** set at 90

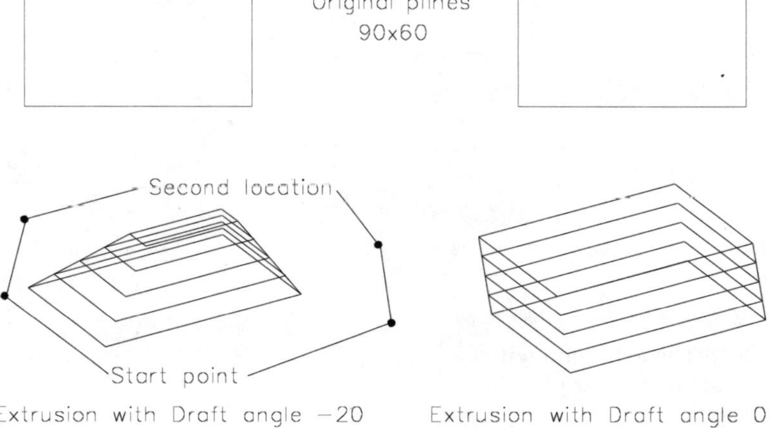

Fig. 3.21 Examples of AutoSurf extrusions with **Fit Angle** set to 90 and using the **Start point** and **Second location** options of the command system

The AutoSurf Revolve command

The AutoSurf command **Revolve** is used to construct AutoSurf solids of revolution from AutoCAD pline, spline and/or arc outlines. Examples of AutoSurf revolved solids are given in Fig. 3.22.

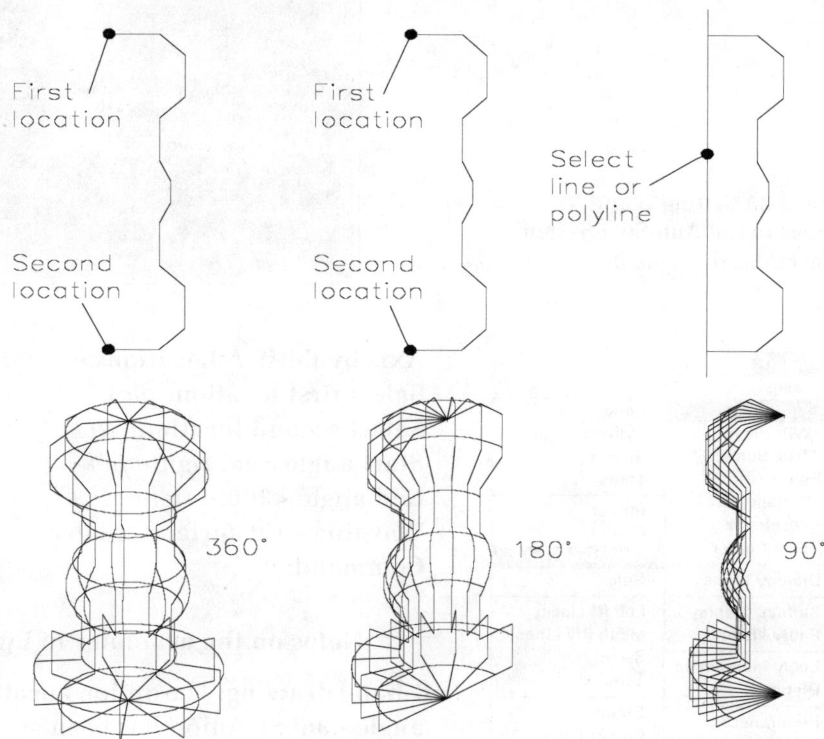

Fig. 3.22 Examples of AutoSurf **revolvesf** 3D models

In the examples given in Fig. 3.22, the pline outlines on which the models are based were drawn in a **UCS FRONT** set in the **UCS Orientation** dialogue box called by selecting **UCS Presets...** in the **View** pull-down menu. The settings for **U Lines** and **V Lines** in the **AutoSurf System Variables** dialogue box were set to 10 and 8 for these examples (Fig. 3.23). This allows the circularity of the revolved surface to show more clearly, but is not really fully necessary.

After setting the **FRONT UCS** and drawing the pline outlines, either select **Revolve** from the **AutoSurf** pull-down menu (Fig. 3.24) or, at the command line:

Command: *enter* revolvesf *right-click*
To invoke advanced options enter '??'...
Select profile curves: *pick* the pline outline

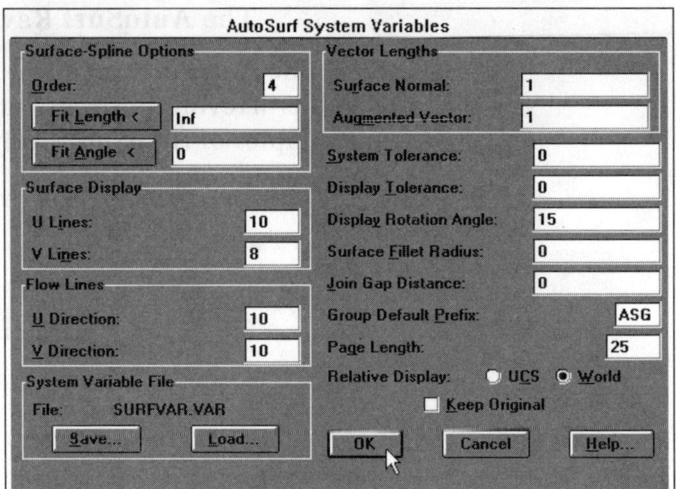

Fig. 3.23 Setting **U** and **V Lines** in the **AutoSurf System Variables** dialogue box

AutoSurf
Create
Surface
Wireframe
Trim Surface
Edit
Surface
Wireframe
Trim Border
Display Views
Surface Display...
Entity Visibility
Entity Information
Distance
Preferences...
Utility

Cone
Cylinder
Sphere
Torus
Planar
Extrude
Revolve
Rule
Loft (U Lines)
Mesh (UV Lines)
Swept
Tubular
Blend
Corner Fillet
Fillet
Offset
Acad to Surface

Fig. 3.24 Selecting **Revolve** from the **AutoSurf** pull-down menu

Axis by Entity/<Locations>: *right-click*
Select first location: *pick*
Select second location: *pick*
Start angle <0>: *right-click*
End angle <360>: *right-click*
Warning – C0 surface created.
Command:

Notes on the examples in Fig. 3.22

Left-hand drawing: The option **Locations** has been used and the **End angle <360>:** option has been accepted.

Centre drawing: The option **Locations** has been used and the **End angle <360>:** option has been changed by *entering* 180 as a response.

Right-hand drawing: The option **Axis by Entity** has been used by *entering* e as a response to this option and the **End angle <360>:** option has been changed by *entering* 90 as a response.

Note that the **U Lines** in each of these examples are all 10 in number, whether the rotation angle is 360°, 180° or 90°.

Two examples of revolved models

First example

1. Select **UCS Presets...** from the **View** pull-down menu and *pick* **FRONT**.
2. **Zoom** to 1.
3. Select **Preferences...** from the **AutoSurf** pull-down menu.

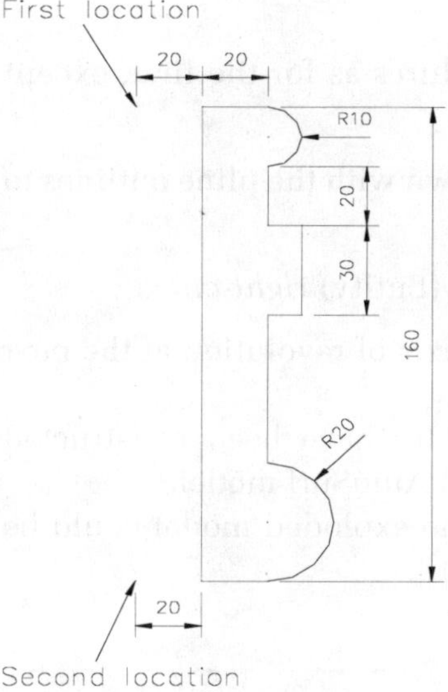

Fig. 3.25 The pline outline for the first example

4. Set **U Lines** at 10 and **V Lines** at 8. This allows the circularity of the revolved surface to show more clearly, but is not really fully necessary.
5. Draw the pline outline as shown in Fig. 3.25.
6. Either select **Revolve** from the **AutoSurf** pull-down menu or, at the command line:

   Command: *enter* revolvesf *right-click*
   To invoke advanced options enter '??'...
   Select profile curves: *pick* the pline outline
   Axis by Entity/<Locations>: *right-click*
   Select first location: *pick*
   Select second location: *pick*
   Start angle <0>: *right-click*
   End angle <360>: *right-click*
   Warning – C0 surface created.
   Command:

7. **UCS WORLD**.
8. **Zoom** to 1.
9. Call **Display** and *enter* i (Iso) *right-click*.
10. The resulting 3D revolved model is shown in Fig. 3.26.
11. If desired the model can now be surface meshed (Fig. 3.27) and also rendered, as shown in Fig. 3.28.

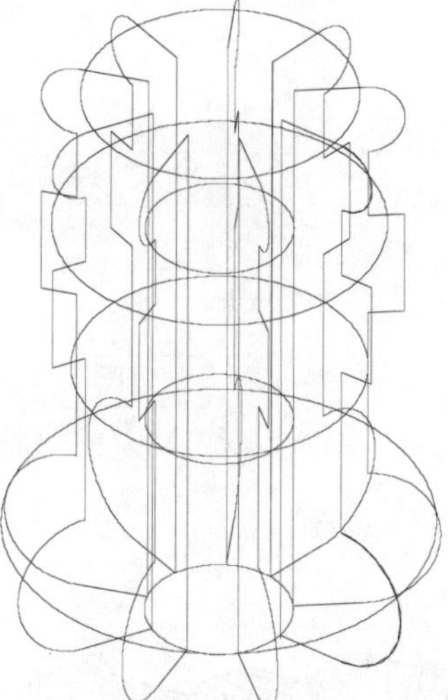

Fig. 3.26 The completed 3D model of the first example

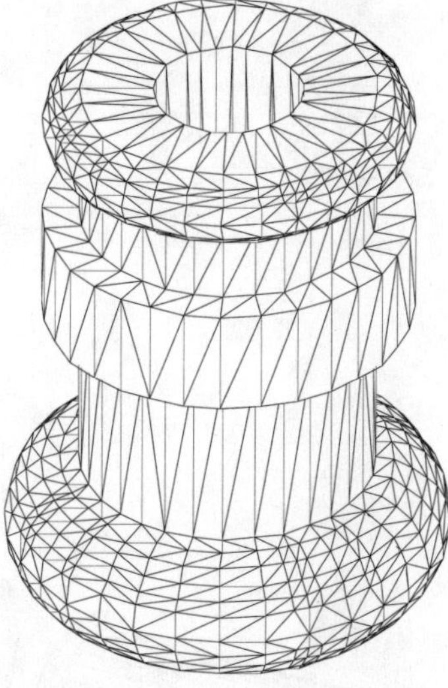

Fig. 3.27 The surface-meshed model

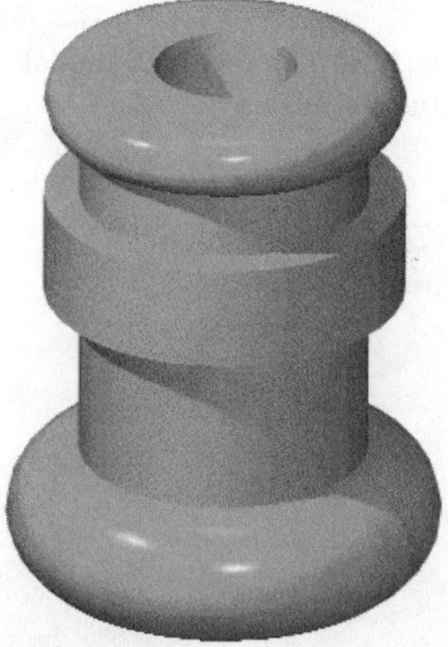

Fig. 3.28 The rendered model

Second example

This example follows the same procedures as for the first, except that:

1. As shown in Fig. 3.29, a line was drawn with the pline outlines to be used at the prompt:

   Axis by Entity/<Locations>: *enter* e (Entity) *right-click*

   followed by *picking* the line as the axis of revolution at the next prompt.
2. The three parts of the revolved solid have been constructed separately, so as to form an exploded AutoSurf model.
3. After calling **revolvesf** (Fig. 3.30), the exploded model could be surface meshed as shown in Fig. 3.31.

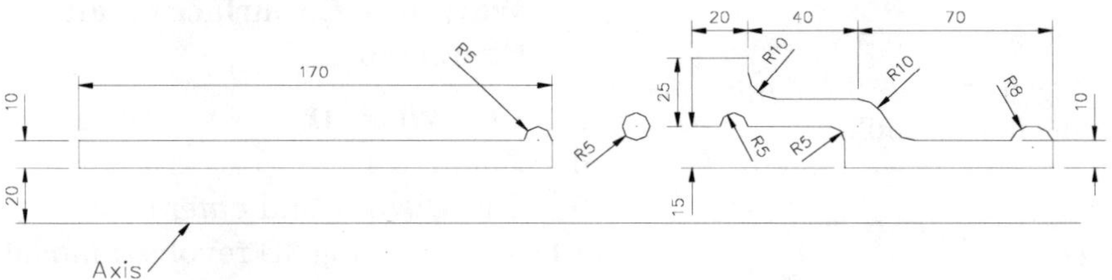

Fig. 3.29 The 3 plines for the second example

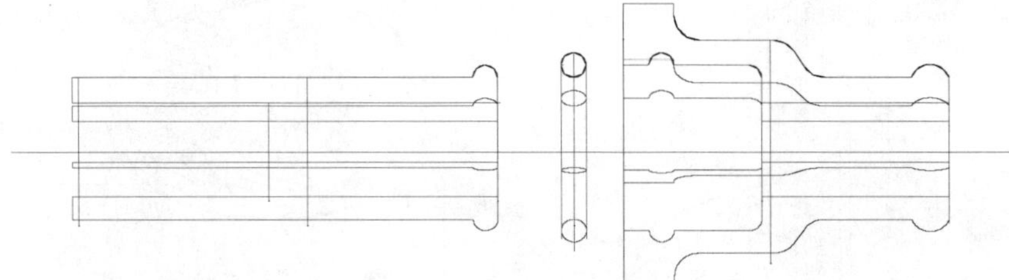

Fig. 3.30 The revolved model from the plines

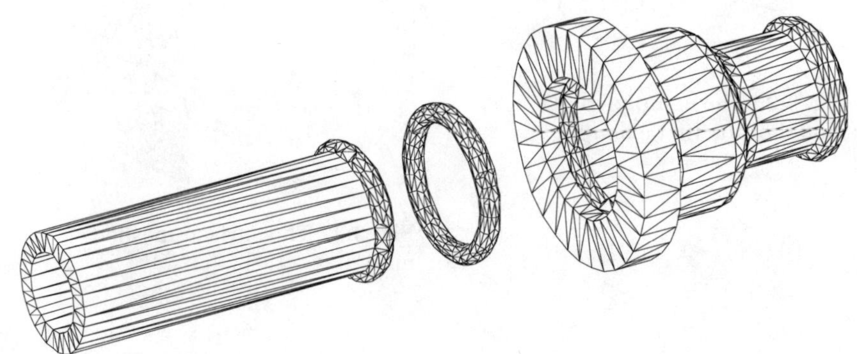

Fig. 3.31 The second example after surface meshing

A half revolution model

Figure 3.32 shows the same AutoSurf model, but this time in response to the prompt **End angle <360>:** the figure 180 was entered. The resulting half model requires its open edges to be surfaced using **planesf** as shown in Fig. 3.32. Failure to surface mesh the open edges would result in an unfinished AutoSurf model.

Figure 3.32 shows the half model in an assembly. This model is of a pipe join which includes an O ring. A rendering of the half model is given in Fig. 3.33.

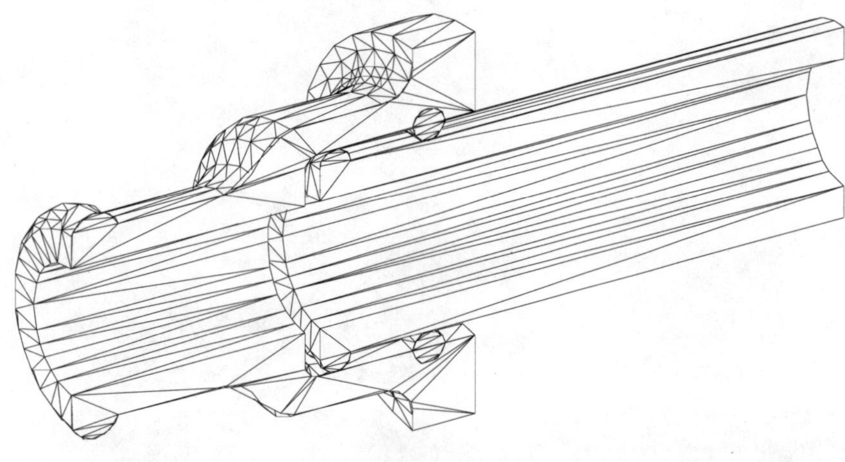

Fig. 3.32 A half model which has been surface meshed. Note that open surfaces have had a **planesf** surface added

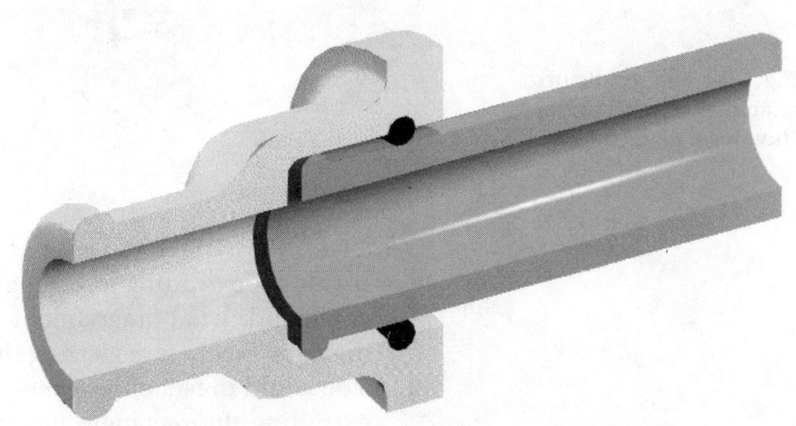

Fig. 3.33 A rendering of the half model in three different materials

Notes on Fit Length and Fit Angle for revolved models

The **Revolvesf** dialogue box, called to screen when ?? is *entered* in response to the first option of the **revolvesf** command system, requests the same two settings as does the **Extrudesf** dialogue box.

These two settings are:

Fit Length – with a default of **Inf**
Fit Angle – with a default of **0**.

When revolving pline outlines with straight lines, make sure that the settings in the **Revolvesf** dialogue box are suitable for the outline being revolved. Figure 3.34 shows the differences in the resulting models from straight line pline outlines when the **Revolvesf** dialogue box settings are accepted at the default of **Inf** and **0** and when the settings are changed to **Fit Length** of less than the shortest pline and **Fit Angle** of **90**.

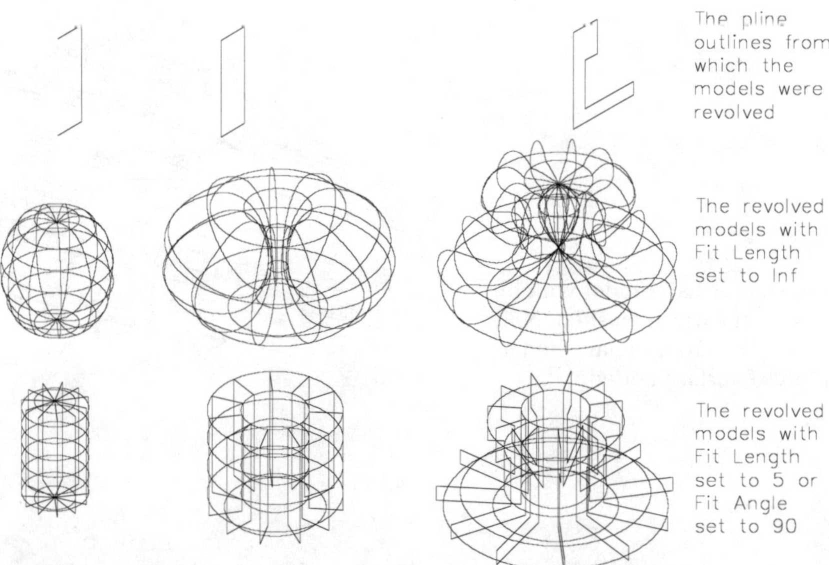

Fig. 3.34 The results of changing settings in the **Revolvesf** dialogue box

Questions

1. If you are extruding a rectangle drawn with the aid of the pline command, what amendment will be required in the **Extrudesf** dialogue box before starting the extrusion?
2. You could in fact choose one of two possible amendments when extruding the rectangle mentioned in Question 1. What is the second possibility?
3. What happens when extruding a pline rectangle when the option **Draft angle <0>:** is set at –30?
4. Why have the illustrations in Fig. 3.22 been produced after setting **U Lines** to 10 and **V Lines** to 8 and not with the default settings of 5 and 3?

5. Why was the first example of an extrusion (Figs 3.6 to 3.14) constructed on a number of different layers?
6. When using the **revolvesf** command system to produce 90° and 180° models of revolution, why is it necessary to add surfaces constructed with **planesf** if you wish to surface mesh and then render the model?
7. The sequence of construction of the second example of an extrusion (Figs 3.15 to 3.19) started with placing the AutoCAD window in a **FRONT UCS**. Why was this necessary?
8. What is the purpose of the option **<Start point>:** in the options of the **extrudesf** command system?
9. How are the settings for **U** and **V Lines** changed from the default of 5 and 3 to a new setting?
10. Have you experimented with bringing up the AutoSurf toolbars? If not go back to page 5 and bring them on screen now. Then use the toolbars to construct an AutoSurf model.

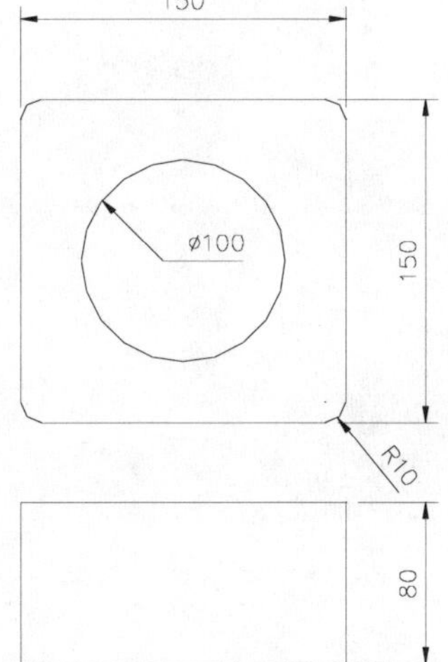

Fig. 3.35 Exercise 1. A dimensioned two-view third-angle projection

Exercises

The first four of the following exercises are comparatively simple examples of AutoSurf models mostly constructed with the aid of the commands **extrudesf** and **revolvesf**. These four exercises allow the reader to practise the use of these two commands. The last two exercises are more difficult, but it is suggested that the reader makes some attempt at answering them. All the exercises are illustrated with dimensioned orthographic projections, the resulting surface-meshed solids and, in addition, rendering is included. There is no

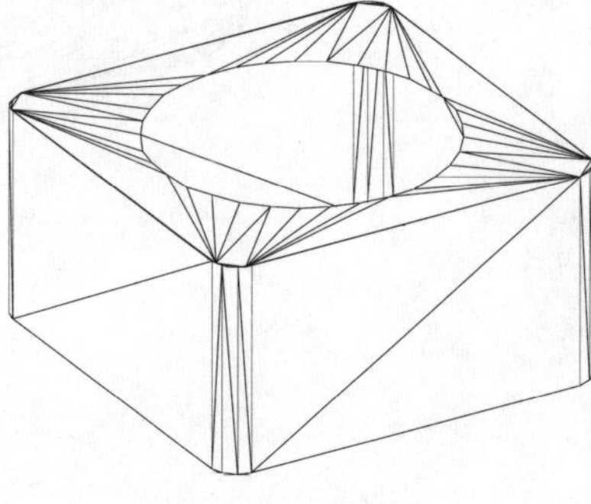

Fig. 3.36 Exercise 1. Left hand. The surface-meshed model

Fig. 3.37. Exercise 1. Right hand. The rendering of the model

need at this stage for the reader to attempt the rendering, but if his/her drawings answering the exercises are saved to disk, an attempt at rendering them can be made at a later stage.

1. Figure 3.35 is a two-view third-angle projection showing the sizes to be used for this exercise – a box with a circular hole cut in its top. Construct an AutoSurf 3D model to the given sizes. Figure 3.36 shows the surface-meshed model of the completed answer and Fig. 3.37 a rendering of the model.
2. Figure 3.37 shows the dimensions of the pline outline from which the model – a file handle – has been revolved. Figure 3.38 shows a surface meshing of the model and Fig. 3.39 a rendering. Construct a revolved AutoSurf model to the dimensions given.

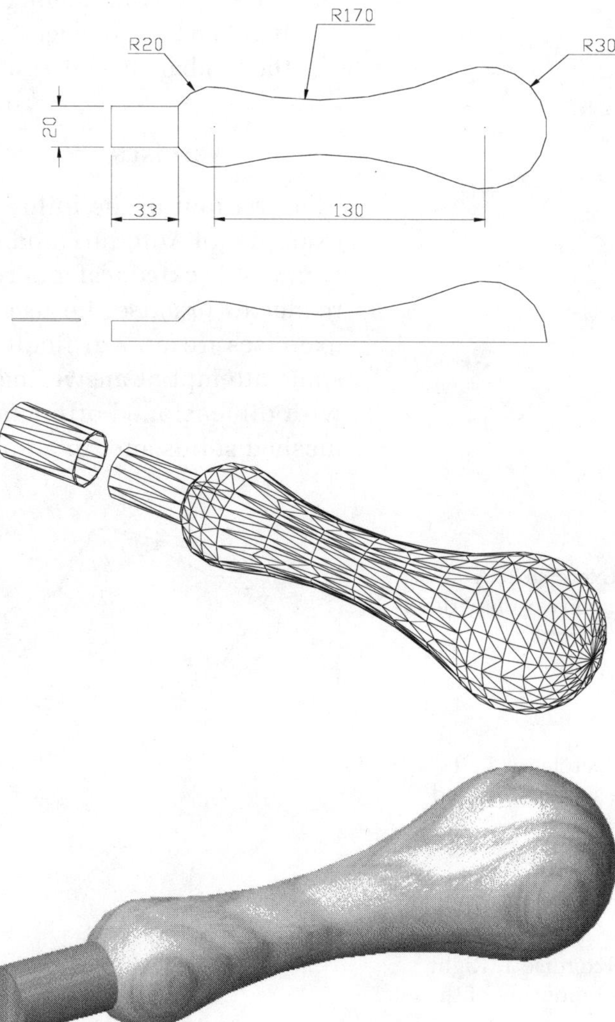

Fig. 3.38 Exercise 2. Details of the pline outline to be revolved

Fig. 3.39 Exercise 2. The surface-meshed model

Fig. 3.40 A rendering of the model

3. Figure 3.41 is a first-angle projection of the two parts of a timer clock – its body and its rotating face. Figure 3.42 is an exploded surface-meshed AutoSurf model of the clock and Fig. 3.43 a rendering of the two parts. Construct the model to the details given.

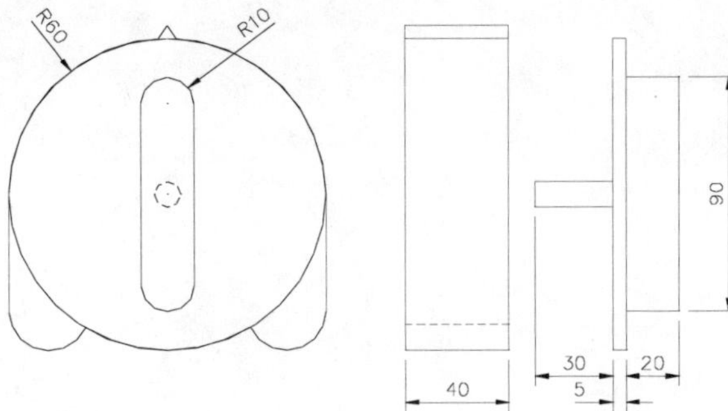

Fig. 3.41 Exercise 3. A first-angle projection of the two parts of the clock showing sizes

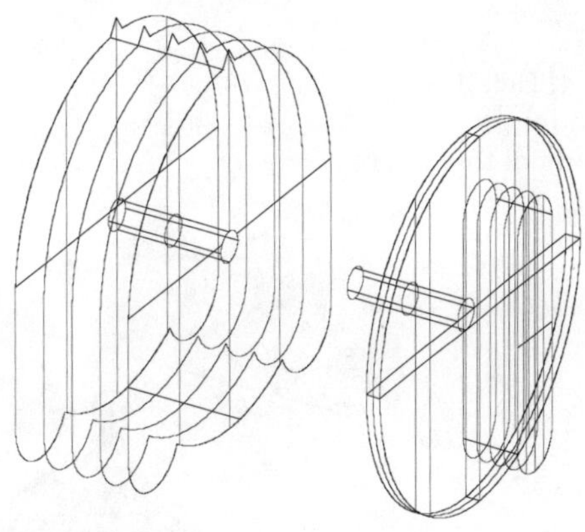

Fig. 3.42 Exercise 3. The extruded parts of the body and face of the clock

Fig. 3.43 Exercise 3. A rendering of the two parts of the clock

4. Figure 3.44 shows details of a 180° revolved AutoSurf model of a small wall decoration. Figure 3.45 shows the surface-meshed model against a rectangular **planesf**. Figure 3.46 is a rendering of the model against a rendering of the **planesf** in a wood finish. Construct the model to the sizes given.

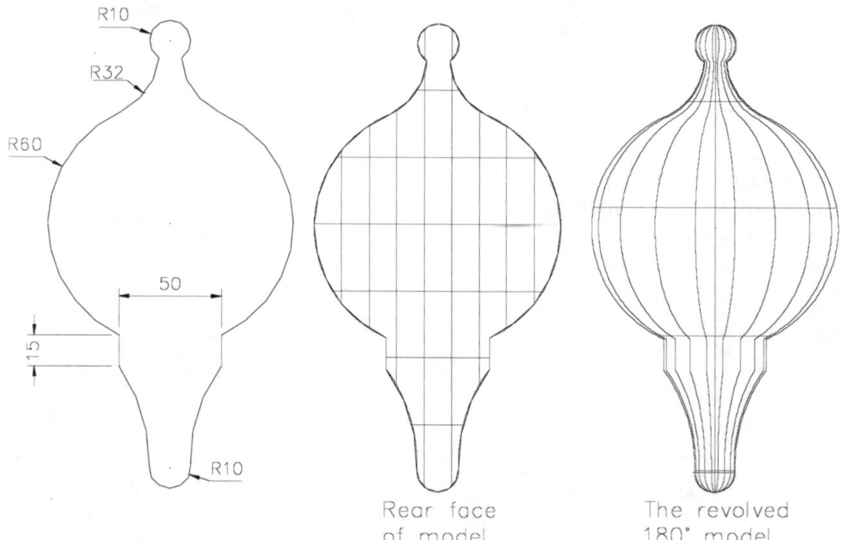

Fig. 3.44 Exercise 4. Details of the sizes of the model, together with details of the model as revolved

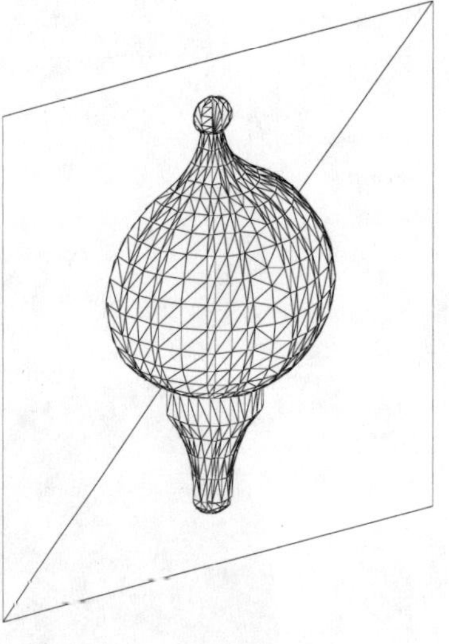

Fig. 3.45 Exercise 4. Left hand. The surface-meshed model against a **planesf** background

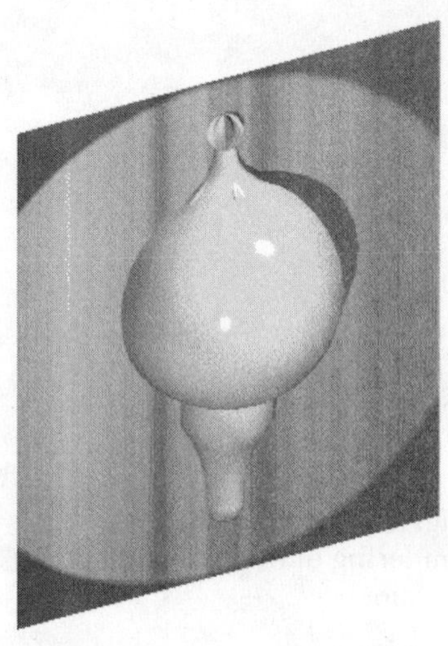

Fig. 3.46 Exercise 4. Right hand. A rendering of the model

5. This is a more difficult revolved AutoSurf model. Figure 3.47 shows the sizes and shape of the pline outline for the revolved model. Figure 3.48 shows the surface-meshed model and Fig. 3.49 a rendering of the model. Construct the model to the details given. Note that the representation of a screw thread in this model is not a true one because no helix has been formed.

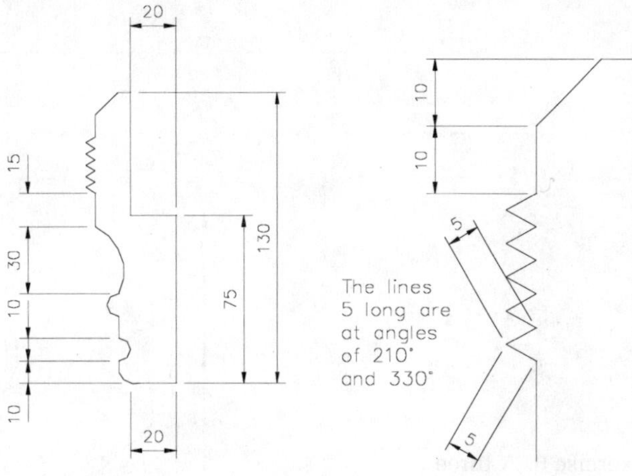

Fig. 3.47 Exercise 5. Details of the pline outline for the revolved model

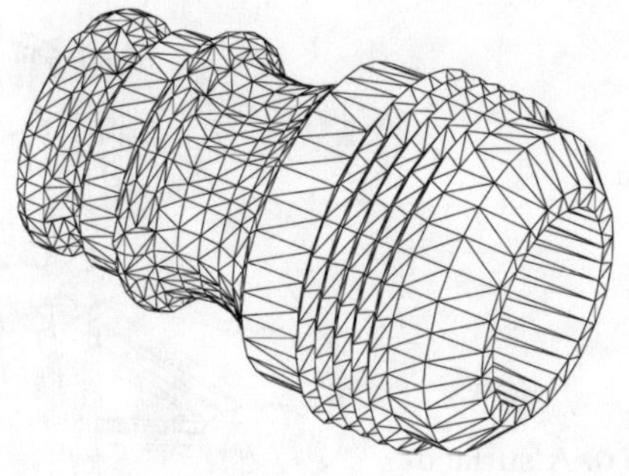

Fig. 3.48 Exercise 5. The surface-meshed model

Fig. 3.49 Exercise 5. A rendering of the model

6. Figure 3.50 is a three-view orthographic projection of an engineering component. Figure 3.51 is a surface-meshed model of the component and Fig. 3.52 a rendering. Construct the model of the component to the details given in the three illustrations.

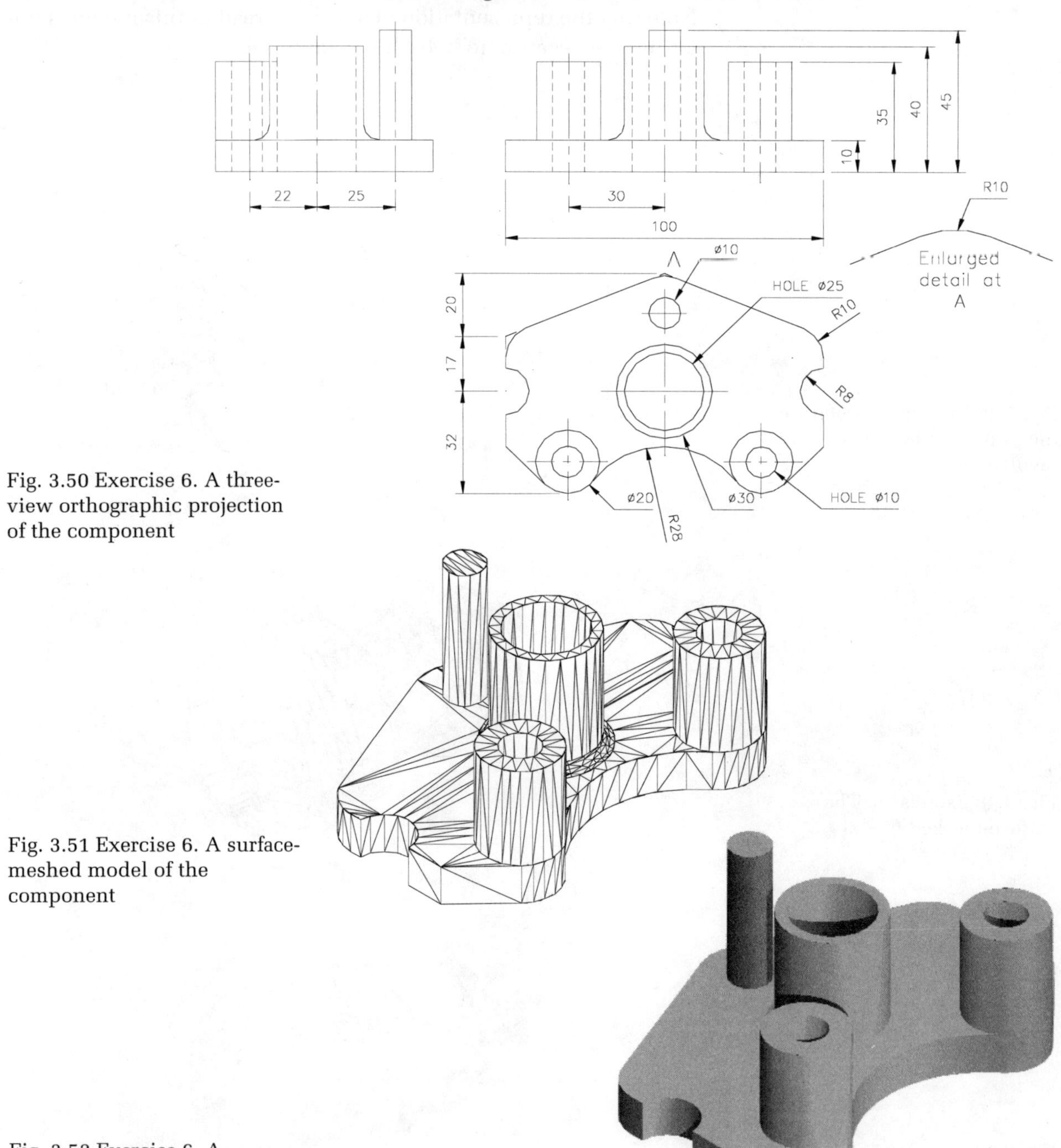

Fig. 3.50 Exercise 6. A three-view orthographic projection of the component

Fig. 3.51 Exercise 6. A surface-meshed model of the component

Fig. 3.52 Exercise 6. A rendering of the model

CHAPTER 4

Other free-form surfaces

Introduction: free-form surfaces

AutoSurf 'free-form' surfaces are those which are derived from wireframes made up of lines, plines and/or curves. AutoSurf includes seven free-form surface command systems. In Chapter 3 examples of two types of free-form surfaces were shown and the methods of constructing them were described. These were surfaces derived from wireframes which were either extruded with the aid of **extrudesf** or revolved surfaces constructed with the aid of **revolvesf**. The other five AutoSurf command systems for constructing free-form surfaces are described in this chapter. These are surfaces constructed from lines and curves with the aid of the commands:

sweepsf – for constructing swept surfaces
rulesf – for constructing ruled surfaces
tubesf – for constructing tubular surfaces
meshsf – for constructing surfaces from previously constructed U and V Lines.
loftsf – for constructing surfaces from previously constructed U Lines.

Using the User Coordinate System (UCS)

In order to be able to construct the wireframes on which free-form surfaces are based, the operator needs to be conversant with the AutoCAD UCS system which allows the XY plane to be set at any angle to the original XY plane which appears when AutoCAD is first loaded onto screen. Throughout this book, lines and arcs on which AutoSurf surfaces will be based, are constructed on UCS planes set by first selecting **UCS Presets...** from the **View** pull-down menu, followed by selecting UCS **FRONT** or UCS **RIGHT** from the **UCS Orientation** dialogue box which appears on screen. Another UCS which will frequently be employed here are UCS **3point** planes, obtained by either selecting or *entering* 3 *x,y,z* coordinates. An example is:

At the command line:

Command: *enter* ucs *right-click*
Origin/ZAxis/3point/OBject/View/X/Y/Z/Prev/Restore/Save/Del/?/<World>: *enter* 3 (3point) *right-click*
Origin point: *enter* 150,75 *right-click*
Point on positive portion of the X-axis<151,75,0>: *enter* 250,75 *right-click*
Point on positive Y-portion of the UCS XY plane<150,76,0>: *enter* .xy *right-click*
(need Z): *enter* 1 *right-click*
Regenerating drawing.
Command:

Note that *entering* 150,75 (an *x,y* coordinate) is the same as *entering* 150,75,0 (an *x,y,z* coordinate).

It is assumed the reader is familiar with these methods of obtaining new UCS planes which are different from the XY plane (the **World** UCS) which appears when AutoCAD is opened.

The command sweepsf

An example of a swept surface is given in Fig. 4.1. This surface was obtained from the curves shown in Fig. 4.2. To construct the curves, in a **FRONT** UCS construct two arcs – the front arc and the centre arc. Then change to the **World** UCS and move the centre arc to its correct position and copy the front arc to the position for the rear arc. Then place the three arcs in the ISO viewing position of the **Display** command options.

To construct the curves joining the ends of the three arcs call the AutoSurf command **spline3d** and, with the aid of the **endpoint** osnap construct splines to form the two curves. To do this either select **Spline** from the **AutoSurf** pull-down menu (Fig. 4.3) or, at the command line:

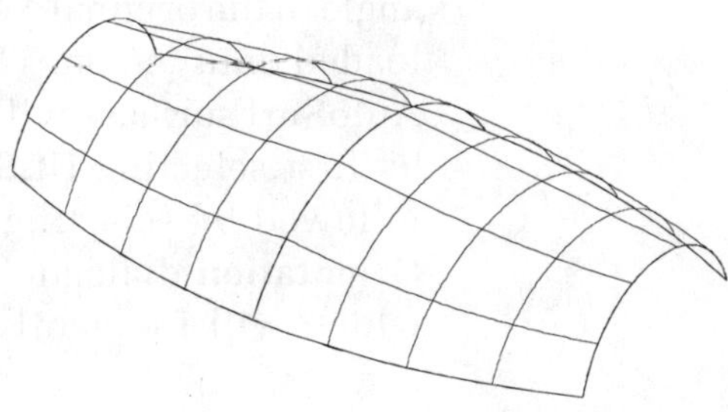

Fig. 4.1 An example of a swept surface

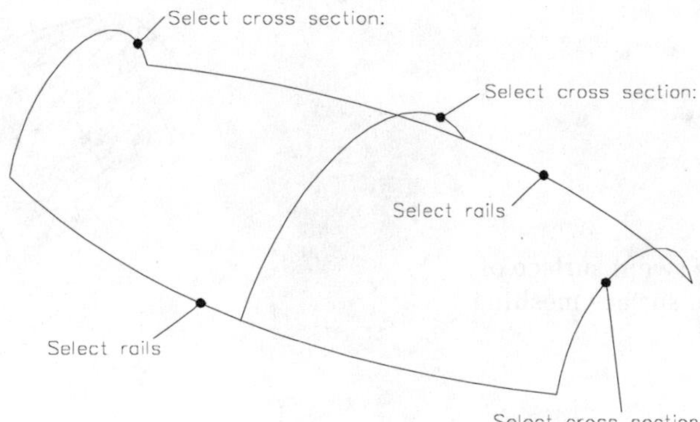

Fig. 4.2 The curves from which the swept surface (Fig. 4.1) was obtained

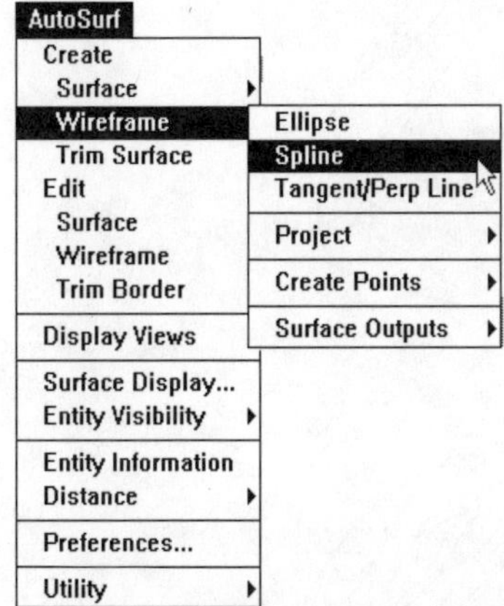

Fig. 4.3 Selecting **Spline** from the **AutoSurf** pull-down menu

Command: *enter* spline3d *right-click*
Create spline by entities/<Locations>: *right-click*
Locate point: *pick* one end of the front curve
Locate point: *pick* one end of the centre curve
Locate point: *pick* one end of the rear curve
Locate point: *right-click*
Command:

Now the wireframe can be formed into a swept surface. For the purpose of the illustration (Fig. 4.1), **U Lines** and **V Lines** were set to 9 and 6 respectively. However, the default values of 5 and 3 could be accepted if wished. To form the surface, either select **Swept** from the **Surface** sub-menu of the **AutoSurf** pull-down menu or, at the command line:

Command: *enter* sweepsf *right-click*
To invoke advanced options enter '??'...
Select cross sections: *pick* **1 found**
Select cross sections: *pick* **1 found**
Select cross sections: *pick* **1 found**
Select cross sections: *right-click*
Select rails: *pick*
Select rails: *pick*
Warning–C0 surface created.
Command:

At this stage do not bother too much about the message **Warning–C0 surface created.** C0, C1 and C2 surfaces will be described later (see pages 116–119).

Figure 4.4 shows the swept surface after surface meshing.

A second example of a swept surface obtained using identical methods is shown in Figs 4.5 to 4.7.

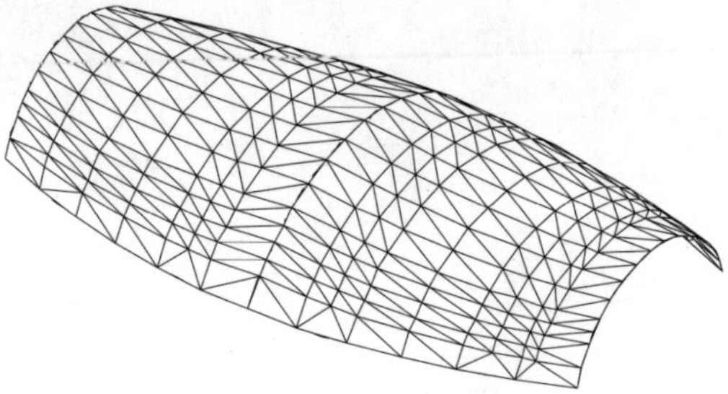

Fig. 4.4 The swept surface of Fig. 4.1 after surface meshing

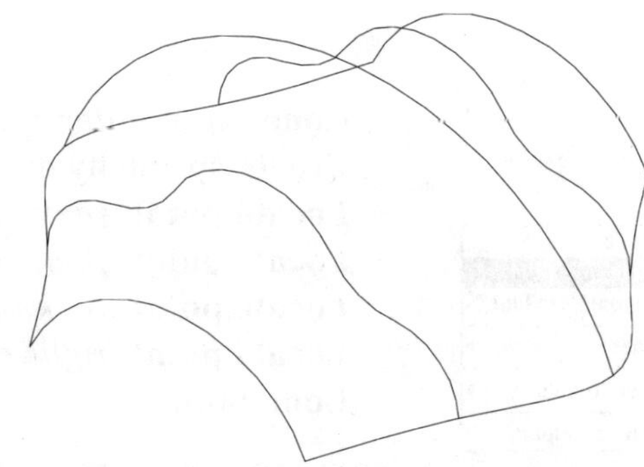

Fig. 4.5 The wireframe for the second example of a swept surface

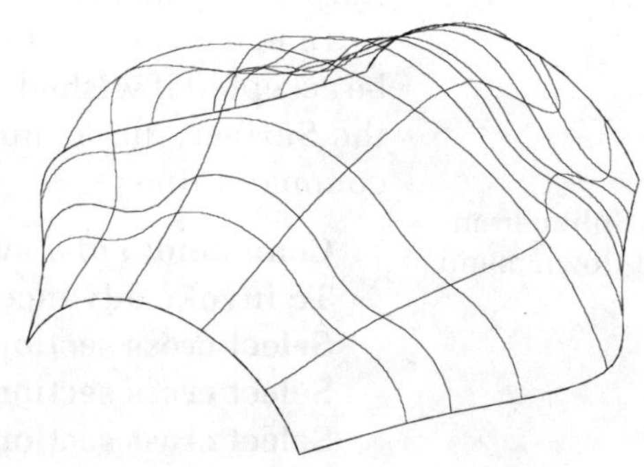

Fig. 4.6 The wireframe of Fig. 4.5 after **sweepsf**

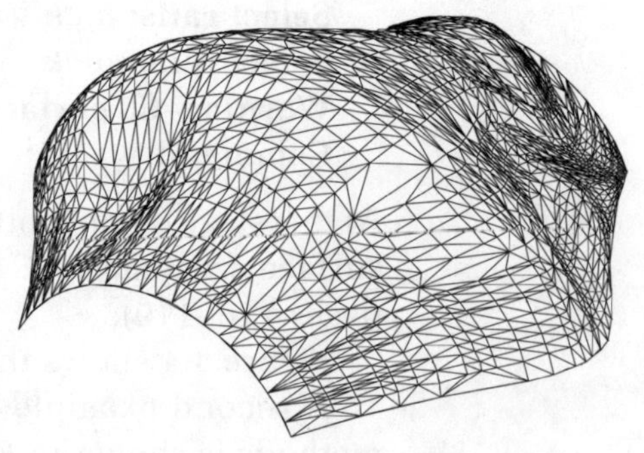

Fig. 4.7 The swept surface after surface meshing

Two examples of models involving swept surfaces

First example

Figures 4.8 to 4.13 show the sequence of stages in constructing this example from the wireframe constructed in AutoCAD (Fig. 4.8) to the surface-meshed model (Fig. 4.13).

When a wireframe had been constructed – the cross-section outlines in **FRONT** and **World** UCS, followed by the ends of the cross-section outlines being joined with the aid of **spline3d** as shown in Fig. 4.8, the single wireframe was surfaced with the aid of **sweepsf**.

The single surface was then mirrored (Fig. 4.9), then copied and the resulting four surfaces placed into the form of a box (Fig. 4.10).

Front and back **planesf** surfaces were added, resulting in the surface model shown in Fig. 4.11. With the aid of **UCS 3point** the model was placed in a UCS onto which an outline of a hole to be cut in the front of the model could be drawn. This outline is indicated in Fig. 4.11 as **Outline for projectsf**.

By projecting this outline onto the front **planesf** surface with the aid of the AutoSurf command **projectsf**, a hole the shape of the

Fig. 4.8 Left. The wireframe outline for the first example

Fig. 4.9 Right. The single wireframe mirrored

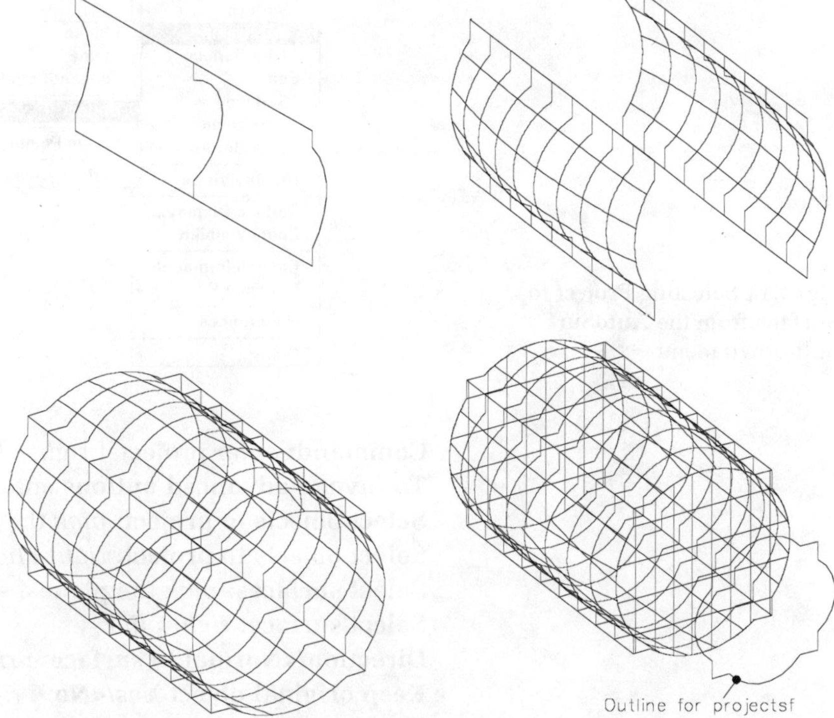

Fig. 4.10 Left. The box outline for the first example after copying and rotating

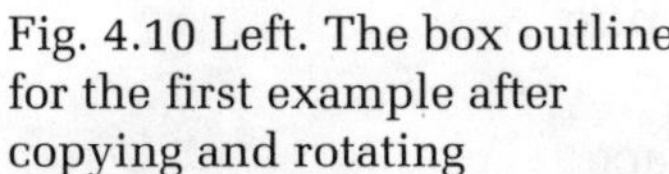
Fig. 4.11 Right. Front and back **planesf** surfaces added and the outline for **projectsf** drawn

outline is cut into and trimmed in the front **planesf** surface as shown in Fig. 4.12. Finally the model is surface meshed as shown in Fig. 4.13.

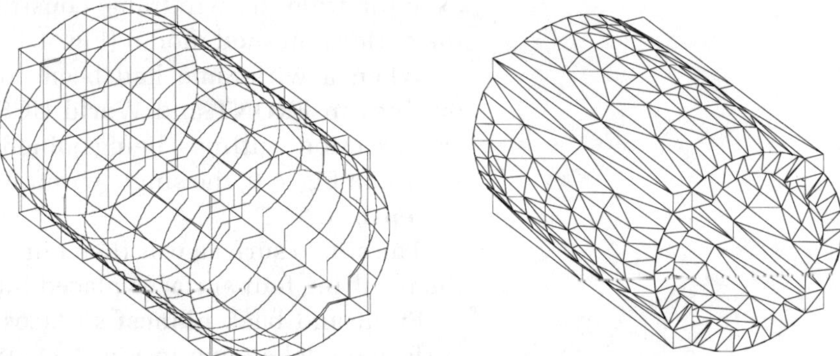

Fig. 4.12 Left. The hole cut in the front of the model with the aid of **projectsf**

Fig. 4.13 Right. The model after surface meshing

To call the **projectsf** command either select **Wireframe/Project** from the **AutoSurf** pull-down menu, followed by selecting **Project to Surface** in the sub-menu which appears (Fig. 4.14) or, at the command line:

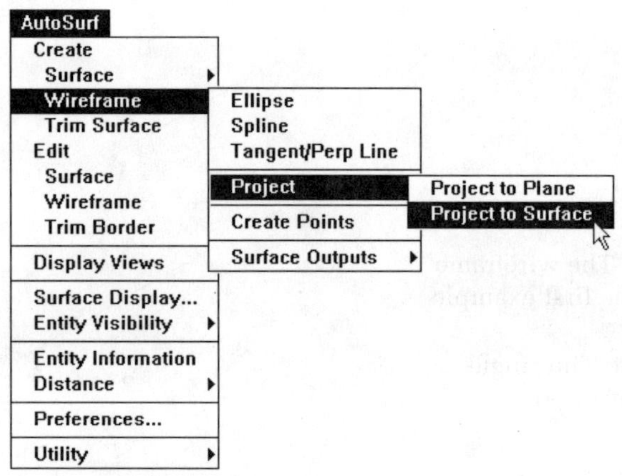

Fig. 4.14 Selecting **Project to Surface** from the **AutoSurf** pull-down menu

Command: *enter* projectsf *right-click*
To invoke advanced options enter '??' ...
Select objects to project: *pick* the outline
Select objects to project: *right-click*
Select surfaces: *pick* the planesf surface
Select surface: *right-click*
Direction/<Normal to surface>: *right-click*
Keep original object Yes/<No>: *right-click*
Command:

Note that in order to have the surface inside the hole trimmed, *enter* ?? when asked and set the options within the **Project** dialogue box which appears as shown in Fig. 4.15.

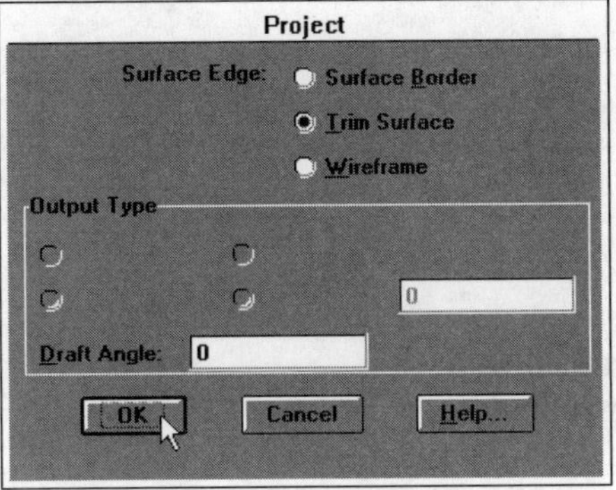

Fig. 4.15 Setting **Trim Surface** in the **Project** dialogue box

Second example

This second example is more complex than the first, but the reader is advised to attempt constructing the model to the descriptions given. Do not bother too much about sizes; the methods of construction using AutoSurf commands are more important. The stages in constructing the model were:

1. Construct a series of ellipses and semi-ellipses as shown in Fig. 4.16, using the UCS **FRONT**, the UCS **World** and UCS **3points** to ensure that the ellipses are accurately drawn. They must be in contact with each other. Figure 4.17 shows the resulting wireframe in three orthographic views.
2. Using the AutoCAD tool **Trim**, trim the ellipses until just one quarter of the wireframe is left. In the **World UCS** add a circle at the bottom of the trimmed ellipses and trim that to a quarter circle.

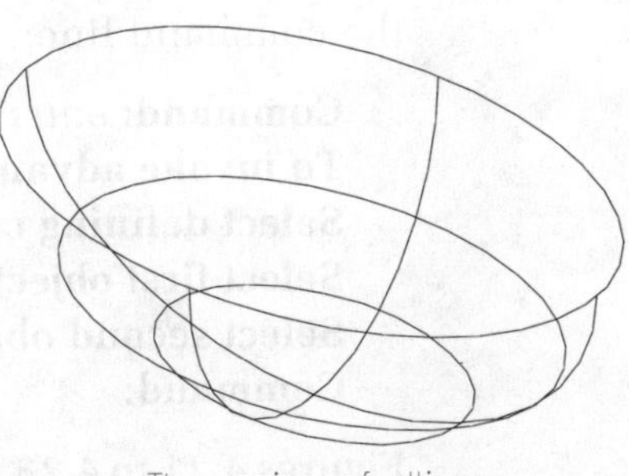

Fig. 4.16 The ellipses upon which the wireframe of the second example is based

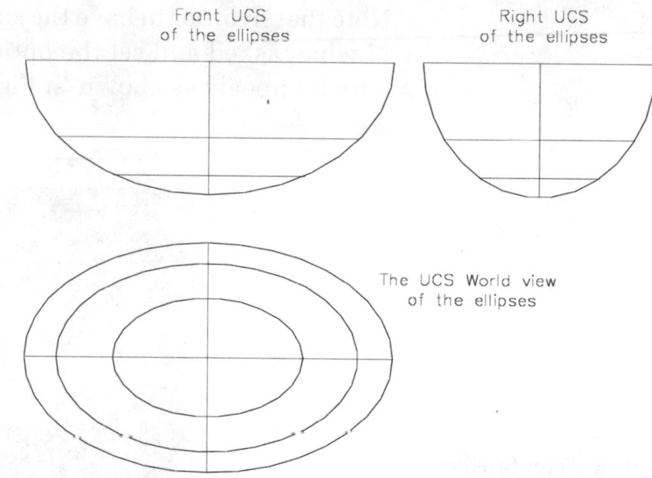

Fig. 4.17 Three orthographic views of the wireframe for the second example

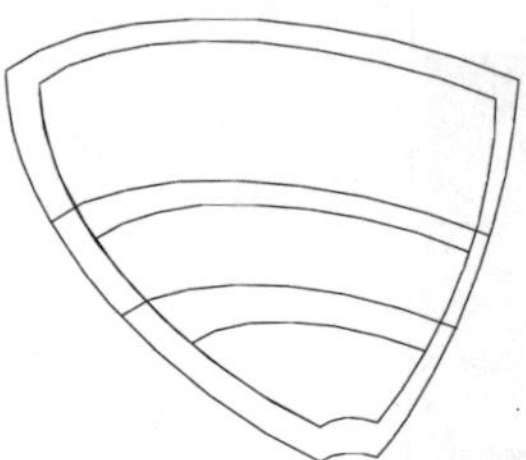

Fig. 4.18 The quarter ellipses and circle for the wireframe outlines

3. With the AutoCAD tool **Offset** offset each part of the wireframe by 10 units as shown in Fig. 4.18.
4. With **sweepsf** form the two swept surfaces as shown in Fig. 4.19.
5. Using AutoCAD **Mirror** complete the bowl as shown in Fig. 4.20.

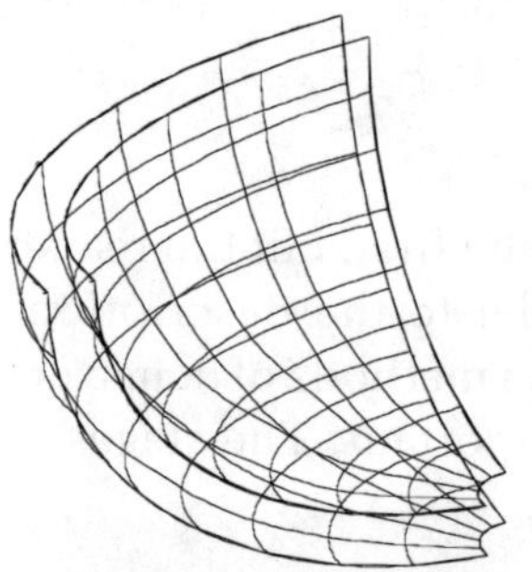

Fig. 4.19 The wireframes after **sweepsf**

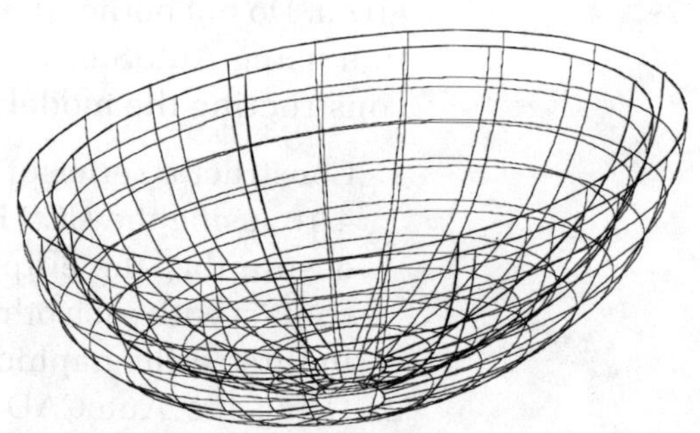

Fig. 4.20 The completed bowl

The command rulesf

Either select **Surface/Rule** from the **AutoSurf** pull-down menu or, at the command line:

Command: *enter* rulesf *right-click*
To invoke advanced options enter '??'...
Select defining curves ...
Select first object: *pick* **1 found**
Select second object: *pick* **1 found**
Command:

Figures 4.21 to 4.23 show the results of using **rulesf** on a wireframe consisting of two arcs. Fig. 4.21 shows the two arcs in AutoCAD space. Figure 4.22 the results of calling **rulesf** and Fig. 4.23 the surface after surface meshing. Figure 4.24 shows the **Ruled Surface** dialogue box called by *entering* **??** in response to the first prompt of the command line sequences when the command is called.

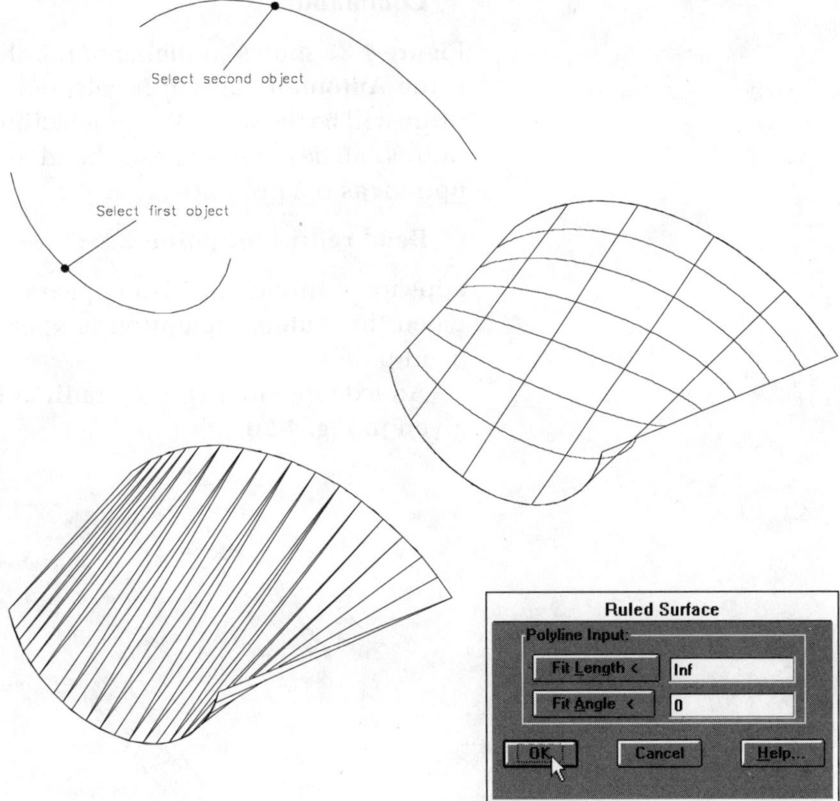

Fig. 4.21 Left. The two objects on which the **rulesf** example are based

Fig. 4.22 Right. The surface after calling **rulesf**

Fig. 4.23 Left. The surface (Fig. 4.22) after surface meshing

Fig. 4.24 Right. The **Ruled Surface** dialogue box

The command tubesf

Before calling the command **tubesf** a line or a pline must first be drawn around which the tubular surface will generate. Only a pline on an XY plane (i.e. any UCS XY plane) can be used as the centre of a tubular surface for the command **tubesf**. Any attempt to form a tubular surface along an arc will fail. However, tubular surfaces can be formed along single lines in 3D space (note – not plines).

To call the **tubesf** command, either select **Surface/Tubular** from the **AutoSurf** pull-down menu or, at the command line:

Command: *enter* tubesf *right-click*
Select a line or polyline: *pick* the pline or line around which the tube is to be formed

Tube diameter <1>: *enter* 20 *right-click*
Automatic/<Manual>: *right-click*
Bend radius for point <20>: *enter* 30 *right-click*
Bend radius for point <20>: *enter* 30 *right-click*
Bend radius for point <20>: *enter* 30 *right-click*
Command:

Figure 4.25 shows a number of tubular surfaces formed in this way. If the **Automatic** option is selected, the radius at all points in the pline will be the same. When selecting the **Manual** option a different radius can be *entered* at each bend in the polyline. With the **Manual** option, as the prompt:

Bend radius for point<20>:

appears, a tiny circle also appears at the defined bend point. But when the **Automatic** option is operating, no circles appear at the bend points.

An example of a varying radii at bend points of the polyline is given in Fig. 4.26.

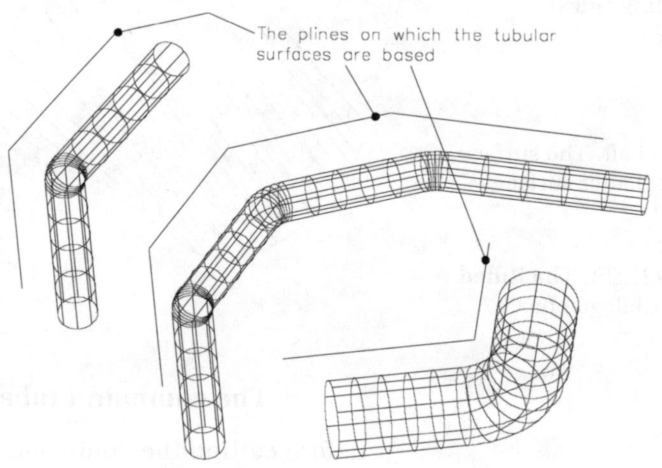

Fig. 4.25 Tubular surfaces formed with the **Automatic** option of **tubesf**

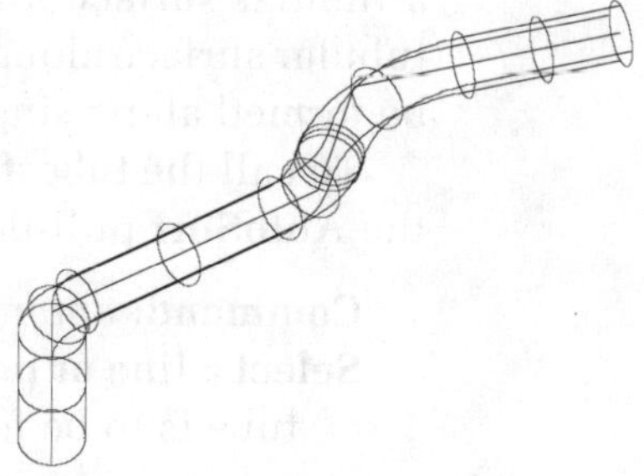

Fig. 4.26 An example of a tubular surface with different radii at bend points

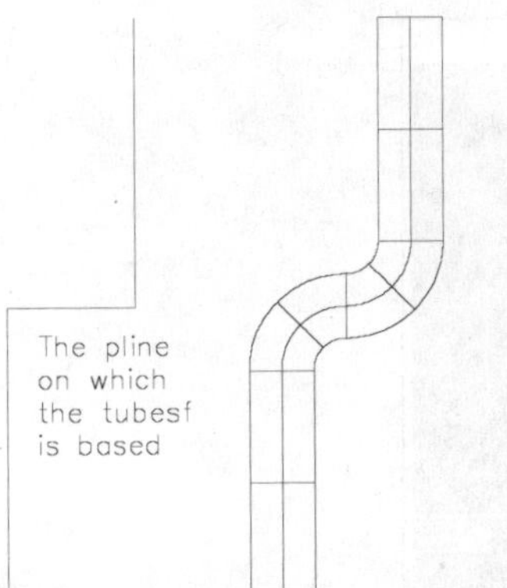

Fig. 4.27 The tubular surface for the first example

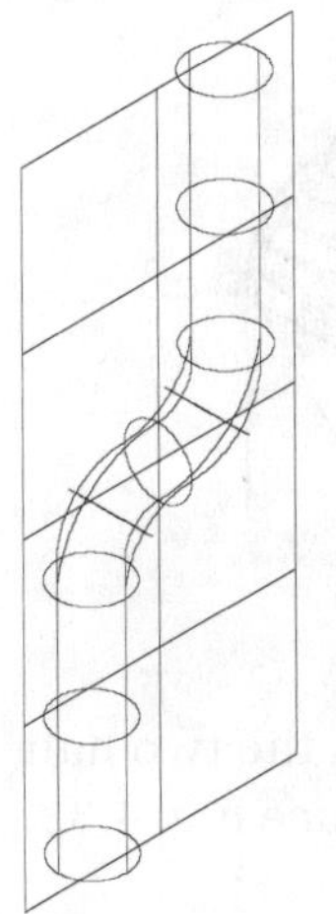

Fig. 4.28 Adding a planar surface through the centre of the tube

Three examples of models involving tubular surfaces

First example

Although the model for this example could have been constructed as a swept surface, we are using **tubesf** and **rulesf** to demonstrate the use of an AutoSurf **Trim** command.

If the reader is to attempt this example, use any convenient sizes – the methods of construction are more important than the dimensions to which the model will be made. The construction commences with the construction of a tubular surface based on the pline shown in Fig. 4.27. In this example the pline has been moved away from the tube. After all it does not form part of the surface and could be erased if thought fit. Then in a **3point** UCS passing through the vertical centre of the tube create a **planesf** rectangle as shown in Fig. 4.28.

Remembering that the tube consists of three separate surfaces – the two straight parts and the bend – trim away one half of the tube using the command **intersf**. To call this command, either select **Intersect/Trim** from the **AutoSurf** pull-down menu (Fig. 4.29) – the settings in the **Surface Intersection** dialogue box are shown in Fig. 4.30 – or, at the command line:

Command: *enter* intersf *right-click*
To invoke advanced options enter '??' ...
Select two surfaces ...
Select first object: *pick*
Select second object: *pick*
Command:

and the surface will be trimmed as shown in Fig. 4.31.

Now place the trimmed tube into the **World** UCS and mirror the half tube so that the two halves so formed are some distance apart.

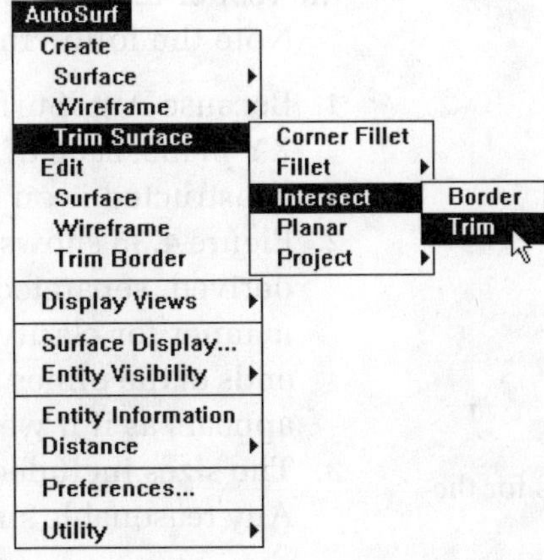

Fig. 4.29 Selecting **Trim** from the **Trim Surface/Intersect** sub-menus of the **AutoSurf** pull-down menu

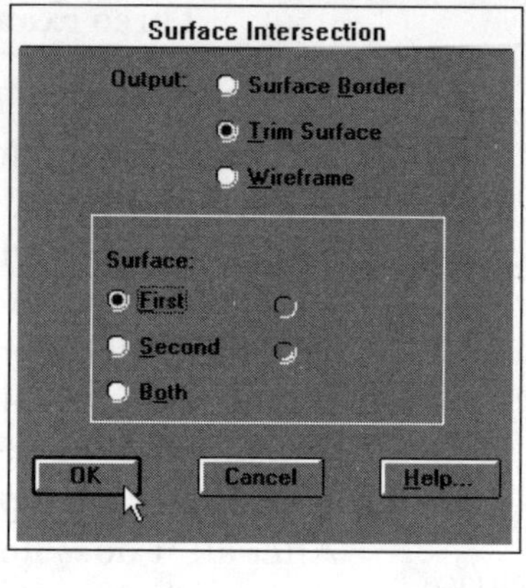

Fig. 4.30 The settings in the **Surface Intersection** dialogue box for the first example

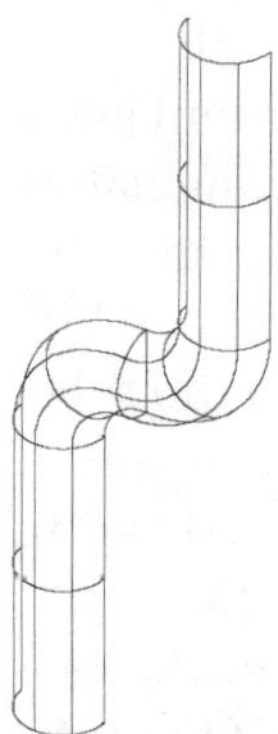

Fig. 4.31 The tube after trimming to the planar surface

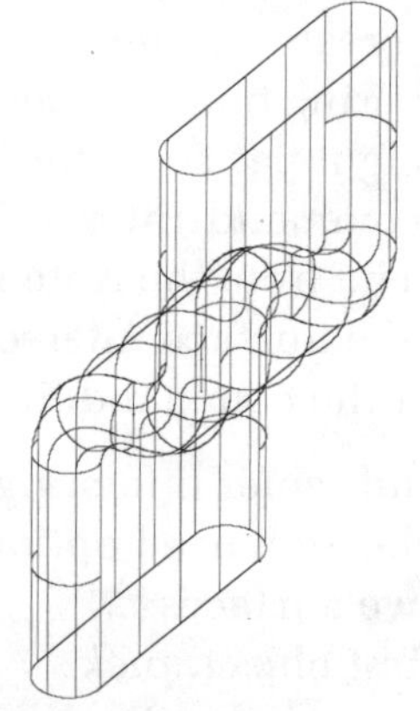

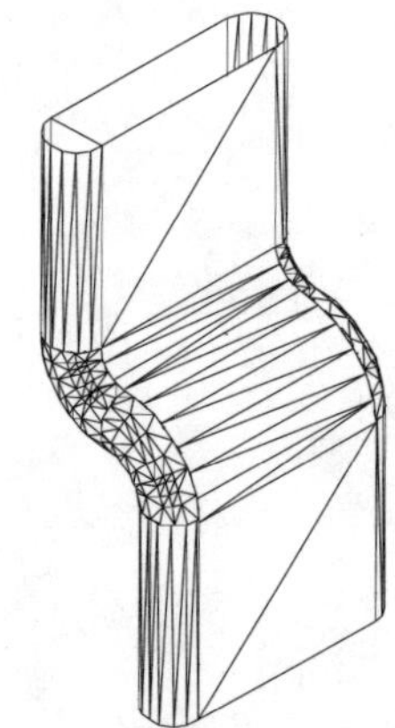

Fig. 4.32 Left. The surfaces of the first example

Fig. 4.33 Right. First example after surface meshing

With the command **rulesf** form ruled surfaces between the two half tubes as shown in Fig. 4.32. Now surface mesh to produce Fig. 4.33.

Second example

This example is an AutoSurf model of a chair constructed from tubular surfaces. Sufficient details are given in Figs 4.34 to 4.36 for the reader to be able to construct the example.

Note the following:

1. Because AutoSurf tubular surfaces can only be constructed in an XY plane, each of the plines from which the parts of the chair are constructed is on a separate UCS plane.
2. Figure 4.35 shows the plines, from which the tubular surfaces are derived, separated from each other. They are only shown in this manner for clarity. When the surfaces are being constructed, the ends of the plines should be touching, so that the pline framework appears as if it were a single entity.
3. The sizes included with Fig. 4.34 are included only for guidance. Any reasonable sizes would be suitable. This example is included

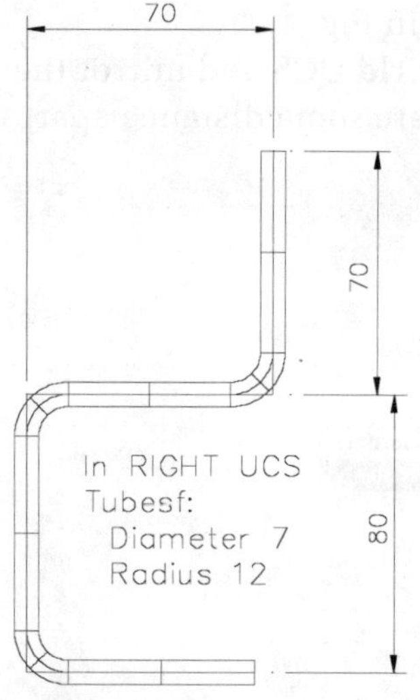

Fig. 4.34 Dimensions for the second example

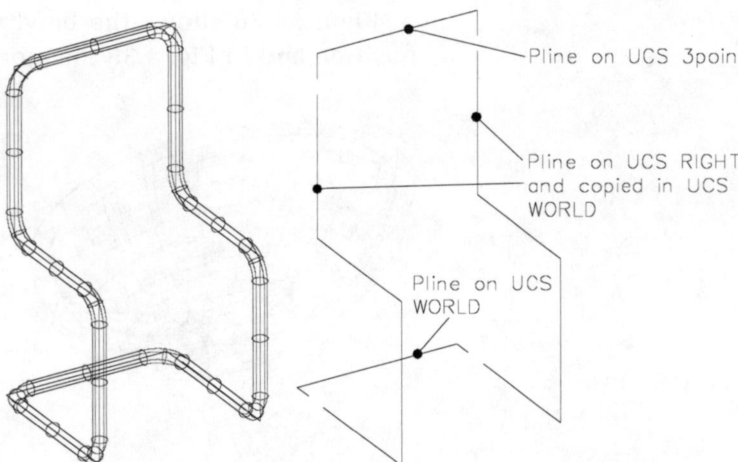

Fig. 4.35 The tubular surfaces for the chair and the plines on which the surfaces were developed

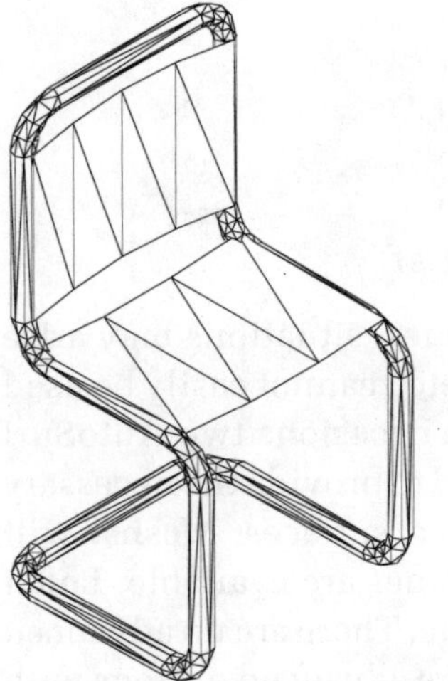

Fig. 4.36 A surface meshing of the chair

to enable the reader to practice the construction of tubular surfaces.

4. The seat and back of the chair, as shown in Fig. 4.36, are ruled surfaces each based on two arcs.

Third example

This example adds an S-bend pipe as a tubular surface to the bowl shown in Fig. 4.20 on page 60. First place the bowl in the **World** UCS, then in a **3point** UCS which cuts through the centre of the bowl. In this **3point** UCS draw a pline on which the tube is to be based. Then call **tubesf** and develop the tubular surface to an appropriate diameter and corner radii. Details of this are shown in Fig. 4.37, with the pline placed to one side of the S bend (remember that such plines are not an essential part of a tubular surface).

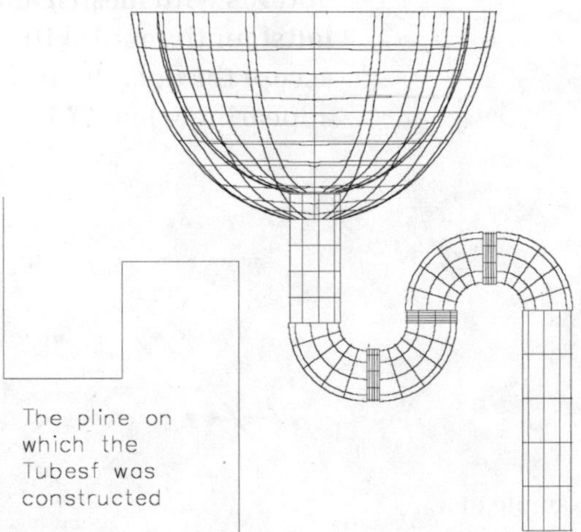

Fig. 4.37 Constructing the tubular surface for the S bend of the bowl

Figure 4.38 shows the bowl with its S bend in a **Display** Iso position and in Fig. 4.39 the model has been surface meshed.

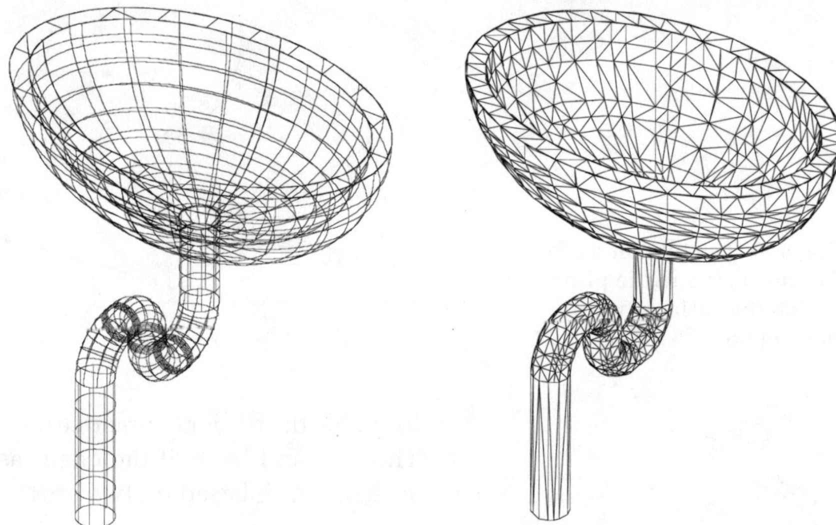

Fig. 4.38 Left. The bowl with its S bend

Fig. 4.39 Right. Fig. 4.37 after surface meshing

The commands meshsf and loftsf

When constructing surfaces from wireframes, situations may arise when commands such as **sweepsf**, **rulesf**, etc., cannot easily be used to produce a satisfactory surface. On such occasions two AutoSurf commands, **meshsf** and **loftsf**, may be found to provide the necessary command systems to produce the required surfaces. **Meshsf** will form surfaces when both U Lines and V Lines are available. **Loftsf** can be used when only U Lines are available. There are no advanced options with **meshsf** and, although there are advanced options with **loftsf**, until more skill is acquired in using AutoSurf, it is as well to accept the default options found in the **Lofted Surface** dialogue box appearing when **??** is *entered* at the first prompt of the command.

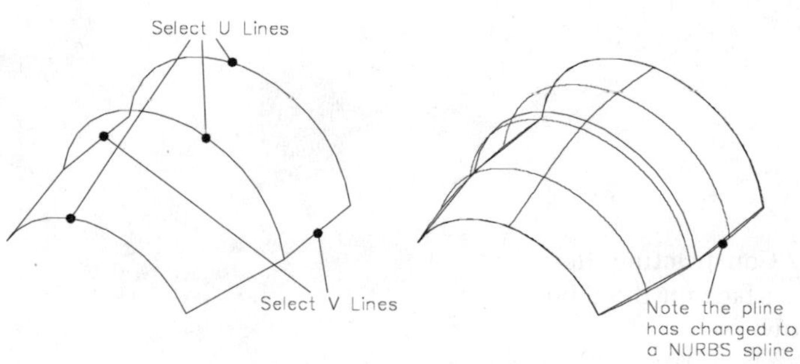

Fig. 4.40 An example of a meshed surface

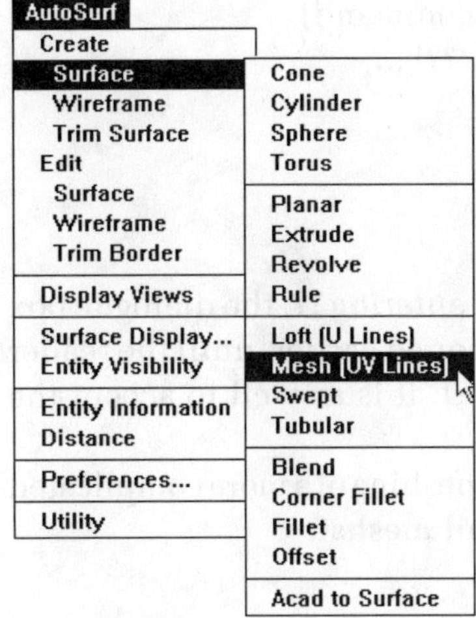

Fig. 4.41 Selecting **Mesh (U/V Lines)** from the **AutoSurf** pull-down menu

An example of a simple meshed surface is shown in Fig. 4.40. A wireframe from three arcs and two plines has been drawn (left-hand drawing). After **meshsf** a surface was formed as shown in the right-hand drawing.

To call the command, either select **Mesh (U/V Lines)** from the **AutoSurf** pull-down menu (Fig. 4.41) or, at the command line:

Command: *enter* meshsf *right-click*
Select U Lines: *pick*
Select U Lines: *pick*
Select U Lines: *pick*
Select U Lines: *right-click*
Select V Lines: *pick*
Select V Lines: *pick*
Select V Lines: *right-click*
Command:

and the meshed surface forms. Notes that the plines forming the V Lines have been changed to NURBS splines (shown in Fig. 4.40).

Now mesh surface the same wireframe constructed without the V Lines, as indicated in Fig. 4.42. Now mesh the surface with the aid of **loftsf**.

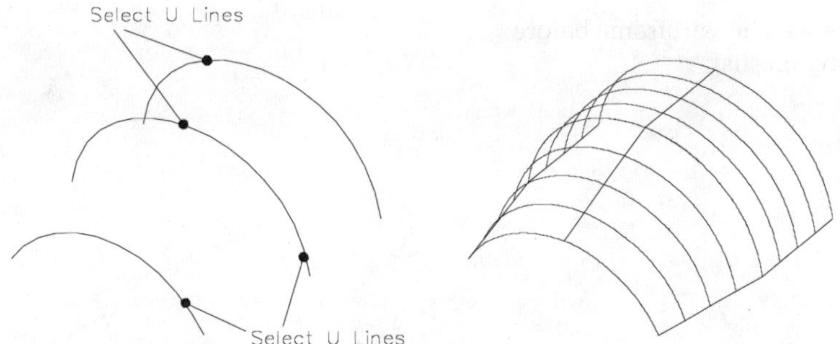

Fig. 4.42 Using **loftsf** to form a surface

To form the surface shown in the right-hand drawing of Fig. 4.42, form the mesh in two stages, first with the front two U Lines, followed by a second stage involving the two rear U Lines.

To call **loftsf**, either select **Loft (U Lines)** from the **AutoSurf** pull-down menu or, at the command line:

Command: *enter* loftsf *right-click*
To invoke advanced options enter '??' ...
Select U Lines: *pick*
Select U Lines: *pick*
Select U Lines: *right-click*

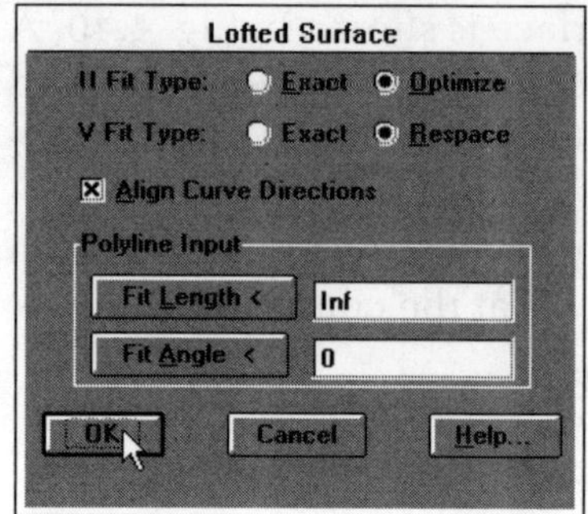

Fig. 4.43 The **Lofted Surface** dialogue box

Command: *right-click* (repeats the command)
To invoke advanced options enter '??' ...
Select U Lines: *pick*
Select U Lines: *pick*
Select U Lines: *right-click*
Command:

If the advanced options are invoked by *entering* **??**, the dialogue box as shown in Fig. 4.43 appears. As mentioned earlier, until the reader becomes more expert in using AutoSurf, it is as well to accept the default settings in this dialogue box.

Figures 4.44 to 4.46 show the surface meshing of a more complicated wireframe with the aid of the command **meshsf**.

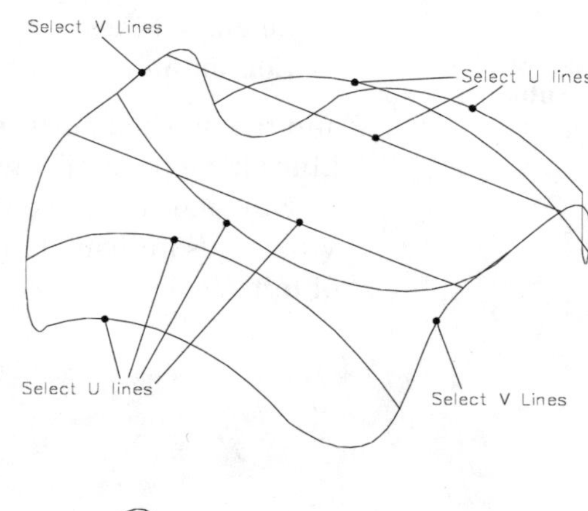

Fig. 4.44 The wireframe before calling **meshsf**

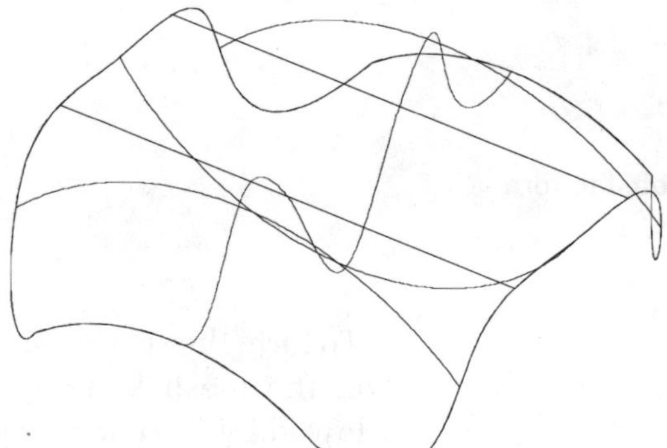

Fig. 4.45 The meshed surface derived from the wireframe

Some further examples of lofted surfaces

It will be remembered that it is not possible to form a surface with the aid of **sweepsf** if the U Lines are from enclosed entities (see page 54).

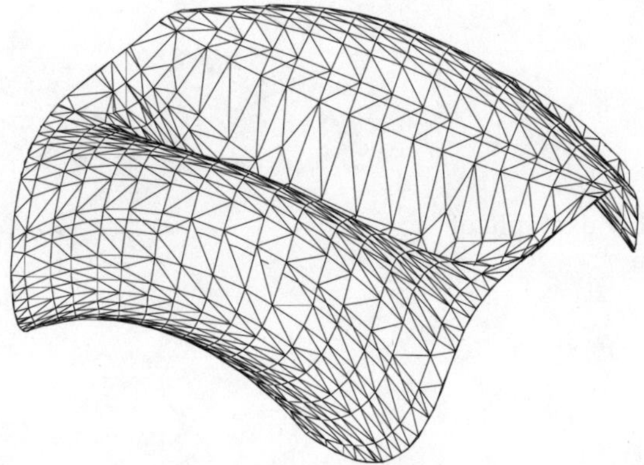

Fig. 4.46 The surface after surface meshing

Providing the settings in the **Lofted Surface** dialogue box are correct, it is possible to form lofted surfaces from U Lines consisting of enclosed entities. The U Lines must be single entities such as plines. Thus for the lofted surface shown in Fig. 4.47, the settings in the **Lofted Surface** dialogue box were amended as shown in Fig. 4.48.

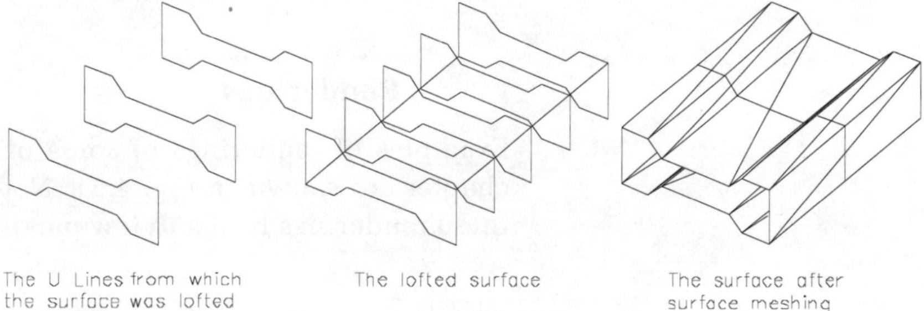

Fig. 4.47 The three stages of producing a lofted surface from U Lines

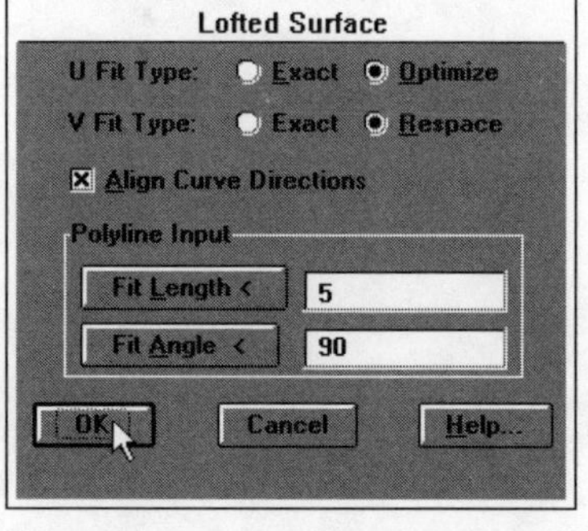

Fig. 4.48 The settings in the **Lofted Surface** dialogue box for the lofted surface of Fig. 4.47

Two further examples of lofted surfaces are shown in Figs 4.49 and 4.50. For Fig. 4.50 the default settings in the **Lofted Surface** dialogue box were accepted.

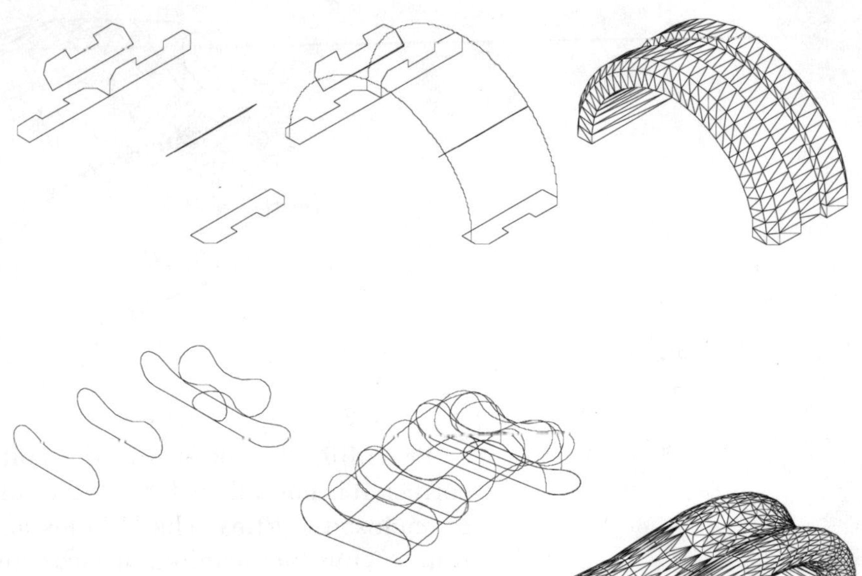

Fig. 4.49 Another example of a lofted surface

Fig. 4.50 A further example

Renderings

Examples of renderings of some of the models described in this chapter are shown in Fig. 4.51. Note that the bottom left hand of these renderings is of a **dview** perspective model.

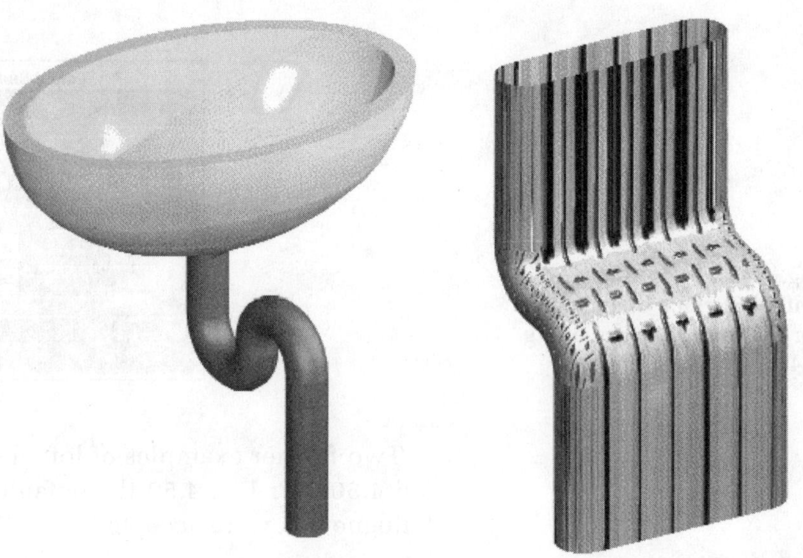

Fig. 4.51 Some examples of renderings of models described earlier in this chapter

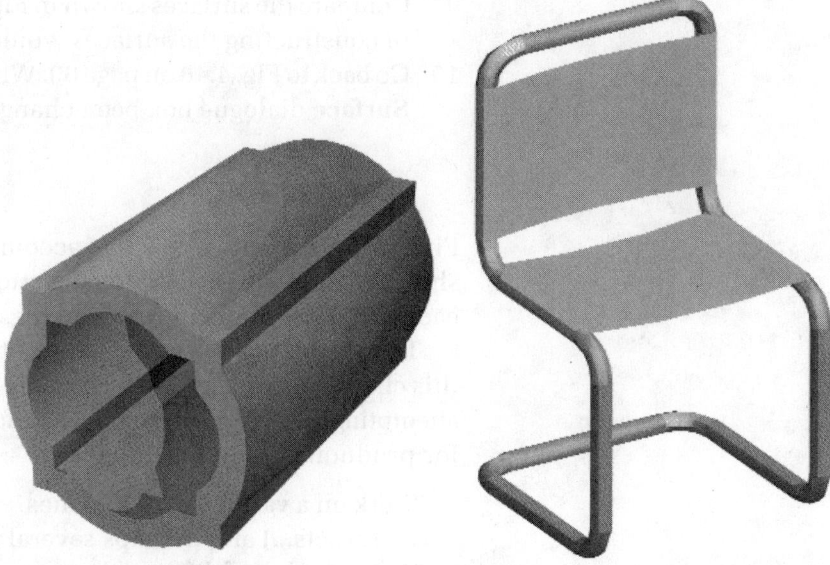

Fig. 4.51 (*Continued*)

Questions

1. Can you name the seven AutoSurf commands for the construction of free-form surfaces?
2. What are the differences between a wireframe for a 3D model, an AutoSurf surfaced model and an AutoSurf surface-meshed model?
3. Why is it important that an operator using AutoSurf is reasonably conversant with using the AutoCAD UCS system if following the methods of constructing AutoSurf models as described throughout this book?
4. It is sometimes not possible to form a surface with the aid of the AutoSurf command **sweepsf** if the U Lines of the wireframe on which the surface is based are closed entities. Is it possible to produce AutoSurf surfaces when U Lines are closed entities? If so which commands are used for the purpose?
5. The command **projectsf** was introduced in this chapter. What is its purpose?
6. The second example of a **sweepsf** surface (a bowl – page 65) required that the ellipses forming the wireframe were trimmed to quarter ellipses. Could the ellipses of the wireframe for bowl have been surfaced in any other manner without having to trim the ellipses to quarters? If so how?
7. If you wish to construct a tubular surface with the radii at bends of varying size, how can this be achieved?
8. The first example of the use of **tubesf** commencing on page 63 could have been constructed using other AutoSurf commands. Can you describe another method of constructing the same surfaces?

9. Compare the surfaces shown in Figs 4.40 and 4.42. Which method of constructing the surfaces would you have used? Give reasons.
10. Go back to Fig. 4.48 on page 69. Why have the settings in the **Lofted Surface** dialogue box been changed from the default values?

Exercises

Five exercises follow. Each is accompanied by a series of drawings showing the sequence of constructions to obtain the final result of each exercise. Some of the drawings include notes.

The reader is advised to attempt the examples given throughout this chapter as well as attempting the exercises in this section. When attempting the exercises remember the following construction techniques for producing AutoSurf models:

Work on a variety of UCS planes – e.g. **FRONT**, **RIGHT** (from **UCS Presets...)** and perhaps several **3point** UCS planes.

Use a number of different layers each of a different colour to enable easier identification of the various surfaces being constructed.

Some of the wireframes illustrated in this section will require the use of the AutoSurf command **spline3d**, which can be used in 3D space. When employing this command, it is best to have the **Osnaps** toolbar showing, so that the **endpoint** osnap can be selected easily.

1. Figures 4.52 and 4.53 show the stages in the construction of this exercise. Working to any convenient sizes, construct the AutoSurf model shown in Fig. 4.53 as Stage 6.
2. Figure 4.54 shows a front view and a plan in first-angle projection of the wireframe on which the surface mesh shown in Fig. 4.55 (Stage 3) is based.

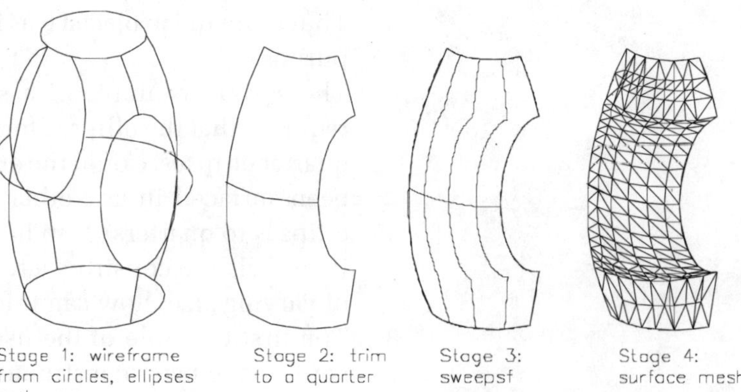

Fig. 4.52 The first four stages in the construction of Exercise 1

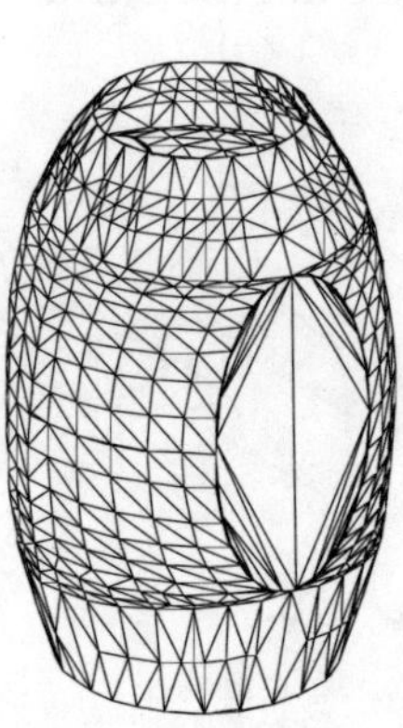

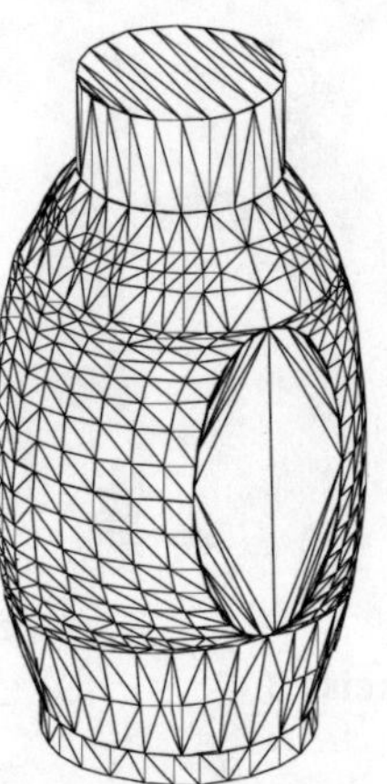

Fig. 4.53 The final two stages in the construction of Exercise 1

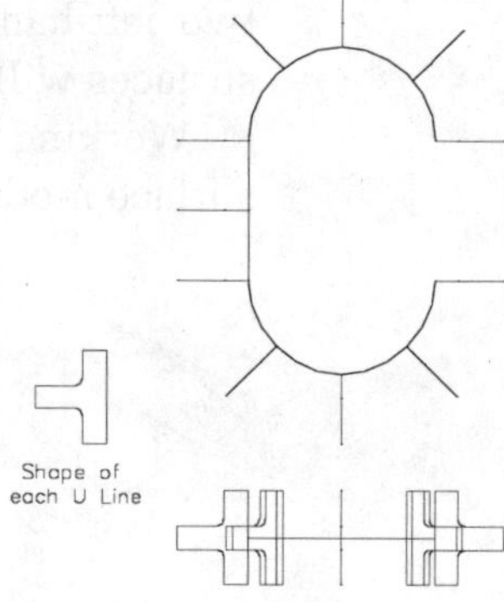

Fig. 4.54 A front view and plan of the wireframe for Exercise 2

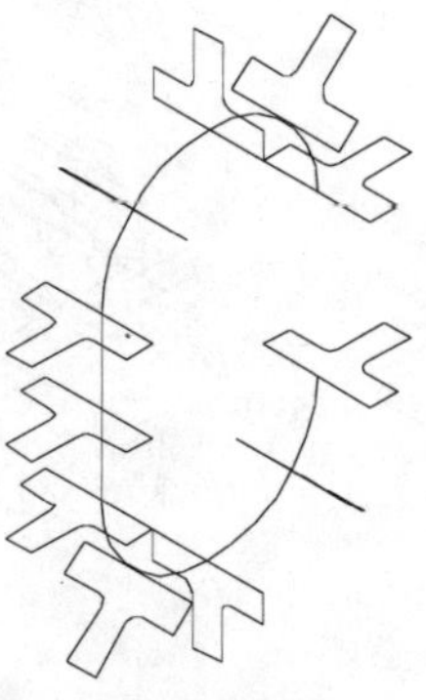

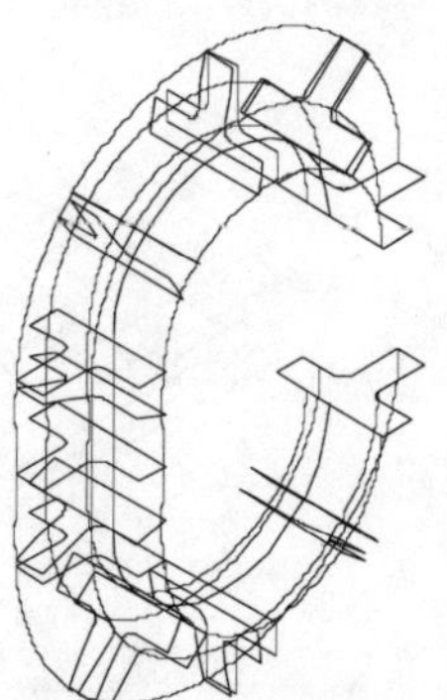

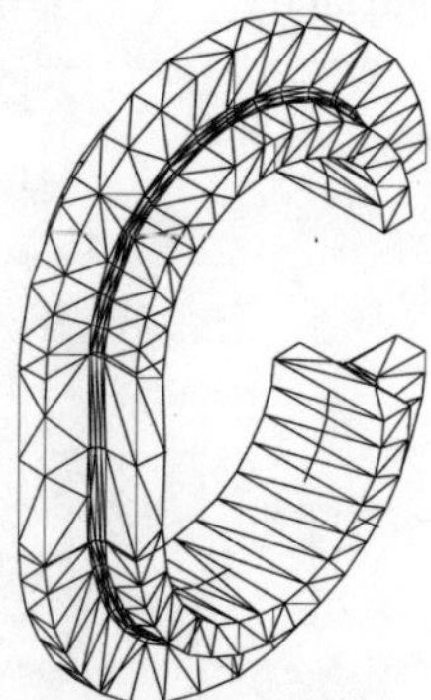

Fig. 4.55 The stages in the construction of Exercise 2

Working to any convenient sizes, construct the wireframe and from it complete the AutoSurf surface mesh of the object.

3. Construct the surface mesh given in Fig. 4.56 (Stage 3).

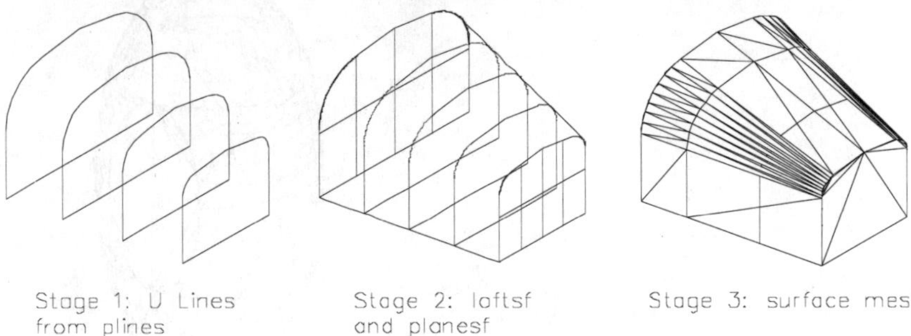

Fig. 4.56 Exercise 3

4. This exercise requires the use of the AutoSurf command **filletsf**. AutoSurf fillets cannot be formed from two **C0** surfaces. Figure 4.57 shows how, in this exercise, C0 surfaces can be avoided. In Fig. 4.57, the left-hand and centre surfaces are **C0**. The right-hand surface is **C2**. To **loftsf** or **sweepsf** from the U Lines as shown in the two left-hand drawings results in a C0 surface. C0, C1 and C2 surfaces will be described later (page 116).

   Working to the details given in Fig. 4.58 construct the meshed surface model shown in Stage 4.

loftsf from 2 closed plines — sweepsf from 2 closed plines — sweepsf from 2 plines

Fig. 4.57 Avoiding a C0 surface

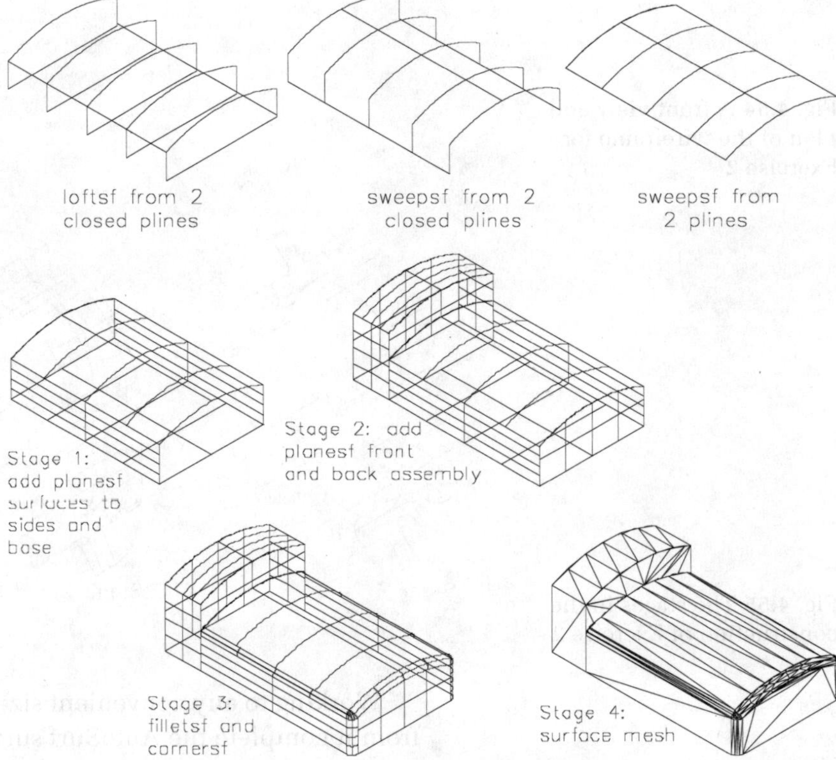

Fig. 4.58 The stages of construction for Exercise 4

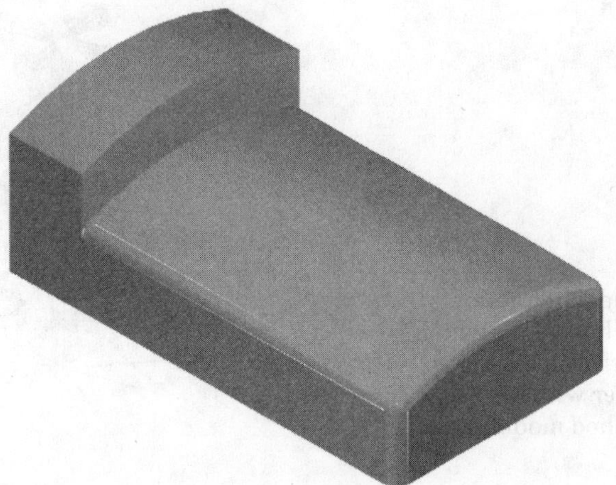

Fig. 4.59 A rendering of the surface-meshed model resulting from Exercise 4

5. This exercise is considerably more difficult than the previous ones, but the reader is advised to attempt it.

   The construction follows the sequence described in Figs 4.60 to 4.62.

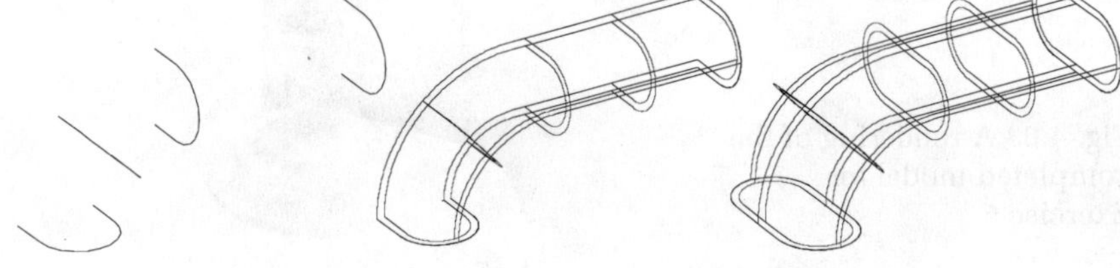

Fig. 4.60 Stages in the construction of the wireframe for the spout

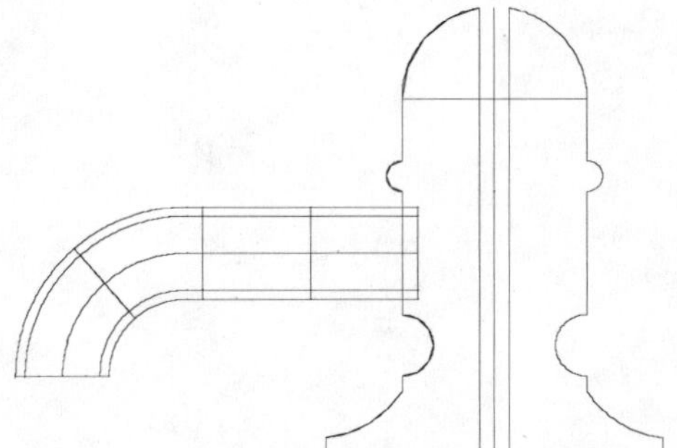

Fig. 4.61 A side view of the wireframe for the **revolvesf** surface of the tap

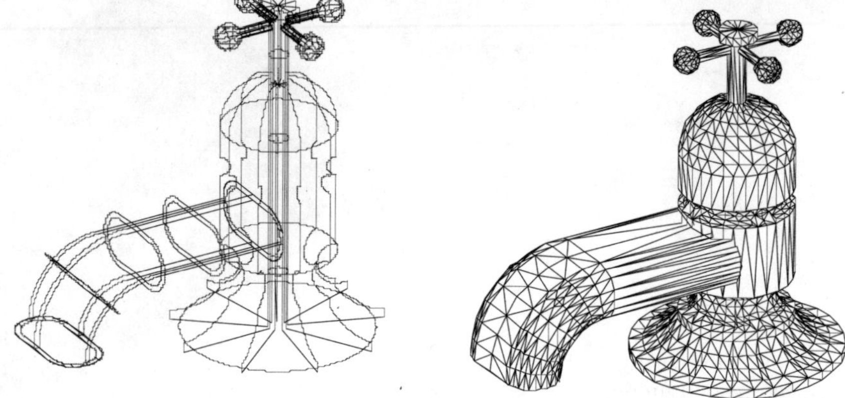

Fig. 4.62 The wireframe, including a handle on which the final surface meshing is base, together with the surface-meshed model

Figure 4.63 shows a rendering of the completed model.

Fig. 4.63 A rendering of the completed model for Exercise 5

CHAPTER 5

Blendsf, projectsf and intersf

Introduction

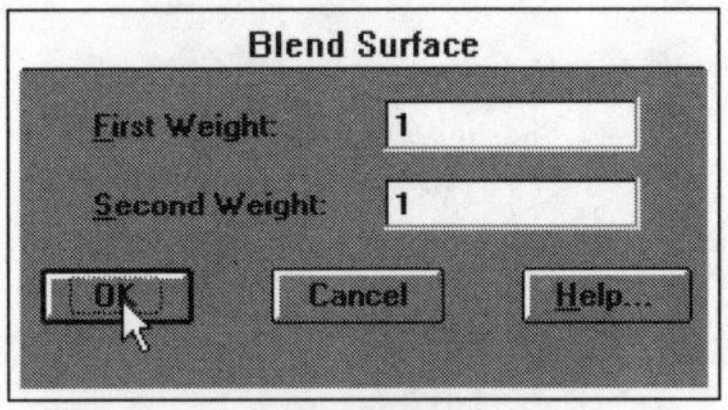

There are a number of commands in the AutoSurf command structure for obtaining new surfaces from existing surfaces and for the editing of existing surfaces. In this chapter we deal with some of these commands systems. **Blendsf** creates new surfaces from existing surfaces; **projectsf** edits existing surfaces to obtain new surfaces; **intersf** edits existing surfaces by a process of trimming. One other command, **joinsf**, will be introduced in this chapter to compare its actions with those of **blendsf**.

Fig. 5.1 The **Blend Surface** dialogue box with its default settings

The command blendsf

The use of this command allows several surfaces to be blended together with surfaces similar to those created with **filletsf**. The curve of the surface generated with its use will be tangential to the existing surfaces. The shape of the blended surface can be affected by **Weight** settings in the **Blend Surface** dialogue box which appears on screen when the response to the prompt **To invoke advanced options enter ?? ...** is to *enter* ??. Figure 5.1 shows the **Blend Surface** dialogue box with default settings.

To call the command, either select **Blend** from the **AutoSurf** pull-down menu (Fig. 5.2) or, at the command line:

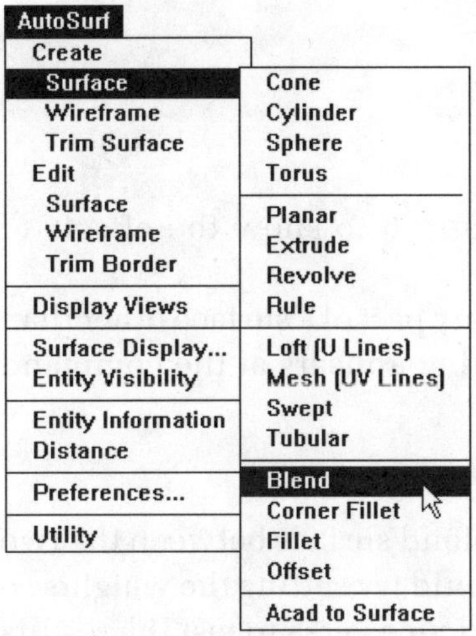

Fig. 5.2 Selecting **Blend** from the **AutoSurf** pull-down menu

Command: *enter* blendsf *right-click*
To invoke advanced options enter '??' ...
Select first object: *pick*
Select first object: *pick*
Select first object: *right-click*
Command:

Figure 5.3 shows the effects of using the command to blend three existing **planesf** surfaces. Figure 5.4 shows the effects of blending surfaces with **Weight 1** set to 1 and **Weight 2** set to 2. In Fig. 5.4, **U**

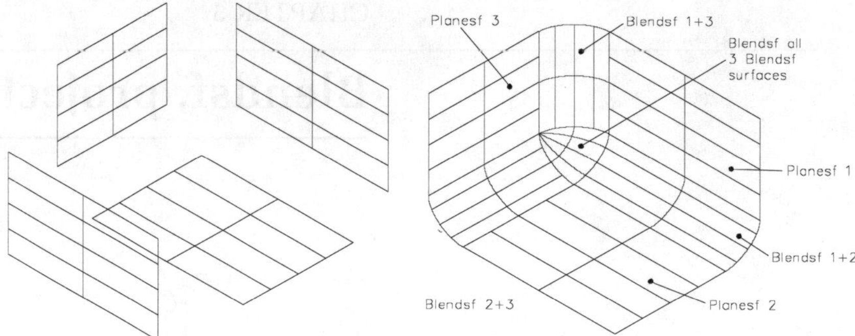

Fig. 5.3 Using **blendsf** to blend existing **planesf** surfaces

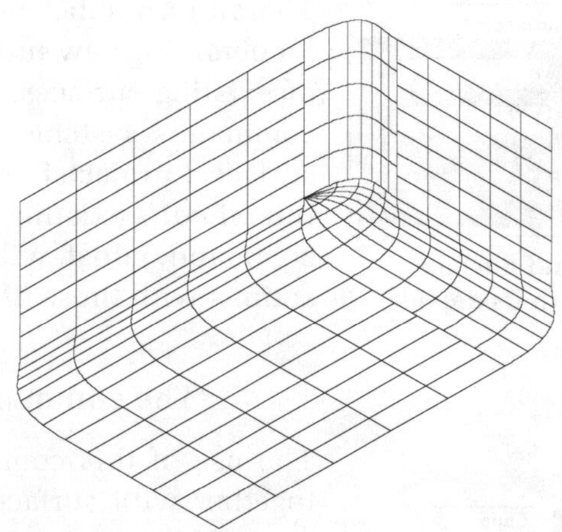

Fig. 5.4 Using **blendsf** with **Weight 1** set to 1 and **Weight 2** set to 3

Lines have been set to 8 and **V Lines** to 6 to show the effects of amending weighting more clearly.

Up to four objects can be picked. If any part of a surface other than an edge is picked, the following warning appears at the command line:

Error – Only slab surface edges may be selected.

Weighting affects the tangency of the blend surface between the two surfaces being blended. The reader should try setting the weights so that **Weight 1** is 2 and **Weight 2** is 1 and vice versa to test the results of amending weights in the **Blend Surface** dialogue box.

Figure 5.5 is an example of a tray constructed from five **planesf** surfaces with corners blended with the aid of **blendsf**. Figure 5.6 shows a box with sides constructed from **sweepsf** surfaces with blended corners.

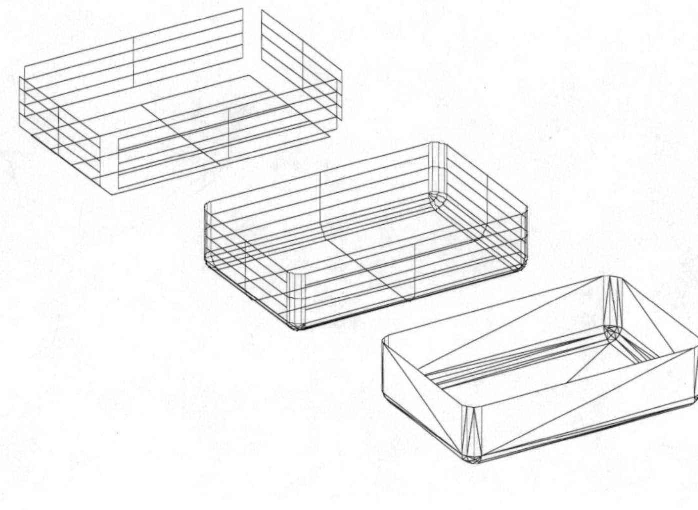

Fig. 5.5 Three stages in constructing a tray from **planesf** surfaces with the aid of **blendsf**

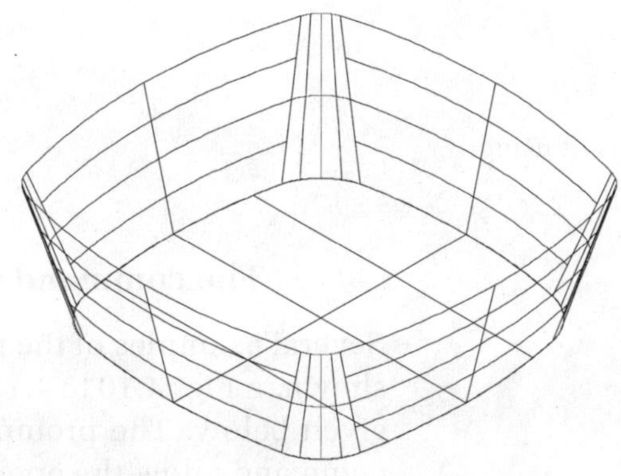

Fig. 5.6 Four **sweepsf** surfaces blended with **blendsf**

The command joinsf

Another AutoSurf command, **joinsf**, appears to have similar results to **blendsf**. However, only two surfaces can be joined with the aid of **joinsf**. Thus, Fig. 5.7 shows that because only two surfaces can be joined, a similar result to that shown in Fig. 5.6 cannot be achieved. Figure 5.7 shows a compromise solution to constructing a box from **sweepsf** surfaces when using **joinsf**.

To call the command either select **Join** from the **AutoSurf** pull-down menu (Fig. 5.8) or, at the command line:

Command: *enter* joinsf *right-click*
To invoke advanced options enter '??' ...
Select surfaces to join: *pick*
Select surfaces to join: *pick*
Select surfaces to join: *right-click*
Select surfaces: *right-click*
Command:

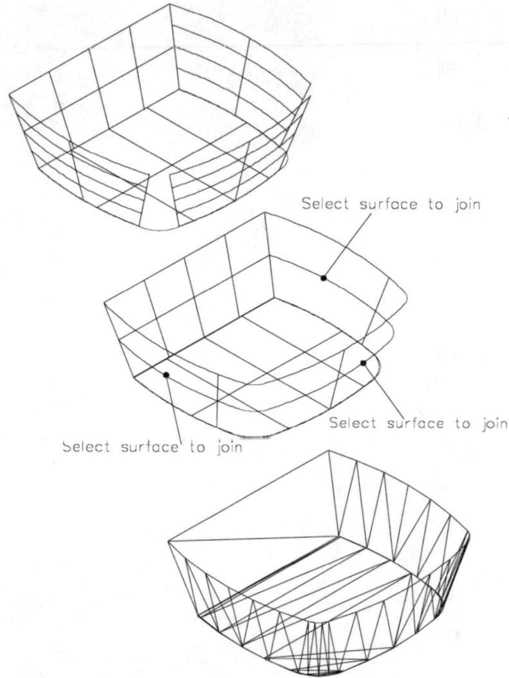

Fig. 5.7 The effects of using **joinsf**

The command projectsf

Several examples of the results of using the command **projectsf** are shown in Figs 4.10 to 4.13 on pages 57 and 58. Further examples are given below. The prompts in the command line sequence for the command allow the operator to project an outline:

To cut a surface.
To allow the outline being projected to be kept or not kept.
To cut through several surfaces.
To cut surfaces in any direction, including the normal (perpendicular) to the surface.
To trim either outside the outline projection or inside the outline projection.

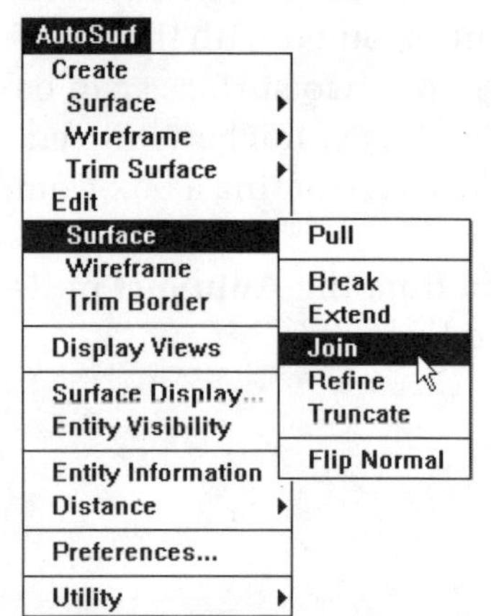

Fig. 5.8 Selecting **Join** from the **AutoSurf** pull-down menu

To call the command either select **Project/Trim** from the **AutoSurf** pull-down menu (Fig. 5.9) or, at the command line:

Command: *enter* projectsf *right-click*
To invoke advanced options enter '??' ...
Select objects to projects: *pick*
Select objects to projects: *right-click*
Select surfaces: *pick*
Select surfaces: *right-click*
Direction/<Normal to surface>: *right-click*

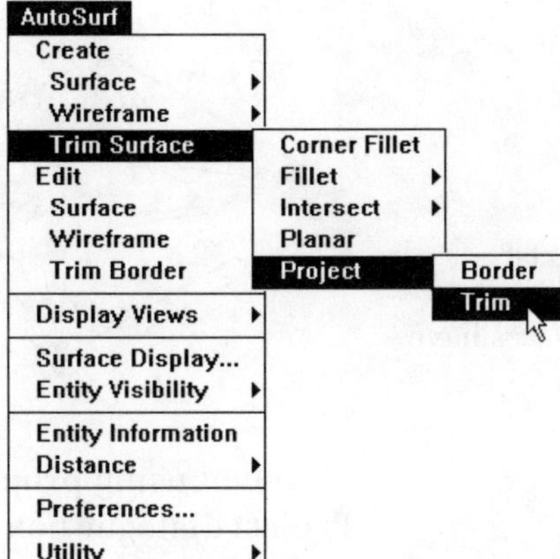

Fig. 5.9 Selecting **Trim** from the **AutoSurf** pull-down menu

Keep original objects: Yes/<No>: *enter* y (Yes) *right-click*
Command:

Figure 5.10 presents outlines to be projected and the surfaces onto which they are to be projected. Figures 5.11 to 5.13 show the results of using **projectsf** on various surfaces.

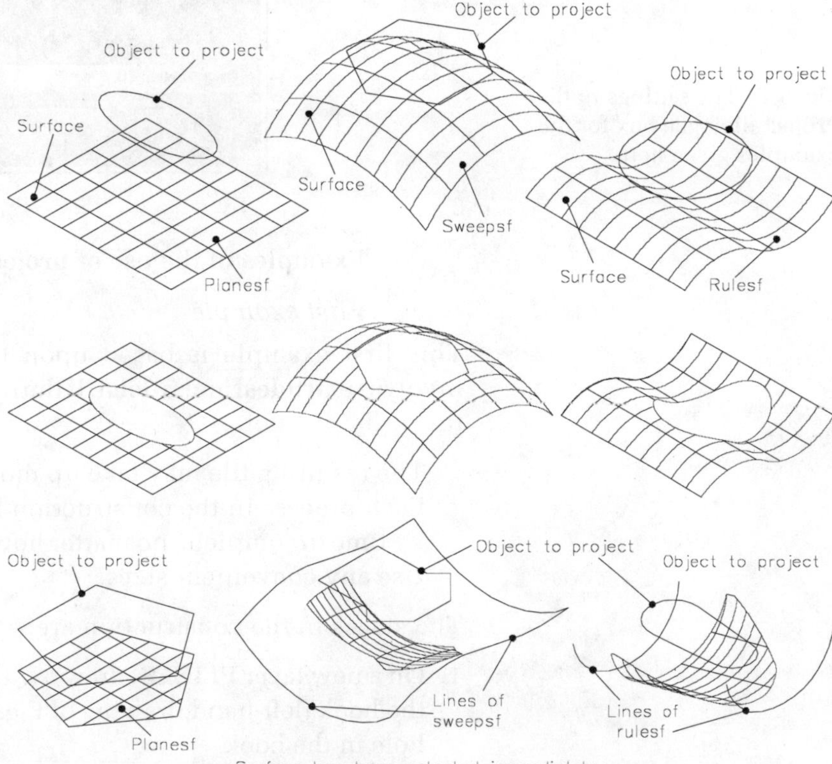

Fig. 5.10 Outlines to be projected and the surfaces on to which they are to be projected

Fig. 5.11 The results of using **projectsf** on the surfaces of Fig. 5.10

Fig. 5.12 The effects of using **projectsf** when the point on the surface has been picked directly below the outline being projected

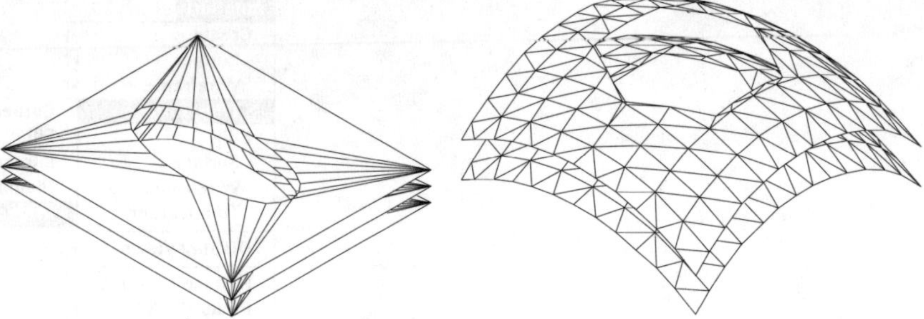

Fig. 5.13 Using **projectsf** through several surfaces. In this example the surfaces have been surface meshed

When using **projectsf** it is advisable to check the settings in the **Project** dialogue box which appears when **??** is *entered* as a response to the first prompt. Figure 5.14 shows the settings for the examples given above.

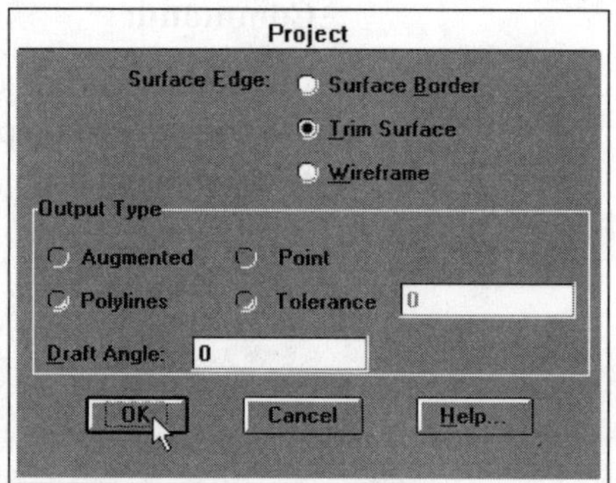

Fig. 5.14 The settings in the **Project** dialogue box for the examples given here

Examples of the use of projectsf

First example

This first example is based upon the use of **projectsf**, but also involves **extrudesf** and **filletsf**. If the reader is attempting to construct this example, note:

The resulting file may take up more than a Mbyte of disk space.
Each process in the construction takes a considerable period of time to complete, no matter how fast the computer being used.
Use any convenient sizes.

The stages in the construction are:

1. On a new layer **PLINES**, draw a pline outline of the outer shape of the hook (left-hand drawing of Fig. 5.15) and add the circle of the hole in the hook.

Plate I Figure 7.6 showing the colours used in a three-viewport screen of the wireframe for an AutoSurf model

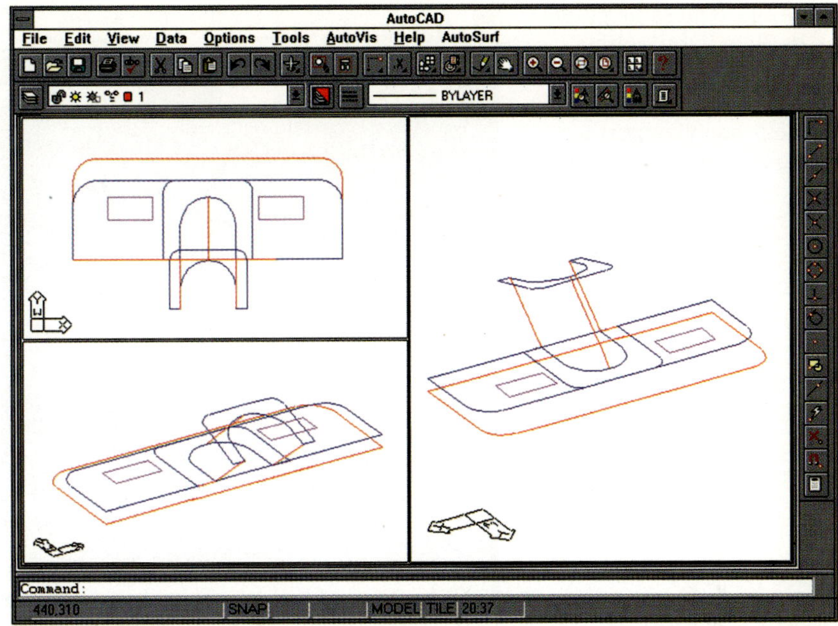

Plate II Figure 7.8 showing the colours used in a four-viewport screen, in which the largest viewport is a rendering of the completed AutoSurf model

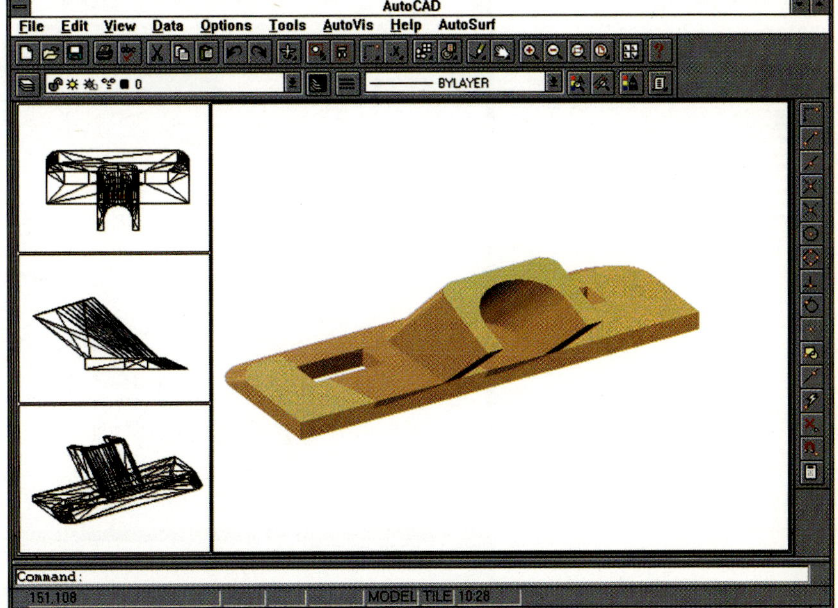

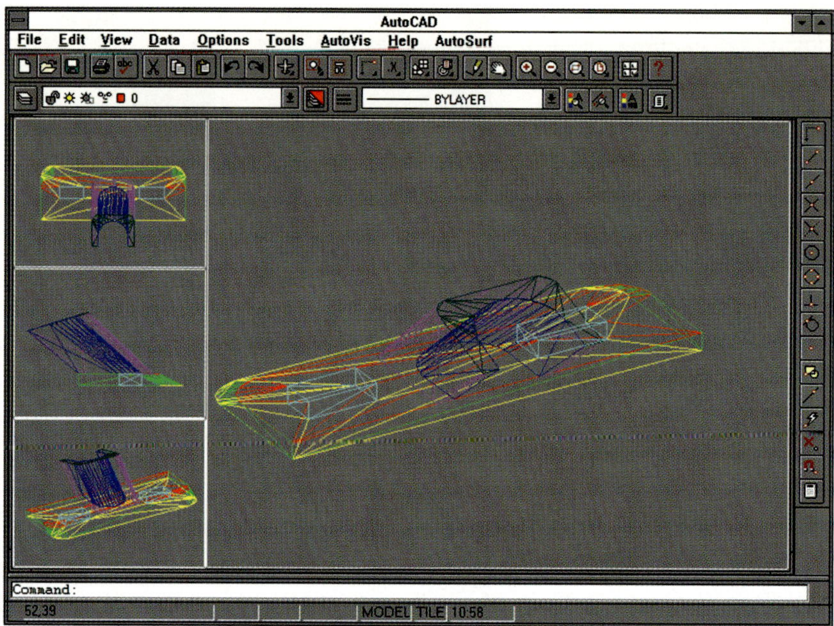

Plate III The same model as in Plate II, but with a different AutoCAD background colour and without one viewport being rendered

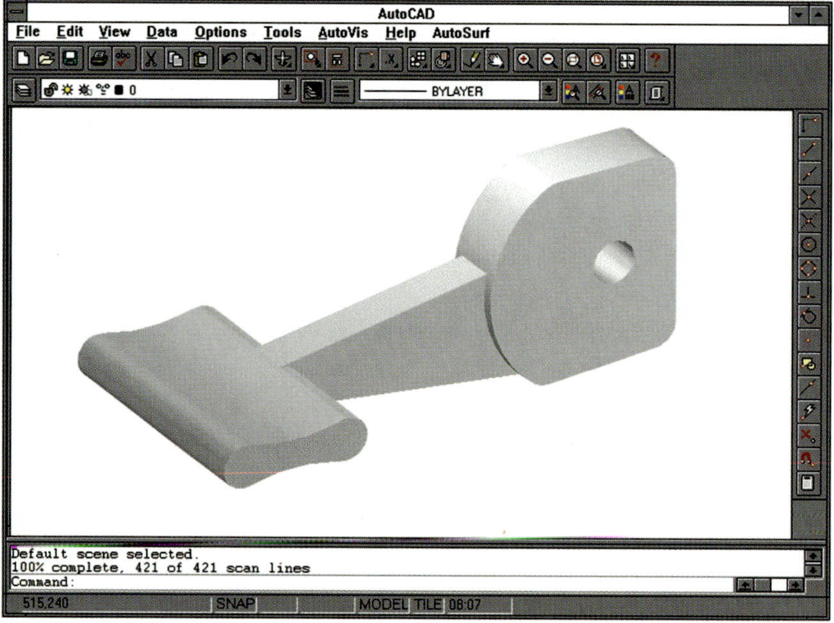

Plate IV The first example of Chapter 9 showing a default rendering without materials

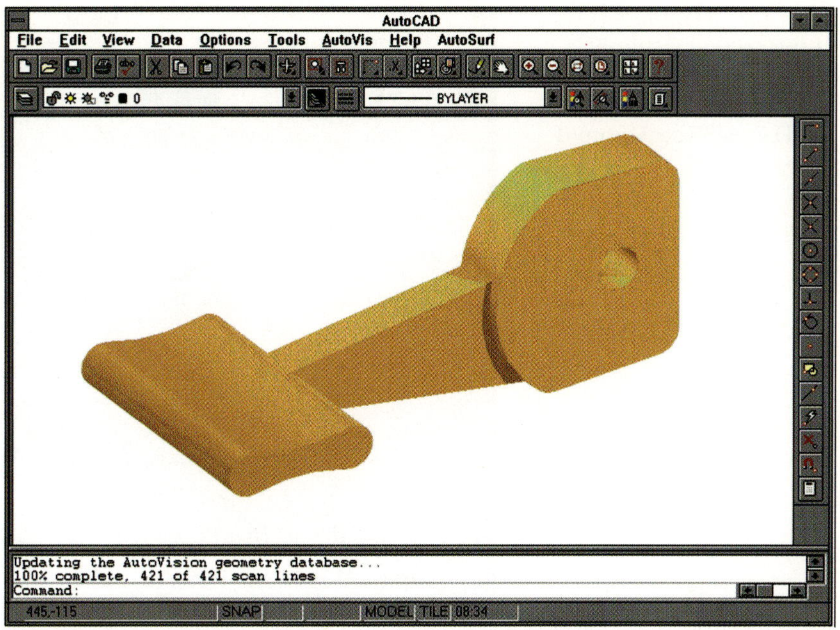

Plate V The first example of Chapter 9 showing a full rendering in the material BRASS GIFMAP

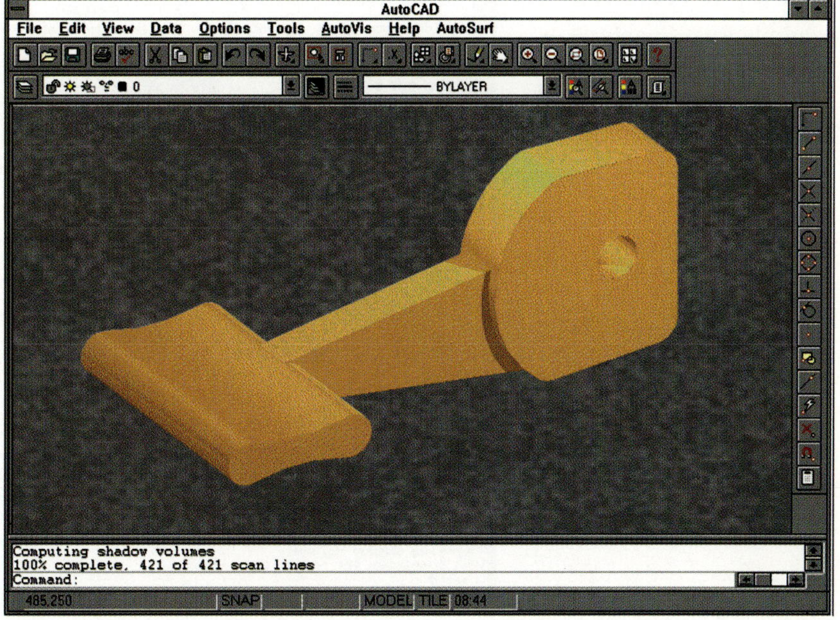

Plate VI The first example of Chapter 9 showing a rendering in BRASS GIFMAP against a CEMENT background

Plate VII The rendering of the second example from Chapter 9 – GREEN GLASS material against a WHITE_ASH background

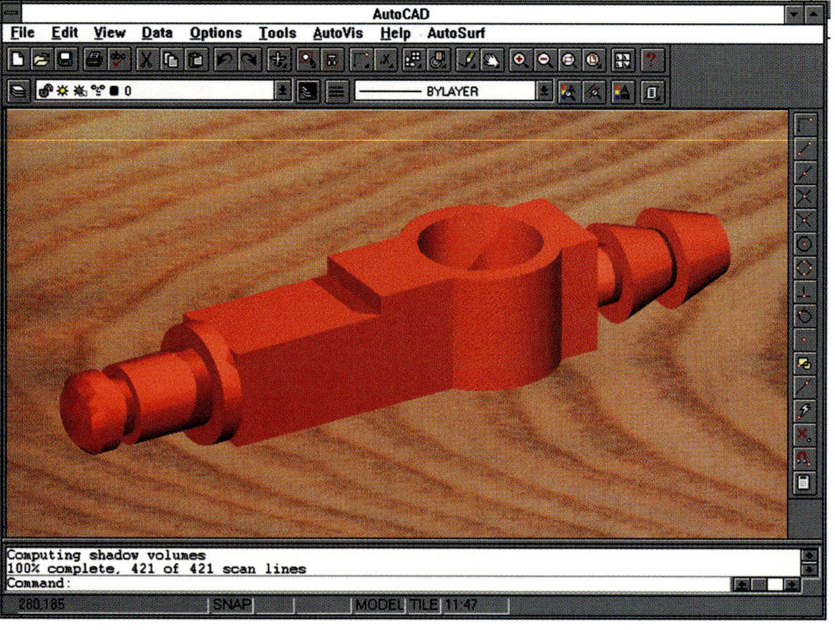

Plate VIII The third example from Chapter 9 – CHERRY RED METAL material against MED_ASH background

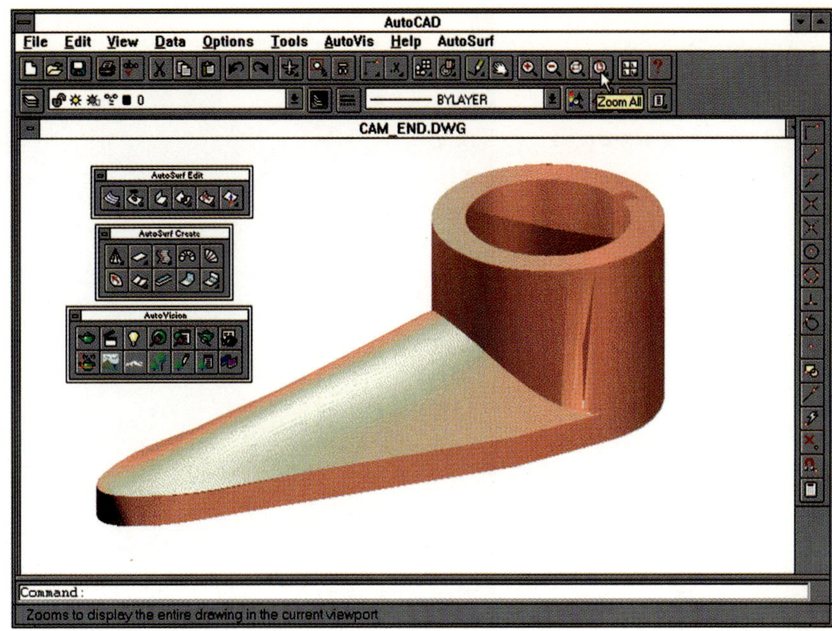

Plate IX A rendering of the model shown in Figure 6.22 – COPPER material. The toolbars for AutoSurf and AutoVision are showing on screen

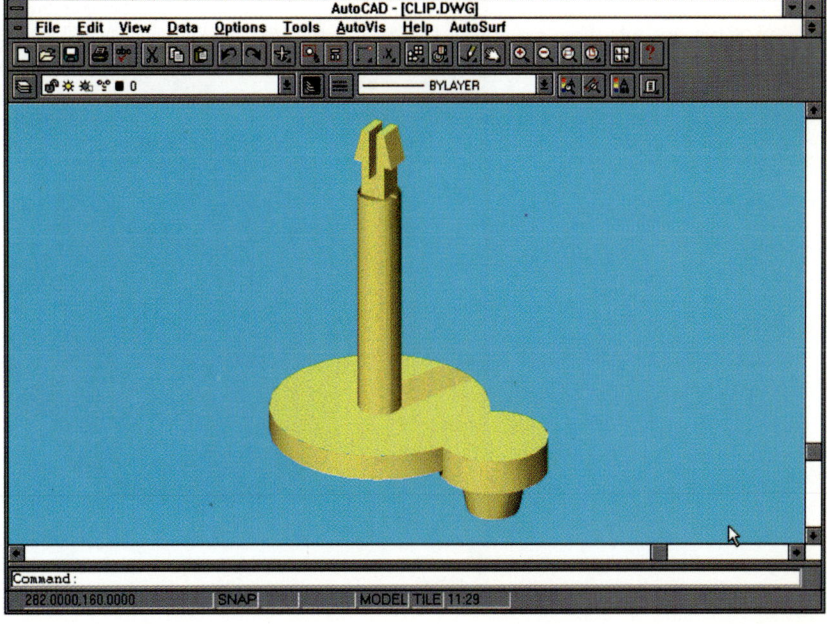

Plate X A rendering of an AutoSurf model of a plastic clip, part of a water-spraying pressure system

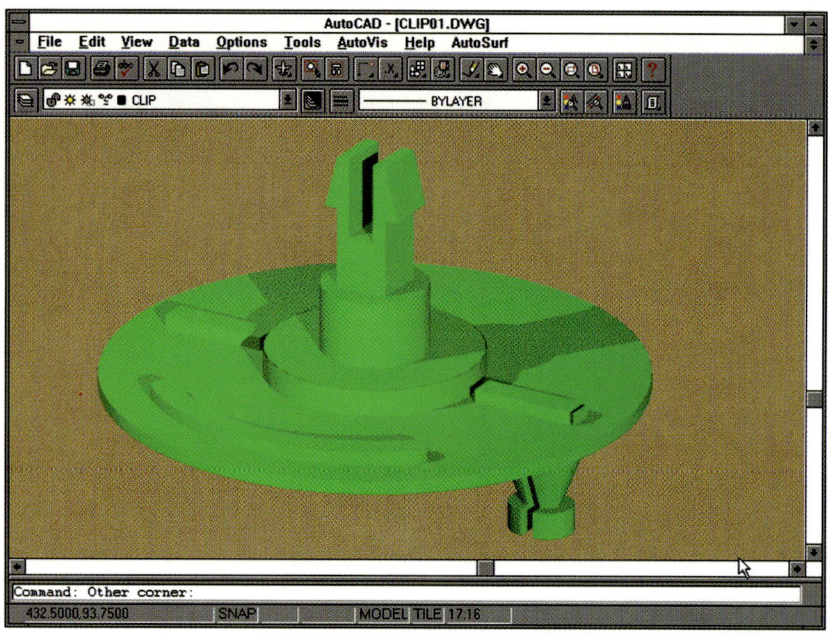

Plate XI A rendering of an AutoSurf model of another part of the water-spraying pressure system, part of which is shown in Plate X

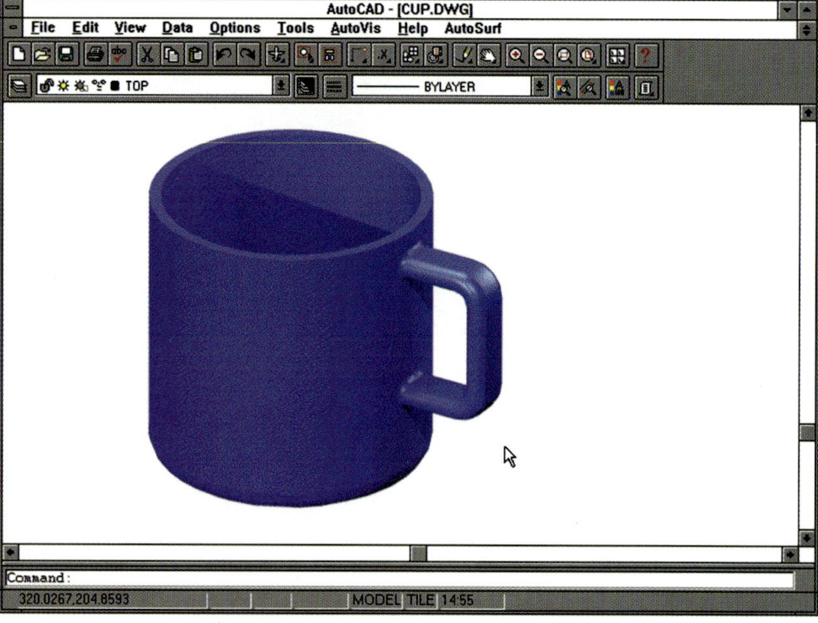

Plate XII A rendering of an AutoSurf model of a plastic cup

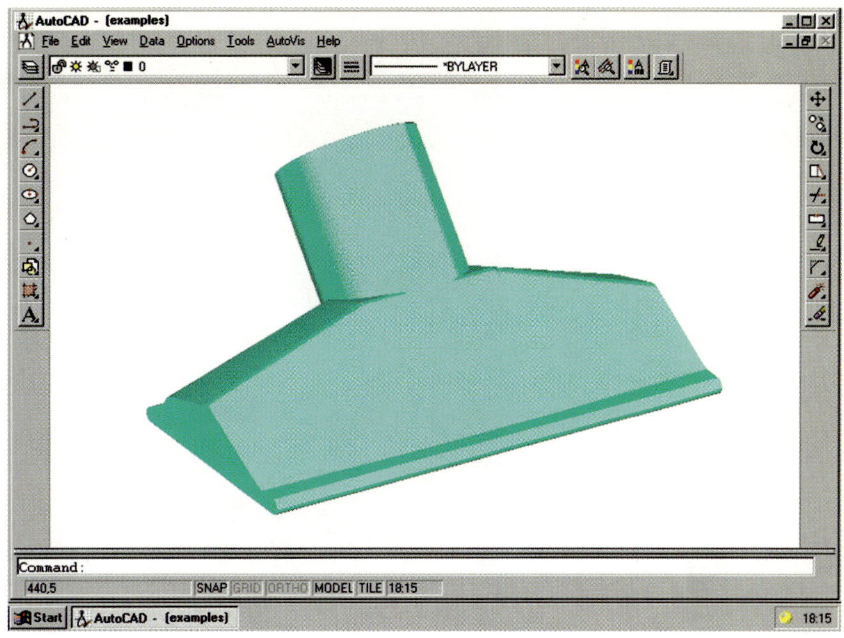

Plate XIII The rendering of Exercise 2, Chapter 7, Fig. 7.23. The model was constructed in AutoSurf Release 3 in Windows 95

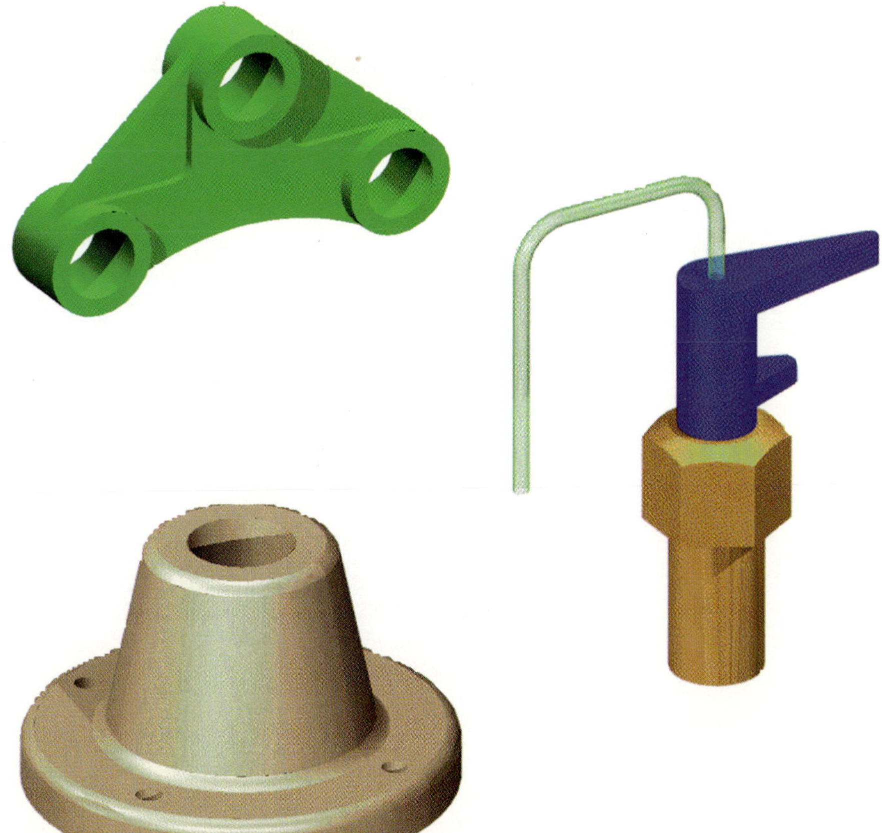

Plate XIV The rendering of Exercise 3, Chapter 7, Fig. 7.25

Plate XV A rendering of the third example, Chapter 10

Plate XVI A rendering of the worked example, Chapter 2

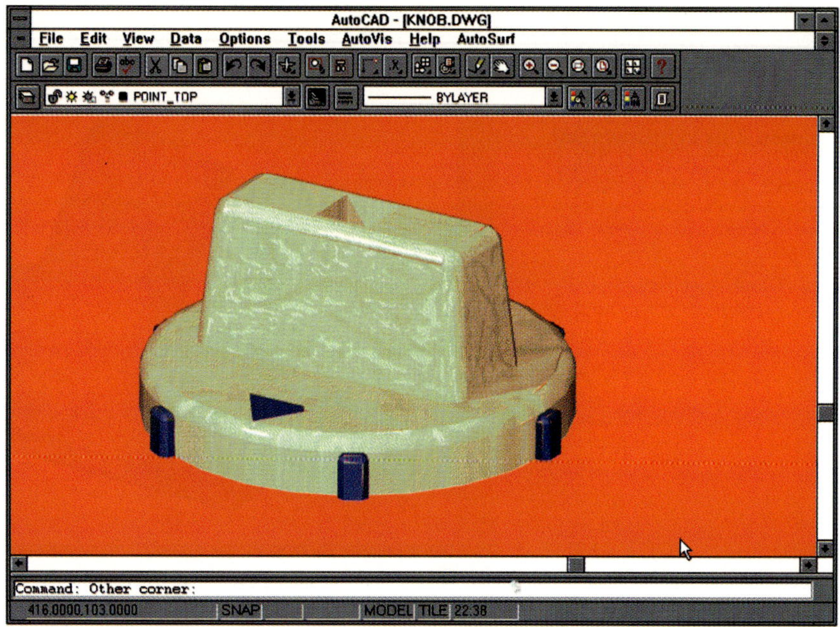

Plate XVII A rendering of an AutoSurf model of a switch for an electronics system against an AutoCAD red background

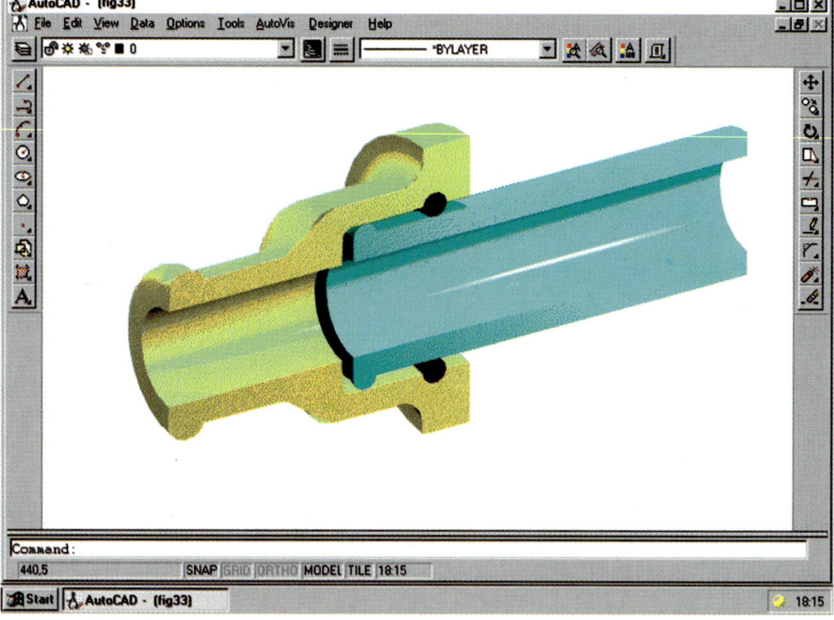

Plate XVIII A rendering of the half-model Fig. 3.33. The model was constructed in AutoSurf Release 3 in Windows 95

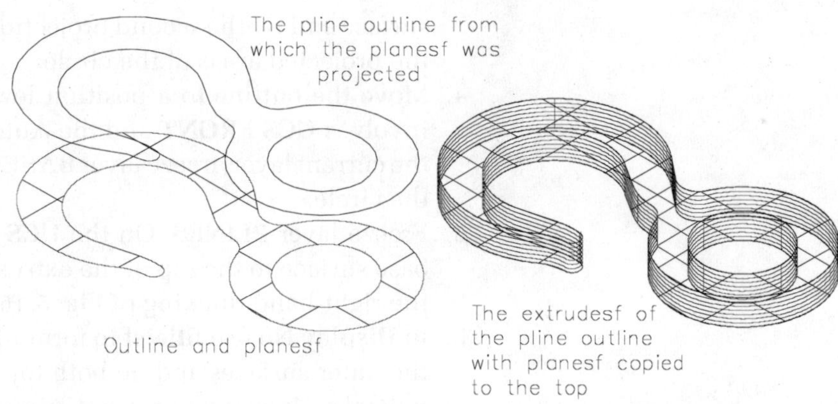

Fig. 5.15 First example. Stages 1 to 5

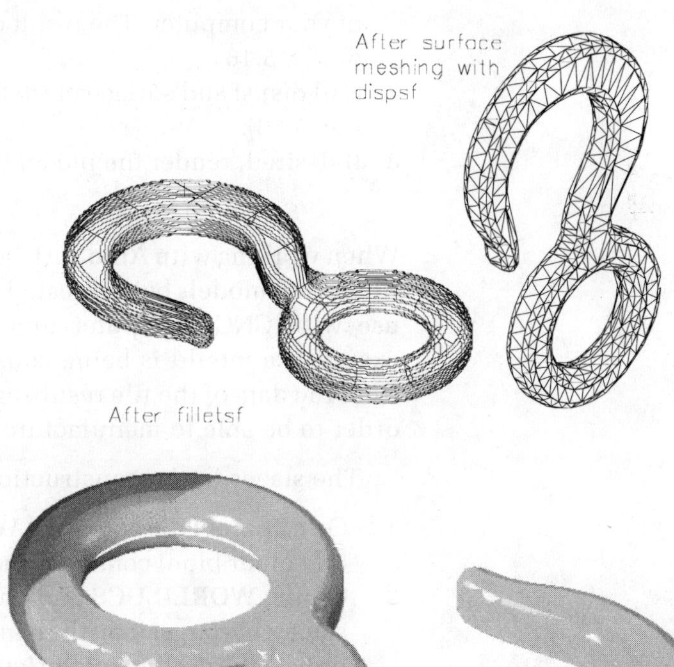

Fig. 5.16 First example. Stages 6 to 7

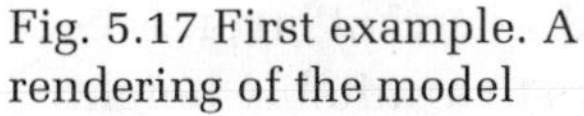

Fig. 5.17 First example. A rendering of the model

2. On a new layer **BASE**, construct a **planesf** rectangle larger than the height and width of the hook outline.
3. With **projectsf**, project the outer outline of the hook onto the **planesf** surface, followed by another **projectsf** of the circle onto the resulting projected hook outline. Note that for the first projection, the point selected must be inside the projection area of the **planesf**

surface and for the second projection the selection must be outside the projected areas of the circle.

4. Move the outline to a position level with the base surface. This involves **UCS FRONT** and the AutoCAD tool **Move**. Make layer **0** the current layer, freeze layer **BASE**. **Extrudesf** both the outline and the circle.
5. Freeze layer **PLINES**. On the **UCS FRONT** use **Copy** to copy the base surface to the top of the extrusions. The results are shown in the right-hand drawing of Fig. 5.15.
6. In **Display** Iso use **filletsf** to form fillets on both top and bottom of the outer surfaces and on both top and bottom of the circle. This will take a long time – several minutes – depending upon the speed of your computer. The result can be seen in the left-hand drawing of Fig. 5.16.
7. Call **dispsf** and surface mesh the model (see right-hand drawing of Fig. 5.16).
8. If desired, render the model (Fig. 5.17).

Second example

When working with AutoSurf, bear in mind that the 3D data from the files of the models being created can be converted to files suitable for use with CNC (computer numerical control) machinery. In this example, a mould is being constructed which could be machined from the data of the file resulting from saving the drawing to disk in order to be able to manufacture mouldings of the name AutoCAD.

The stages in the construction of this model are:

1. On a **3point UCS** above the **World UCS** and on a new layer **NAME** (of colour blue) construct the letters of the name AutoCAD.
2. On the **WORLD UCS** and on layer **0**, construct a **planesf** surface somewhat larger than the name AutoCAD. With the aid of **projectsf** project the outlines of the letters to form the surface shown in Fig. 5.18 (upper drawing).
3. Change to the **FRONT UCS** and move the name AutoCAD to the level of the **WORLD UCS**.
4. Make a new layer **LETTERS** and make it the current layer. Freeze layer **0**. With **extrudesf** extrude the letters to a suitable height.
5. Make a new layer **TOP** and make it the current layer. In the **FRONT UCS** move the letters to the top of the extrusion.
6. Freeze layer **LETTERS** and **planesf** each part of the name AutoCAD.
7. Thaw all layers except **NAME**, which should be frozen.
8. Surface mesh the whole model with the aid of **dispsf**.
9. In the **FRONT UCS** rotate the model through 180° to turn it upside down.

Fig. 5.18 Second example. Stages 1 to 8

Fig. 5.19 Second example. A rendering of the model for the mould

10. Place the model in a **Vpoint** of –0.6,–1,0.6 and render. The result is shown in Fig. 5.19.

The command intersf

When two surfaces of an AutoSurf 3D model require trimming one to the other, or both to each other, the command **intersf** can be used. As its name implies the command is mainly for trimming unnecessary parts of surfaces which cross each other. Either both surfaces or a single surface can be trimmed as indicated in the **Surface Intersection** dialogue box (Fig. 5.20) which appears when **??** is *entered* in response to the first prompt of the command line sequence for the command.

To call the command, either select **Intersect Surface** from the **AutoSurf** pull-down menu (Fig. 5.21) or, at the command line:

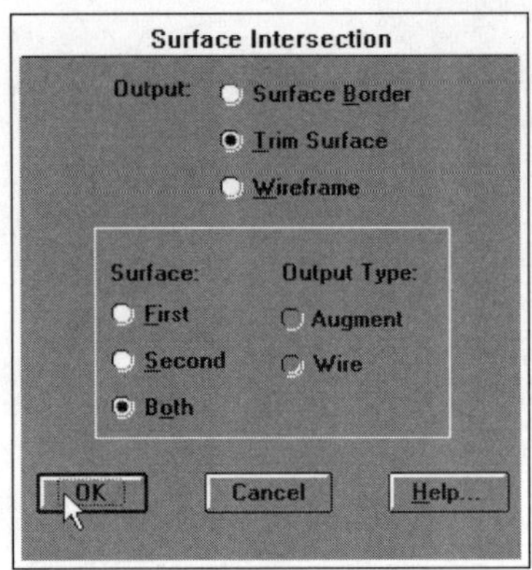

Fig. 5.20 The settings in the **Surface Intersection** dialogue box for the intersections in Fig. 5.22

Command: *enter* intersf *right-click*
To invoke advanced options enter '??' ...
Select two surfaces:
Select first object: *pick*
Select second object: *pick*
Command:

A straightforward example showing the trimming of two intersecting **planesf** surfaces is shown in Fig. 5.22. Both the first and second surfaces to be selected have been trimmed.

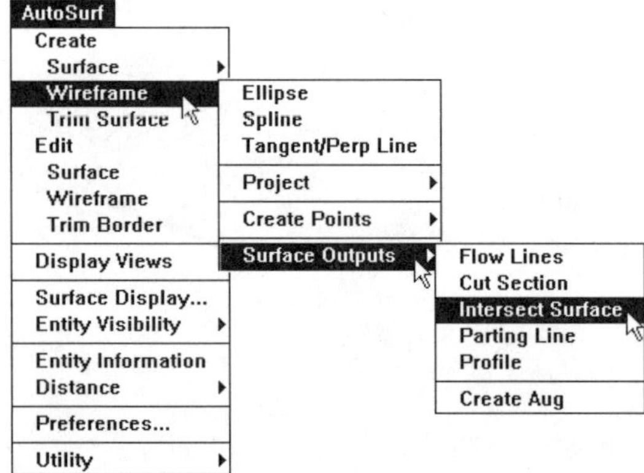

Fig. 5.21 Selecting **Intersect Surface** from the **AutoSurf** pull-down-menu

Note that one must be careful when selecting the intersecting surface to be trimmed, to *pick* on the side of the surface away from the part to be trimmed from the surface. This is shown in Fig. 5.23 in which two surfaces – a **planesf** surface and a **rulesf** surface – are intersecting. In this example (the top two drawings of this illustration), both surfaces have been trimmed – the settings in the **Surface Intersection** dialogue box are as shown in Fig. 5.20.

The lower two drawings of Fig. 5.23 show the trimming when the settings in the **Surface Intersection** dialogue box have been amended to either **First** or **Second Surface**:

Left-hand drawing – trimming of the **First Surface**.
Right-hand drawing – trimming of the **Second Surface**.

Figure 5.24 shows three stages in the trimming of surfaces with the aid of **intersf**:

Left-hand drawing – four **rulesf** surfaces and a **planesf** surface intersect each other.
Central drawing – the trimming completed.
Right-hand drawing – the model has been surface meshed.

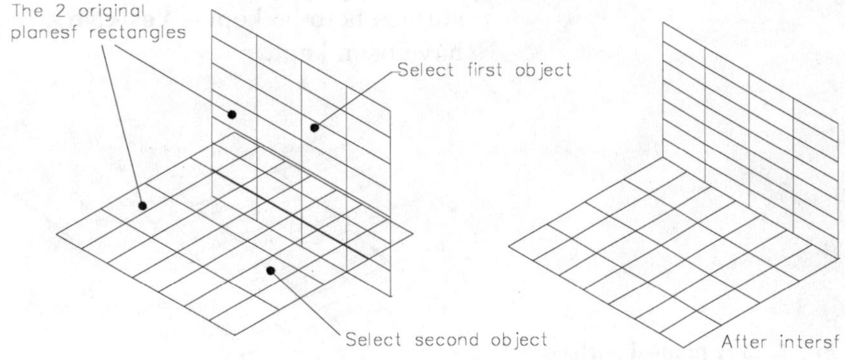

Fig. 5.22 The trimming of two surfaces with the aid of **intersf**

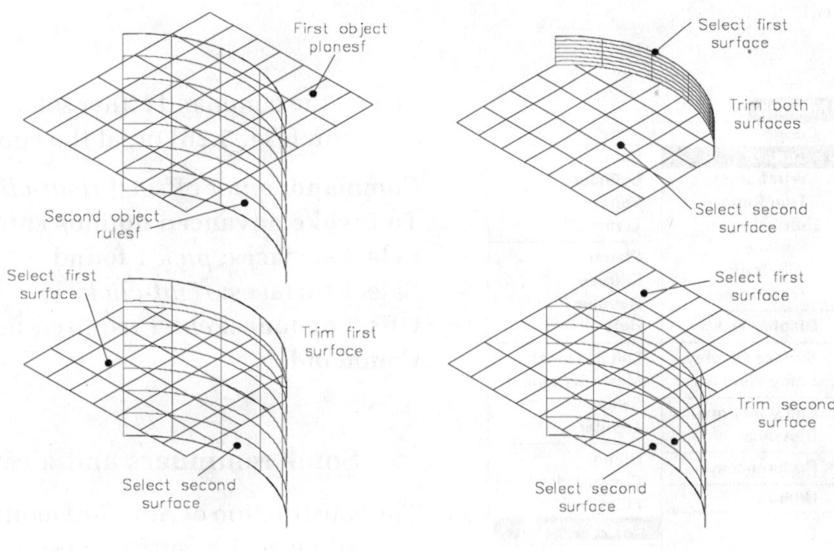

Fig. 5.23 Take care which part of the surface being selected is *picked*

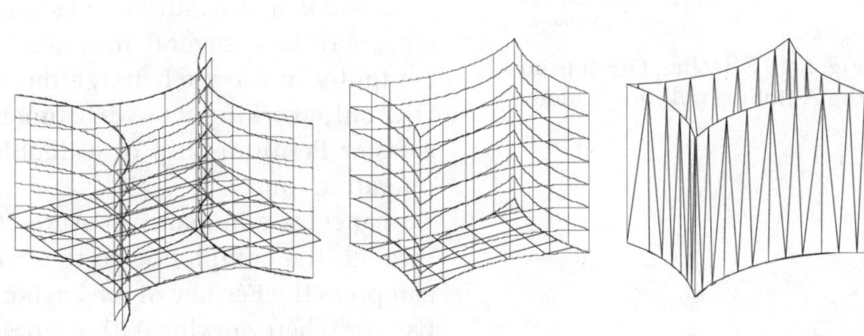

Fig. 5.24 An example of the use of the command **intersf**

The command offsetsf

This is the last command to be dealt with in this chapter. Surfaces can be offset from each other as indicated in the two examples of Fig. 5.25. When calling this command, if ?? is *entered* in response to the first option of the command sequence, a message asks if the original surface is to be kept – **Yes/<No>**. In Fig. 5.25 the original surfaces have been kept.

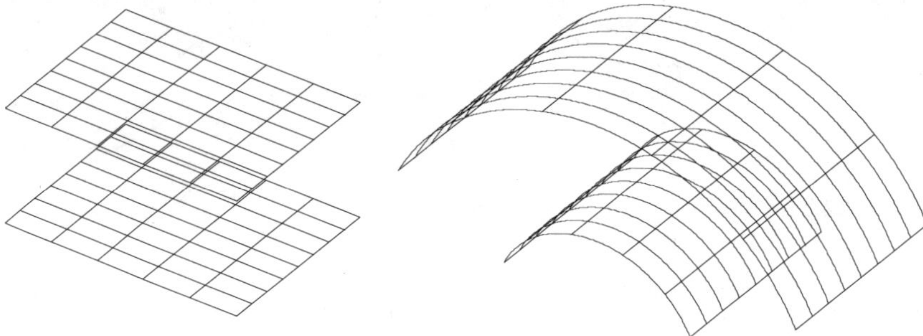

Fig. 5.25 A **planesf** surface offset and a **sweepsf** surface offset

AutoSurf
Create
Surface
Wireframe
Trim Surface
Edit
Surface
Wireframe
Trim Border
Display Views
Surface Display...
Entity Visibility
Entity Information
Distance
Preferences...
Utility

Cone
Cylinder
Sphere
Torus
Planar
Extrude
Revolve
Rule
Loft (U Lines)
Mesh (UV Lines)
Swept
Tubular
Blend
Corner Fillet
Fillet
Offset
Acad to Surface

Fig. 5.26 Selecting **Offset** from the **AutoSurf** pull-down menu

To call the command either select **Offset** from the **AutoSurf** pull-down menu (Fig. 5.26) or, at the command line:

Command: *enter* offsetsf *right-click*
To invoke advanced options enter '??' ...
Select surfaces: *pick* **1 found**
Select surfaces: *right-click*
Offset distance: *enter* required figure
Command:

Some reminders and a revision exercise

1. The construction of AutoSurf models can take a considerable time. Operations such as surface meshing, filleting complicated surfaces, etc., may take several minutes. Because of this, the faster the computer in use the better, although a PC equipped with an Intel DX2 chip working at 66 MHz functions reasonably well. However, a faster Pentium chip or a doubler chip will save considerable operating time.
2. To cancel a command in AutoCAD Release 13 when part way through the completion of the command sequence, the operator can press the **Esc** key of the keyboard. It is not advisable to use the **Esc** key when working with AutoSurf. When in the middle of a long operation, say the filleting of a complicated surface, the operator decides he/she has made a mistake – e.g. *entered* wrong fillet sizes – it is best to wait for the operation to complete and then press the **U** key (**Undo**) to undo the operation. Pressing the **Esc** key when in AutoSurf may cause the system to crash with unexpected results.
3. Use the AutoCAD command **purge** before saving an AutoSurf model drawing to disk. It may in fact be necessary to purge several

times one after the other. Purging results in considerable reduction of drawing file size. When working in AutoCAD Release 13, **purge** can be used at any time during a drawing sequence.

4. The more familiar you are with the AutoCAD **UCS** system, the easier you will find the construction of wireframes (as based on the methods described in this book) for AutoSurf models becomes.

A revision exercise

Figures 5.27 to 5.29 show the sequence of operations required to construct the AutoSurf 3D model of a powder bottle. The reader may care to work this exercise in order to revise some of the command systems dealt with in earlier chapters. The sequence of construction follows a routine such as:

Fig. 5.27 The wireframe on which the model is based

1. Construct a wireframe as shown in Fig. 5.27 – a circle with a number of semicircles at intervals around and tangential to the circle. Note that the top two semicircles are very close together.
2. Left-hand drawing of Fig. 5.28. Using **loftsf** create the surface as shown
3. Central drawing of Fig. 5.28. Add a **primsf** cylinder for the neck of the bottle and, with **filletsf**, fillet the area between the lofted surface and the cylinder.
4. Right-hand drawing of Fig. 5.28. Add a **planesf** surface to circles at back and front of the model so far constructed.

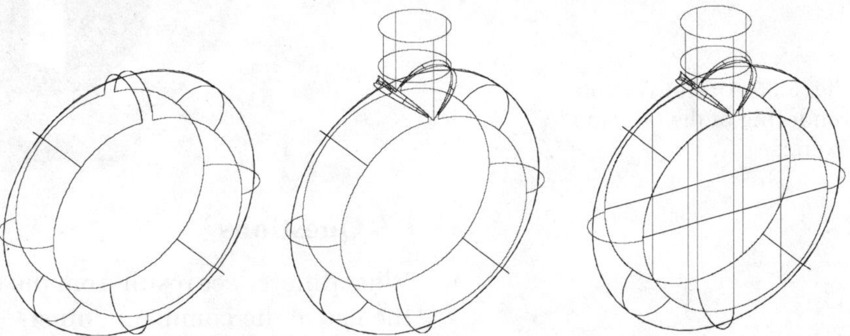

Fig. 5.28 Stages 2, 3 and 4

5. Left-hand drawing of Fig. 5.29. Add a **primsf** cylinder as a cap for the bottle and a **rulesf** base on which the bottle is to stand.
6. Central drawing of Fig. 5.29. Surface mesh the model.
7. Right-hand drawing of Fig. 5.29. Add a **planesf** label to the front of the model.

Figure 5.30 is an AutoVision rendering of the completed model. The material **GREEN GLASS** was used as a surface for the bottle.

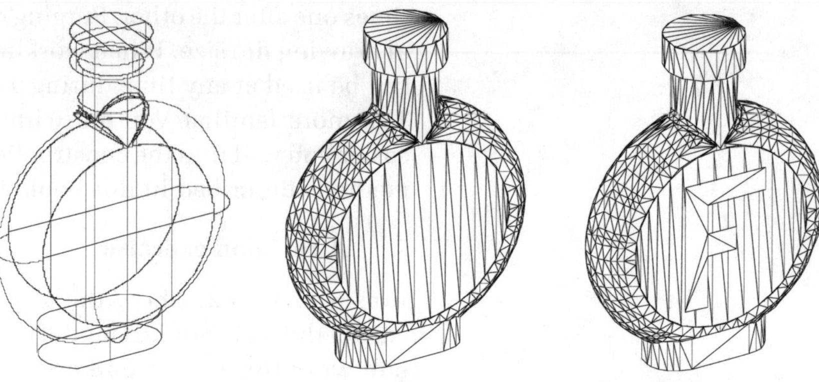

Fig. 5.29 Stages 5, 6 and 7

Fig. 5.30 An AutoVision rendering of the revision exercise.

Questions

1. What differences result from the use of the command **blendsf** and the use of the command **joinsf**?
2. Can part of a wireframe be selected as an object when using the command **blendsf**?
3. When using **projectsf** why is it important to take care when picking the surface onto which an outline is being projected?
4. The first example of the use of **projectsf** given on page 57 shows the outline being projected onto a **planesf** surface. Could not the outline itself be acted upon by **planesf** to produce the same results?
5. Why is it necessary to take care when picking a surface which is to be acted upon by the command **intersf**?

6. When using **intersf** and only one of two surfaces is to be trimmed, how can one ensure that only the one surface is affected?
7. Can a surface be offset with the aid of **offsetsf** just to move the surface?
8. Why is it not advisable to use **Esc** to cancel an AutoSurf command while the command is in operation?
9. Why is it best to use **purge** before saving an AutoSurf model drawing to disk?
10. Why do you think that the commands **blendsf**, **offsetsf** and **joinsf** are said to form 'derived surfaces'?

Exercises

1. Figure 5.31 shows the stages of constructing a box from four **rulesf** vertical surfaces and a **planesf** bottom surface.

   It will be remembered that when using **blendsf** as many as four edges may be selected when forming a required surface.

   Construct the box shown in Fig. 5.31 working to any suitable sizes.

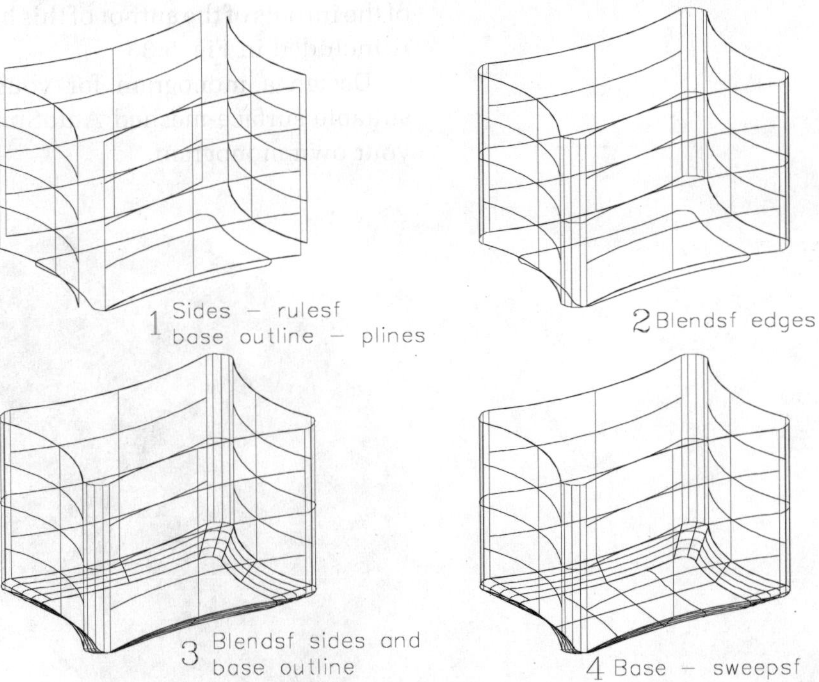

Fig. 5.31 Exercise 1

2. A rendering of an AutoSurf model of a magnifying glass holder is given in Fig. 5.32, together with a dimensioned drawing of the outline from which the model was derived.

Construct a surface-meshed copy of the model to the sizes given. Dimensions not shown are left to your own judgement.

Fig. 5.32 Exercise 2

3. Figure 5.33 shows a rendering of the front of an AutoSurf 3D model for a mould which is to be used to produce copies of the monogram of the initials of the author of this book. An outline of the monogram is included in Fig. 5.33

   Design a monogram for your own initials and construct a suitable surface-meshed AutoSurf model for a mould for casting your own monogram.

Fig. 5.33 Exercise 3

4. Figure 5.34 shows three stages of producing a model of a cylinder which has been shaped at top and bottom with the aid of the AutoSurf command **intersf**. The intersecting surfaces are two **planesf** surfaces and a **rulesf** surface. Construct the cylinder to any convenient sizes.

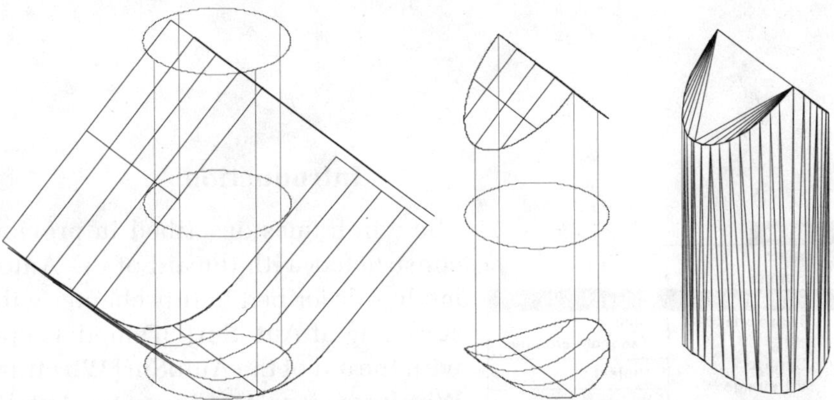

Fig. 5.34 Exercise 4

5. The right-hand drawing of Fig. 5.35 shows a model of an AutoSurf **sphere** which has been intersected by a wavy **sweepsf** surface and then surface meshed. Working to any convenient dimensions, construct a similar model to that shown in the figure.

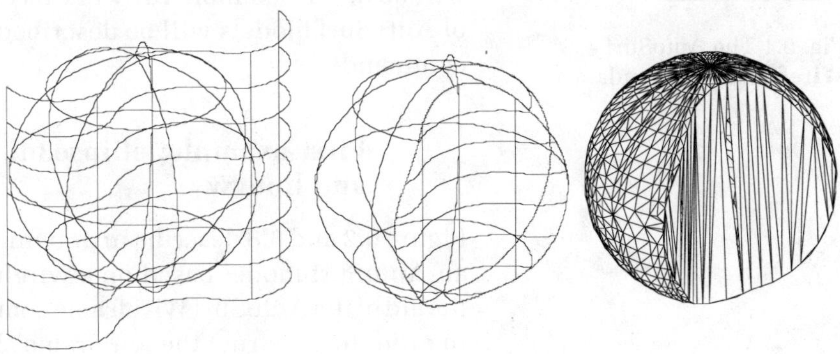

Fig. 5.35 Exercise 5

CHAPTER 6

Further AutoSurf models

Introduction

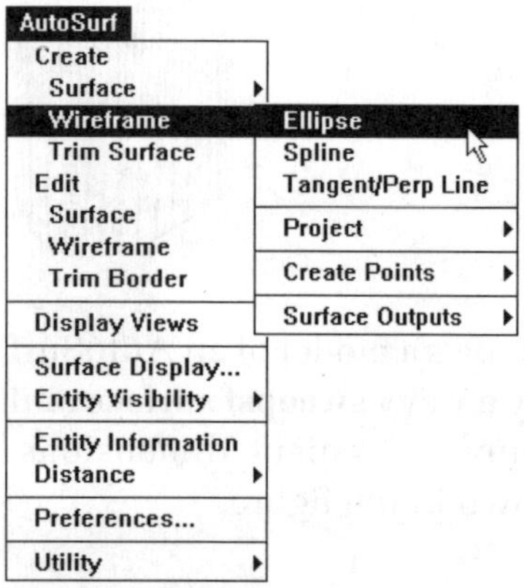

Fig. 6.1 The AutoSurf **Wireframe** commands

The wireframes described in previous chapters have been mostly constructed with the aid of the AutoCAD **Draw** tools. Some of the models described in this chapter will involve the construction and surfacing of AutoSurf 3D models created from wireframes formed with the aid of the AutoSurf **Wireframe** commands, as shown when **Wireframe** is selected from the **AutoSurf** pull-down menu (Fig. 6.1). There are some advantages in using the AutoSurf **Wireframe** commands – as, for example, when *picking* points on 3D splines with the aid of osnaps.

Some of the command systems will have been described in earlier chapters, and only those commands not previously mentioned will be described more fully in this chapter. A number of examples of AutoSurf models will be described to illustrate the actions of the commands.

First example: ellipse3d, spline3d, breakvw, join3d and linevw

Figure 6.2 and 6.8 describe in drawings the sequence of constructing an AutoSurf model based on a wireframe constructed mostly with the aid of the AutoSurf **Wireframe** commands **ellipse3d** and **spline3d**. In order to construct the wireframe shown as drawing 1 in Fig. 6.2, a number of 3point **UCS** planes were created as the construction proceeded. In addition, a number of different layers of varying colours were involved in the construction, these layers being frozen, thawed and made current as the need arose.

The command ellipse3d

To call the command either select **Ellipse** from the **AutoSurf** pull-down menu (Fig. 6.1) or, at the command line:

Command: *enter* ellipse3d *right-click*
Major axis direction: *pick*
Major axis length <240>: *enter* figure *right-click*
Minor axis length <120>: *enter* figure *right-click*
Command:

In all five ellipses were drawn spaced at equal vertical intervals for this example (drawing 1 of Fig. 6.2).

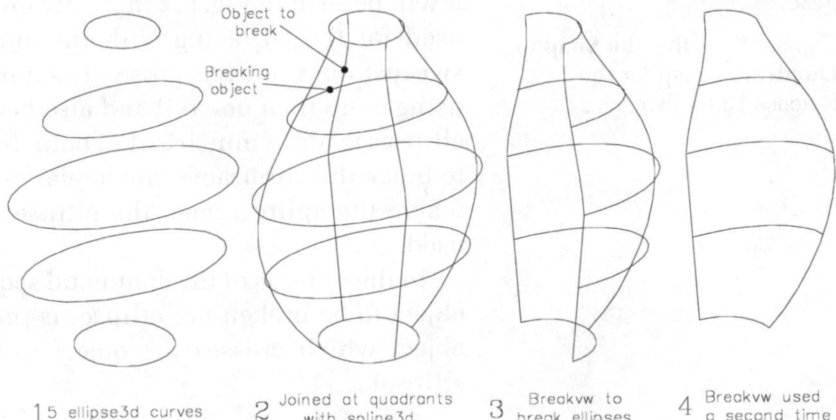

Fig. 6.2 The first 4 stages in the construction of the first example

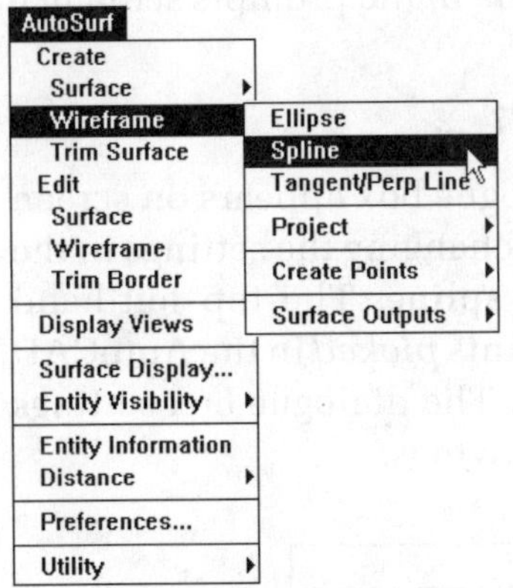

Fig. 6.3 Selecting **Spline** from the **AutoSurf** pull-down menu

The ellipses were then joined at their osnap **quadrant** points with splines drawn with the aid of the AutoSurf command **spline3d** (Fig. 6.3) as shown in stage 2 of Fig. 6.2. One advantage of using the **ellipse3d** command rather than AutoCAD ellipses is that **ellipse3d** recognises the osnap **quadrant** when joined with **spline3d**. The osnap attaches the spline to the ends of the axes of the ellipses. The quadrant osnap can be selected from the AutoCAD R13 **Osnap** toolbar (Fig. 6.4), or the quadrant osnap can be set from the command line:

Command: *enter* osnap *right-click*
Osnaps: *enter* qua *right-click*
Command:

and the quadrant osnap is set until it is unset from the command line by calling osnap and *entering* off.

The command spline3d

To call the command either select **Spline** from the **AutoSurf** pull-down menu (as shown in Fig. 6.3) or, at the command line:

Command: *enter* spline3d *right-click*
To invoke advanced options enter '??' ...

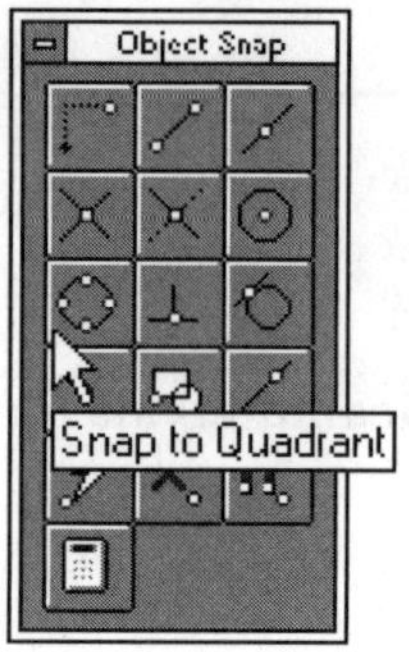

Fig. 6.4 Selecting the **Snap to Quadrant** osnap for the Release 13 toolbar

Create spline by Entities/<Location>: *right-click*
Locate points: _qua of *pick* upper ellipse
Locate points: _qua of *pick* next ellipse
Locate points: _qua of *pick* next ellipse
Locate points: _qua of *pick* next ellipse
Locate points: _qua of *pick* bottom ellipse
Locate points: *right-click*
Command:

It will be seen in Fig. 6.2 that only one quarter of the wireframe was used for the surfacing with the aid of **sweepsf**. This is because **sweepsf** does not recognise closed outlines such as ellipses when using more than one rail and also because the shape formed by the ellipses is not symmetrical in both directions in plan view. In order to break the wireframe into a quarter of its original shape at points where the splines meet the ellipses, the command **breakvw** was used.

In the options of the command sequence for this command, each object to be broken (an ellipse) is *picked*, followed by *picking* the object which crosses the object to be broken (a spline near the ellipse).

Notes on the command spline3d

When the command is called, the first line in the prompts sequence at the command line is:

To invoke advanced options enter '??' ...

Enter **??** in response and the **Spline** dialogue box appears on screen (Fig. 6.5). Figure 6.6 shows the results of changing the settings in the dialogue box when drawing the same spline. The top left-hand drawing of this illustration shows the points *picked* in the AutoCAD editor to form each of the spline curves. The dialogue box settings for each spline are shown inside the drawings.

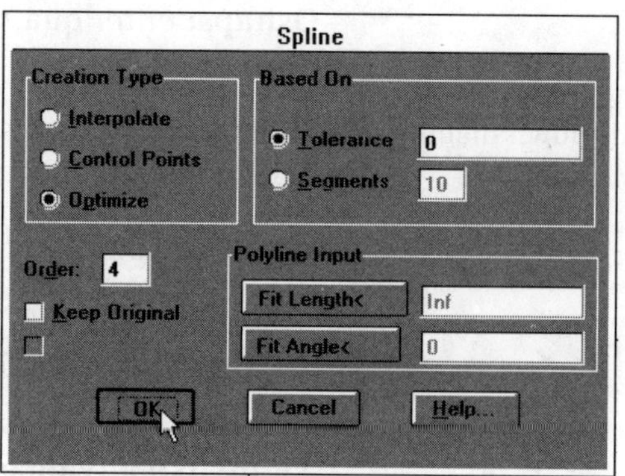

Fig. 6.5 The **Spline** dialogue box

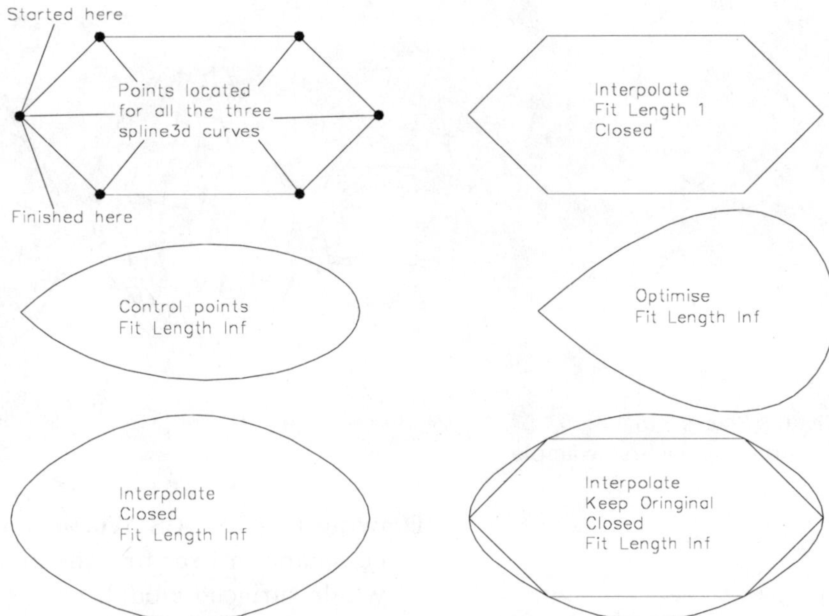

Fig. 6.6 The results of changing the settings in the **Spline** dialogue box

The command breakvw

To call the command either select **Break by View** from the **AutoSurf** pull-down menu (Fig. 6.7) or, at the command line:

Command: *enter* breakvw *right-click*
To invoke advanced options enter '??' ...
Break with Entity/<Locations>: *enter* e *right-click*
Select objects to break: *pick* an ellipse
Select objects to break: *right-click*
Select breaking objects: *pick* spline near ellipse
Select breaking objects: *right-click*
Command:

AutoSurf
Create
Surface
Wireframe
Trim Surface
Edit
Surface
Wireframe
Trim Border
Display Views
Surface Display...
Entity Visibility
Entity Information
Distance
Preferences...
Utility

Edit Spline
Unspline
Break by View
Extend by View
Offset by View
Trim by View
Explode3D
Fillet3D
Join3D
Refine Polyline
Show Direction
Reverse Direction
Augmented Line

Fig. 6.7 Selecting **Break by View** from the **AutoSurf** pull-down menu

If **??** is *entered* in response to the first option of the command sequence, the following further option appears at the command line the advanced option appears:

Break at All/<Closest>:

When all break points have been given to enable three-quarters of the wireframe to be erased, the results of the erasure are as seen in drawing 4 of Fig. 6.2.

Drawings 5 to 8 of Fig. 6.8 show the remaining stages of completing the AutoSurf 3D model:

Drawing 5 – surface the quarter wireframe with the aid of **sweepsf**.

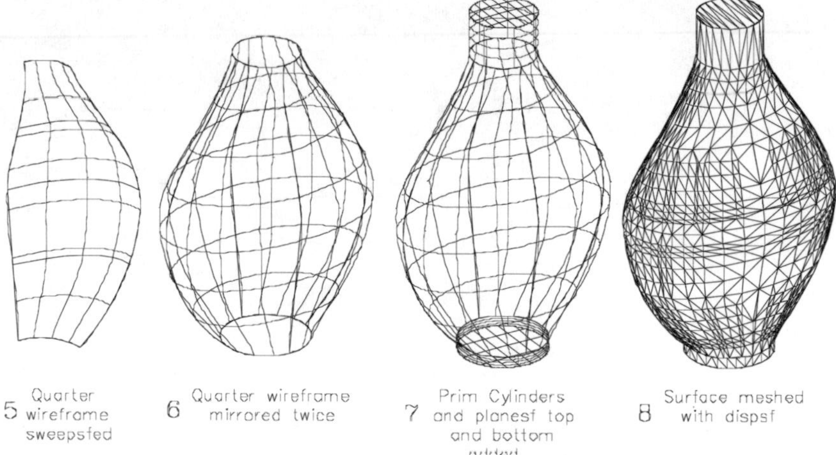

Fig. 6.8 Stages 5 to 8 of constructing the first example

Drawing 6 – in UCS **World**, and with the AutoCAD **mirror** command, mirror first the quarter, then the half to form the whole surfaced model.

Drawing 7 – with **primsf** form cylinders at top and bottom, and with **planesf** surface circles for top and bottom.

Drawing 8 – finally with **dispsf** surface mesh the entire surfaced model.

The command join3d

If, when breaking parts of a wireframe, it is found that an object has been accidentally broken at the wrong point, the break can be repaired with the aid of the AutoSurf command **join3d**. The command may also be of value in other situations where it is necessary to join plines, arcs or splines in a wireframe in order to form a continuous arc, pline or spline from two such objects with touching ends.

To call the command either select **Join3D** from the **AutoSurf** pull-down menu (Fig. 6.9) or, at the command line:

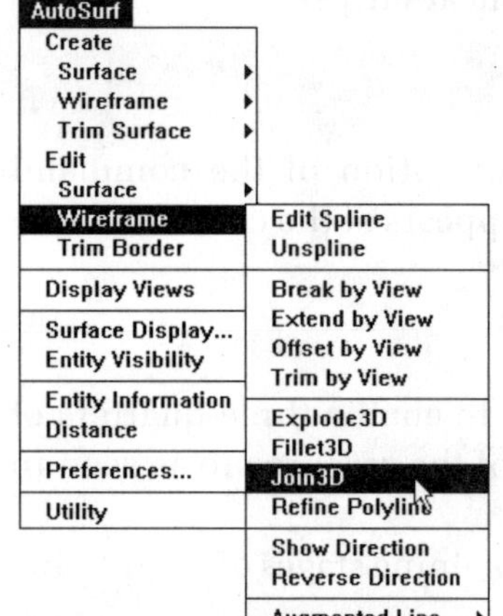

Fig. 6.9 Selecting **Join3D** from the **AutoSurf** pull-down menu

Command: *enter* join3d *right-click*
To invoke advanced options enter '??' ...
Automatic/<Manual>: *right-click*
Select objects: *pick*
Select objects: *pick*
Select objects: *right-click*
Command:

To set the advanced options, *enter* ?? to the first option. Note that when joining 3D splines the **Spline** check circle should be set (Fig. 6.10) if spline curves are to be joined, but if straight splines or

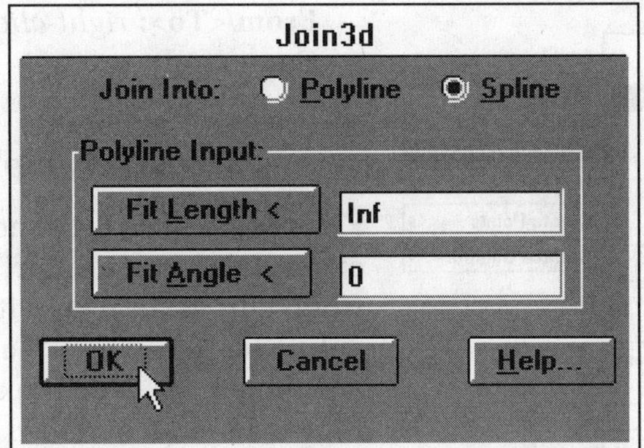

Fig. 6.10 The **Join3d** dialogue box with **Spline** set

polylines in a wireframe are being joined, the **Pline** setting must be active (*left-click* in the **Polyline** check circle) in the dialogue box.

The command linevw

Another AutoSurf command which may prove to be useful when constructing wireframes is **linevw**. Using the command will allow plines to be drawn tangentially to existing **spline3d** curves. An example is given in Fig. 6.11 in which plines have been drawn tangential to a closed, optimised **spline3d** curve with the aid the command. The command may also be used for the drawing of plines or splines perpendicular to existing splines. The command may be used when drawing plines or splines in 3D space.

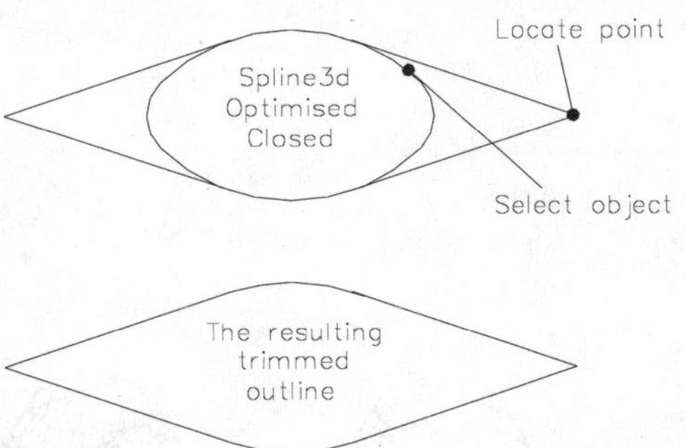

Fig. 6.11 Using **linevw** to draw a pline from points to a closed spline

To call the command either select **Tangent/Perp Line** from the **AutoSurf** pull-down menu (Fig. 6.12) or, at the command line:

Command: *enter* linevw *right-click*
Select objects: *pick* the spline
Select objects: *right-click*
Locate points: *pick* (or *enter* coordinates)
Perpendicular/<Tangent>: *right-click*

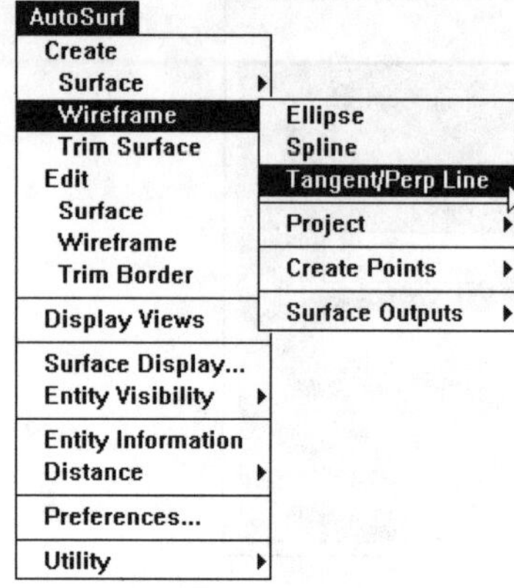

Fig. 6.12 Selecting **Tangent/ Perp Line** from the **AutoSurf** pull-down menu

From/<To>: *right-click*
Command:

Second example to include intersf

Figures 6.13 and 6.14 show the stages in the construction of another example of an AutoSurf 3D model based on a wireframe made up from curves drawn with **ellipse3d** and joined with the aid of **spline3d** (drawings 1 and 2 of Fig. 6.13). In this example, the wireframe has been broken into quarters, as shown in drawing 3 of Fig. 6.13 and surfaced with **sweepsf**. The quarter surface was mirrored to form a half surface (drawing 4 of Fig. 6.13) and to a full surface (drawing 5 of Fig. 6.14). **Projectsf** was then used to cut holes in the recombined surfaces (drawing 5 of Fig. 6.14). Cylinders were added in the holes (drawing 6 of Fig. 6.14) and the intersections between the cylinders and the main surface formed with the aid of the AutoSurf command **intersf** (drawing 7 of Fig. 6.14). Circles for top and bottom of the vertical surface and for the ends of the cylinders were drawn and surfaced with **planesf**. The completed model was surfaced meshed with **dispsf** (drawing 8 of Fig. 6.14).

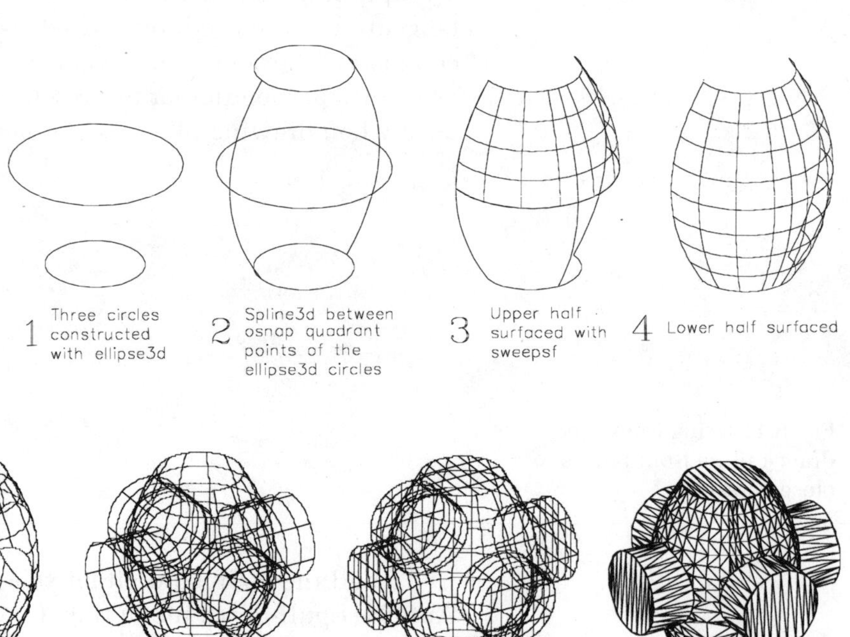

Fig. 6.13 Stages 1 to 4 of the second example

Fig. 6.14 Stages 5 to 8 of the construction for the second example

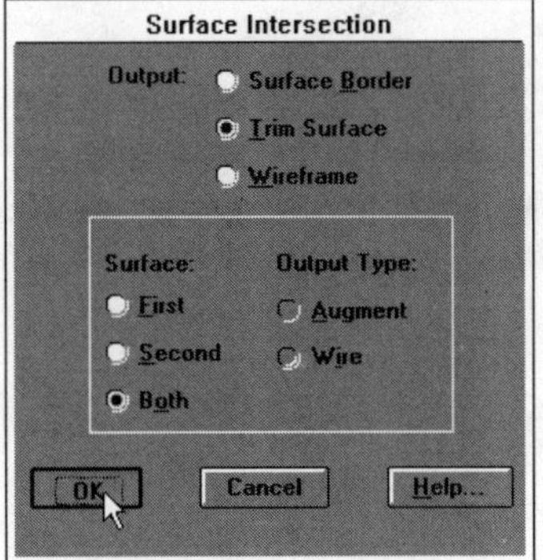

Fig. 6.15 The settings in the **Surface Intersection** dialogue box for the second example

The command **intersf** was used with an earlier example. However, here is the command structure again:

Command: *enter* intersf *right-click*
To invoke advanced options enter '??' ...
Select two surfaces:
Select first object: *pick* one surface
Select first object: *pick* second surface
Command:

and the intersection is formed, but note the settings in the **Surface Intersection** dialogue box (Fig. 6.15).

Third example to include joinsf

Figures 6.16 and 6.17 show the stages in the construction of this third example. The stages in the construction followed the sequence:

1. Drawing 1 of Fig. 6.16. Construct a wireframe with **spline3d.** Note the bottom part of the wireframe, which was constructed from a single **spline3d** which was copied five times and each copy rotated to form a suitable wireframe from which a **loftsf** surface could be formed using the five splines as **U Lines**.
2. Drawing 2 of Fig. 6.16. The two parts of the wireframe were surfaced with the aid of **sweepsf** and **loftsf**. The **U** and **V Lines** for this stage were set at 8 and 5 respectively.
3. Drawing 3 of Fig. 6.16. The two surfaces were mirrored to form a complete handle. Remember at this stage that the surface is in four parts.

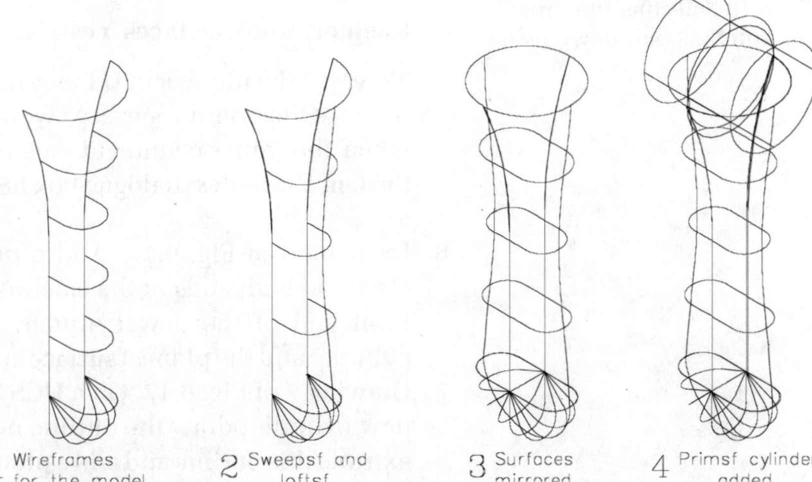

Fig. 6.16 Stages 1 to 4 of the construction for the third example

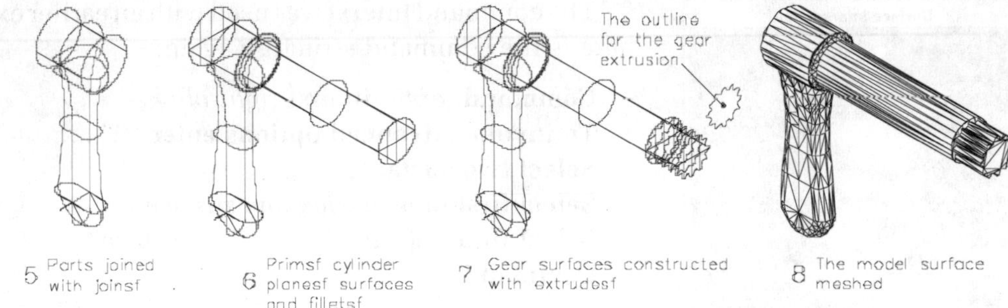

Fig. 6.17 Stages 5 to 8 of the construction for the third example

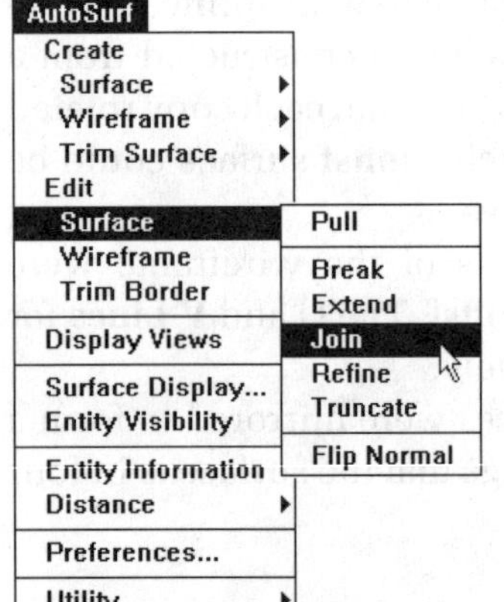

Fig. 6.18 Selecting **Join** from the **AutoSurf** pull-down menu

4. Drawing 4 of Fig. 6.16. A **primsf** cylinder was added at the top of the existing surface.
5. Drawing 5 of Fig. 6.17. All four parts of the wireframe for the handle were joined together with the aid of **joinsf**.

   To call the command either select **Join** from the AutoSurf pull-down menu (Fig. 6.18) or, at the command line:

   Command: *enter* joinsf *right-click*
   To invoke advanced options enter '??' ...
   Select surfaces to join: *pick* one surface
   Select surfaces to join: *pick* another surface
   Select surfaces to join: *pick* another surface
   Select surfaces to join: *pick* another surface
   Select surfaces to join: *right-click*
   Command:

   The advanced options for the command do not bring up a dialogue box, but show the following at the command line:

   Keep original surfaces Yes/<No>:

   Note that the number of **U Lines** in the joined surface have changed because the original surfaces were based on a **U Line** of 8, whereas when the **joinsf** command was called, **U Lines** in the **AutoSurf System Variables** dialogue box had been changed to the default of 5.
6. Drawing 6 of Fig. 6.17. Add a **primsf** cylinder and add **planesf** circles at both ends of the existing **primsf** cylinder and also at the front end of the new cylinder. Then **filletsf** between the new cylinder and the **planesf** surface at the front of the existing cylinder.
7. Drawing 7 of Fig. 6.17. On a **UCS 3point** surface at the front of the new cylinder, draw the outline of a 12 tooth gear. With **extrudesf** extrude this outline and add a **planesf** surface to the gear outline for the front of the extruded surface.

8. Drawing 8 of Fig. 6.17. With **dispsf**, surface mesh the model.
9. The completed surface-meshed model could now be rendered if thought necessary as in Fig. 6.19.

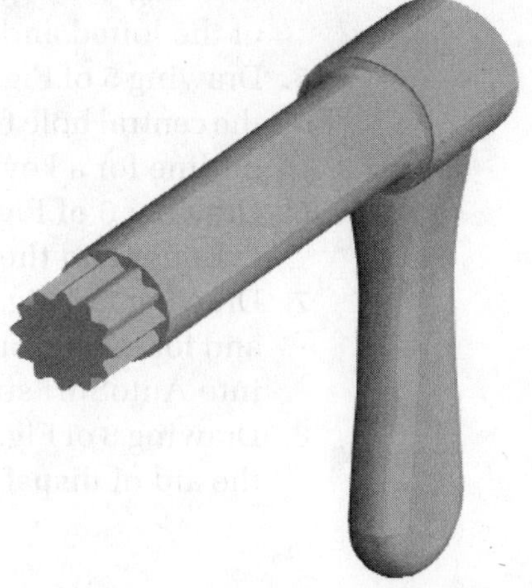

Fig. 6.19 A rendering of the third example

Fourth example: a change switch from a machine

This fourth example again depends upon a wireframe constructed with the aid of the AutoSurf command **spline3d**. Figure 6.20 shows the first six stages in the construction for this example.

1. Drawing 1 of Fig. 6.20. Construct the two wireframes forming the basis for the model from **spline3d** curves.

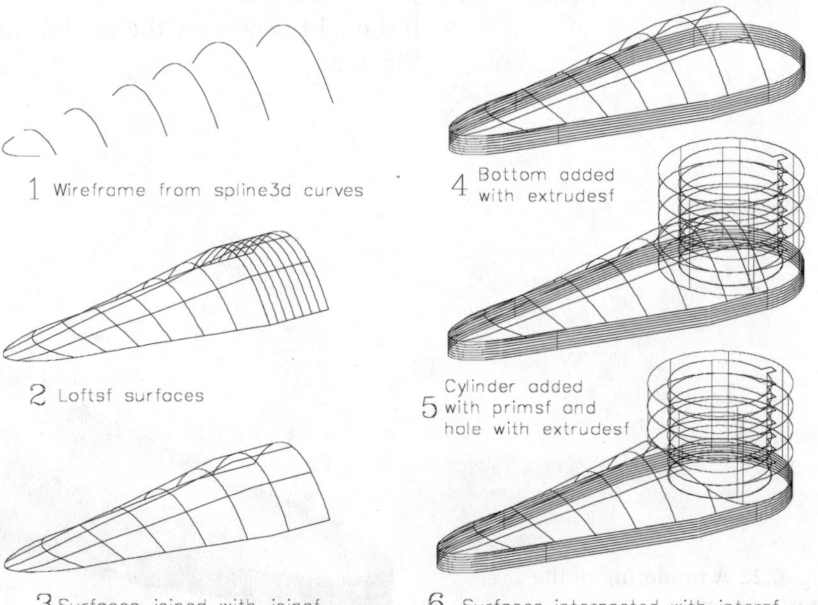

Fig. 6.20 Stages 1 to 6 of the construction for the fourth example

2. Drawing 2 of Fig. 6.20. With **loftsf** form two AutoSurf surfaces from the wireframes.
3. Drawing 3 of Fig. 6.20. With **joinsf** join the two surfaces.
4. Drawing 4 of Fig. 6.20. Draw a pline outline to the shape of a plan of the lofted and joined surface and **extrudesf** the outline.
5. Drawing 5 of Fig. 6.20. Add a **primsf** cylinder and an **extrudesf** for the central hole from a pline outline, one side of which includes the outline for a keyway.
6. Drawing 6 of Fig. 6.20. Form the line of intersection between the cylinder and the front tongue surface with the aid of **intersf**.
7. Drawing 7 of Fig. 6.21. Construct pline outlines for the base surface and for the top surface of the model and with **planesf** change them into AutoSurf surfaces.
8. Drawing 8 of Fig. 6.21. The model can now be surface meshed with the aid of **dispsf**.

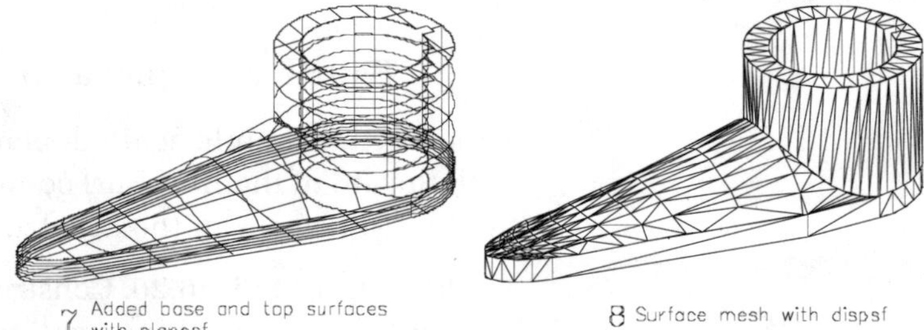

Fig. 6.21 Stages 7 and 8 of the construction for the fourth example

9. If thought necessary the model can now be rendered as shown in Fig. 6.22.

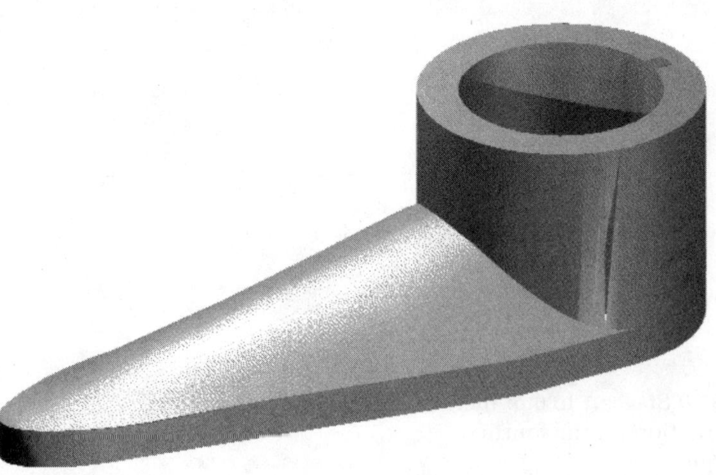

Fig. 6.22 A rendering of the fourth example

The command purgesf

In an earlier chapter the use of the AutoCAD command **purge** was recommended for saving disk space when an AutoSurf model drawing is saved to file on disk. The command should be called several times to completely purge AutoSurf blocks from a drawing.

Another command which can be used to decrease the size of drawing files in **purgesf**. To call the command at the command line:

Command: *enter* purgesf *right-click*
Display/<Memory>: *right-click*
Select/<All>: *right-click*
Command:

If **Display is** the required option the prompt becomes:

Select AutoSurf surfaces: *window* the drawing on screen
18 found. or a similar number depending upon the drawing
Command:

AutoSurf command name endings

The reader will have noted that some AutoSurf commands end with **sf**, some with **3d** and some with **vw**. Some commands look similar because of this – examples are **join3d** and **joinsf**. Be careful you are not calling the wrong command because you have entered the wrong ending.

Questions

1. Do you know the difference between an AutoCAD ellipse and an AutoSurf **ellipse3d**?
2. Why is it sometimes advisable to use AutoSurf **Wireframe** commands to construct a wireframe rather than AutoCAD commands?
3. Have you remembered that it is advisable to work on a number of layers when constructing AutoSurf models?
4. What is the purpose of the AutoSurf command **linevw**?
5. Can you use **breakvw** on an AutoCAD ellipse?
6. What is the difference between the two AutoSurf commands **join3d** and **joinsf**?
7. If you use **joinsf** on a surface which has been constructed with the default **U** and **V Lines** setting of 5 and 3 and the current settings of **U** and **V Lines** is 10 and 7, what happens in the resulting model drawing?

8. When using **joinsf** the advanced option is **Keep original surfaces Yes/<No>:**. Why is the default **No**?
9. There are two commands for decreasing the size of AutoSurf drawing files. Can you name both of them?
10. When using **intersf** what happens if you do not set **Both** in the **Surface Intersection** dialogue box?

Exercises

The following exercises are intended for practising fairly simple AutoSurf 3D models and will allow for revision of preceding chapters. However, the reader is advised to work through the examples in this chapter as well as attempting the exercises below. It will be noted that the exercises in this chapter are based on mechanical engineering parts.

1. Figure 6.23. Construct an AutoSurf 3D model of the handle shown.

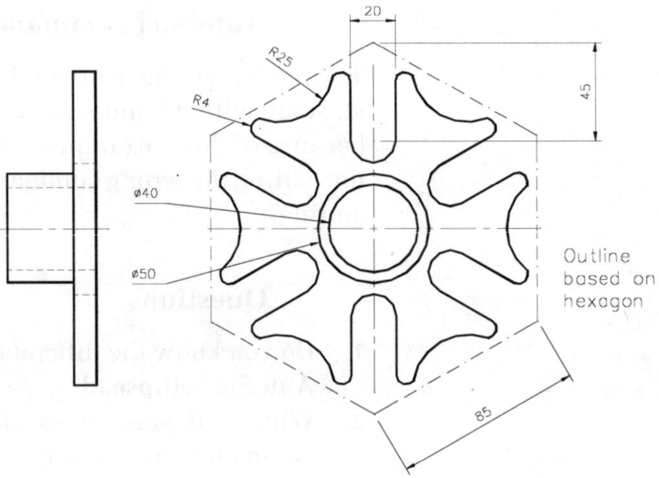

Fig. 6.23 Exercise 1

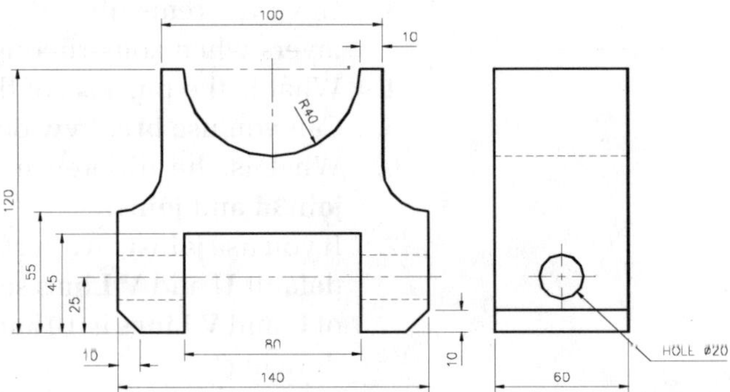

Fig. 6.24 Exercise 2

2. Construct an AutoSurf 3D model of the slide shown in a two-view orthographic projection in Fig. 6.24.
3. Figure 6.25 is a two-view third-angle orthographic projection of a link. Construct an AutoSurf 3D model drawing of the link.

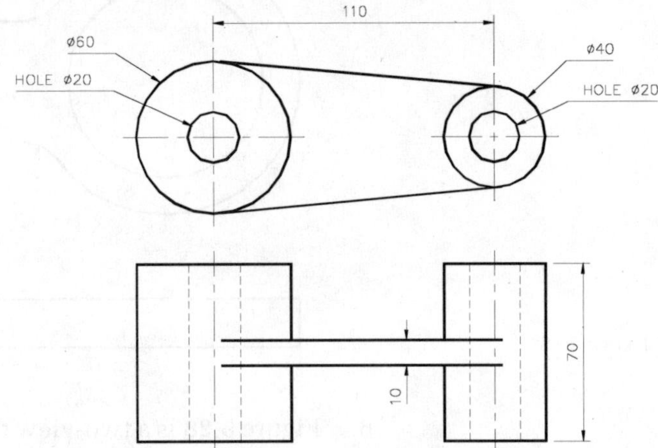

Fig. 6.25 Exercise 3

4. Construct a fully surfaced AutoSurf 3D model of the component shown in the drawings of Fig. 6.26.

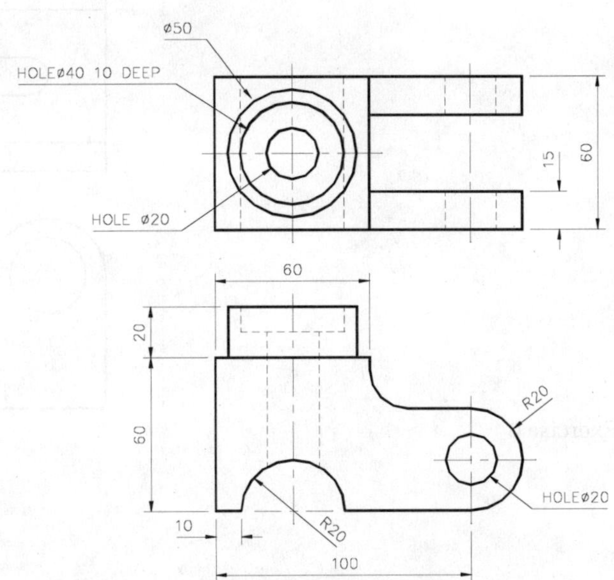

Fig. 6.26 Exercise 4

5. Figure 6.27 shows two orthographic views of part of a tensioning device. Construct a fully surfaced AutoSurf 3D model of the part.

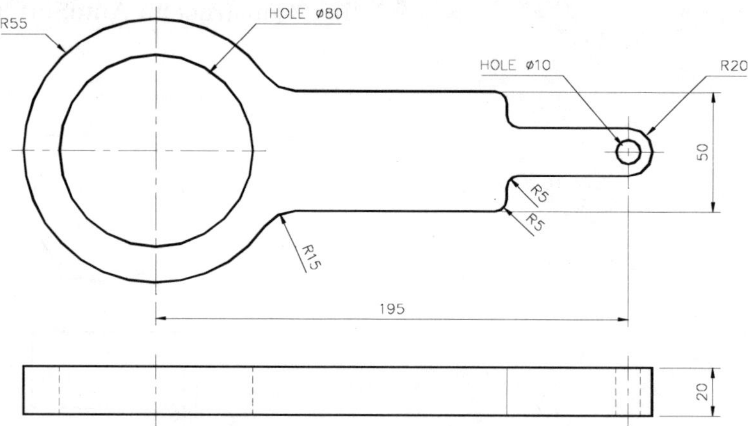

Fig. 6.27 Exercise 5

6. Figure 6.28 is a two-view third-angle orthographic projection of a plate. Construct a fully surfaced AutoSurf 3D model of the plate.

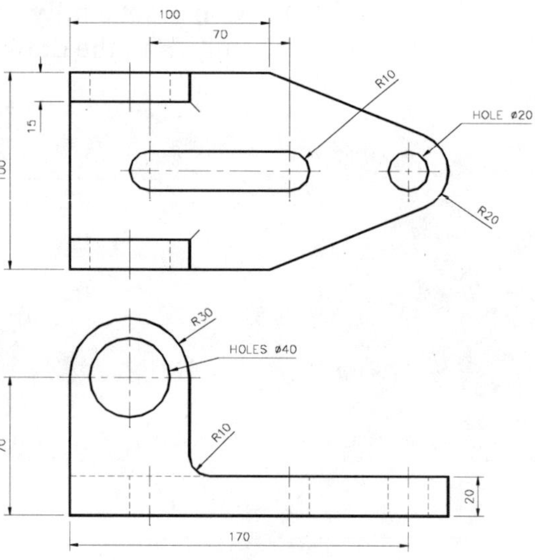

Fig. 6.28 Exercise 6

7. Construct an AutoSurf 3D surfaced model of the slide shown in Fig. 6.29.

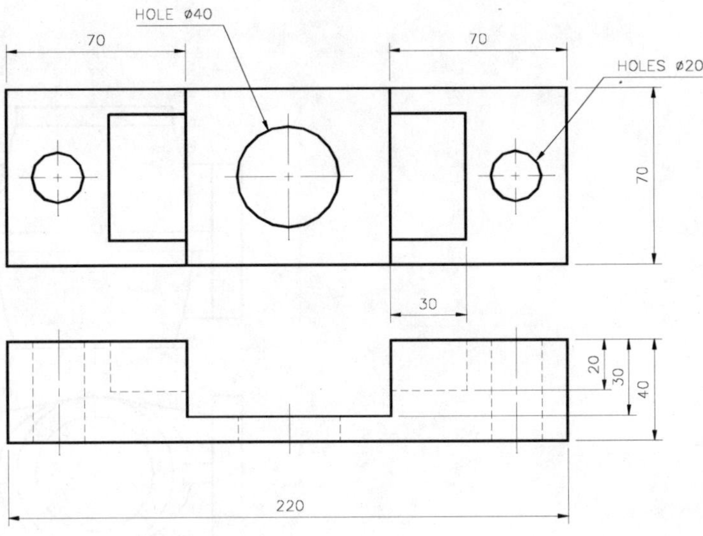

Fig. 6.29 Exercise 7

8. Construct an AutoSurf 3D model of the cap shown in the two views of Fig. 6.30.

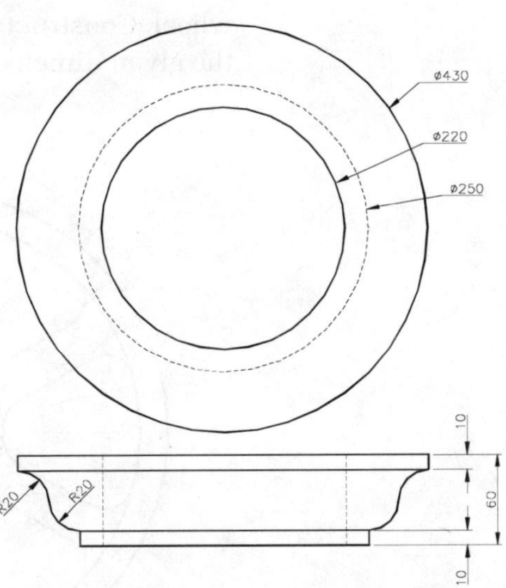

Fig. 6.30 Exercise 8

9. Figure 6.31 shows three first-angle orthographic views of part of a boiler escape valve. Construct an AutoSurf 3D model of the part to the given dimensions.

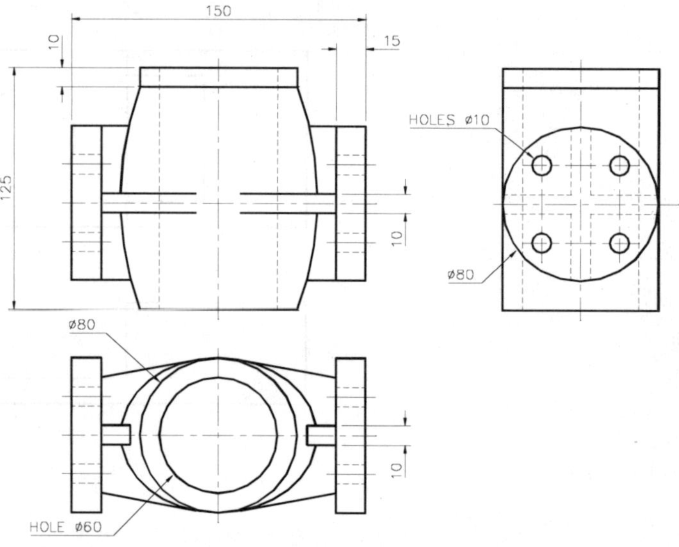

Fig. 6.31 Exercise 9

10. Figure 6.32 is an orthographic projection of a control handle wheel. Construct an AutoSurf 3D model drawing of the wheel to the given dimensions.

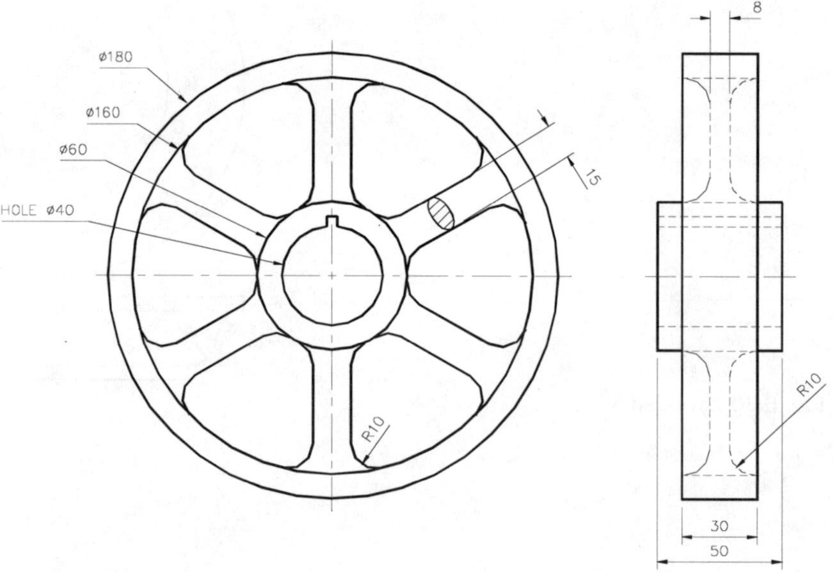

Fig. 6.32 Exercise 10

CHAPTER 7

Other methods of construction

Viewing a 3D model

In earlier chapters, in order to place an AutoSurf model under construction into a good viewing position, we have used the AutoSurf command **Display**. Any 3D model in AutoCAD, including those constructed with the aid of AutoSurf, can be placed in a variety of viewing positions with the aid of two AutoCAD commands **vpoint** and **dview**. The command **dview** is used to *dynamically* place 3D models in any viewing position, including perspective views, hence the **d** of **dview** (dynamic view). **Vpoint** can be used to place a 3D model into any static viewing position.

The AutoCAD command vpoint

New viewing positions can either be set by calling the command from the command line or by selection of **3D Viewing Presets** from the **View** pull-down menu (Fig. 7.1). In addition to orthographic views, the presets are based upon regarding North as the top of the screen and West as the left-hand side of the screen. Thus, as an example, **SW Isometric** is as if viewed from the bottom left-hand side of the screen to produce a 30°,30°,30° isometric view. If calling the command from the command line:

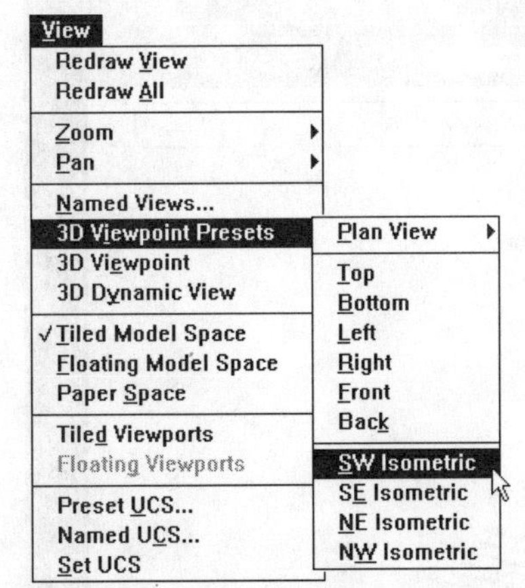

Fig. 7.1 Selection of **3D Viewpoint Presets** from the **View** pull-down menu

Command: *enter* vpoint *right-click*
Rotate/<Viewpoint><0,0,1>: *enter* (e.g.) 1,1,1 *right-click*
Regenerating drawing.
Command:

and the model regenerates in a position as if viewed from the direction of +ve X, +ve Y and +ve Z, i.e. from the North East of and 30° above the screen. Other settings would be:

−1,−1,1 as if from the South West and 30° above.
1,1,−1 as if from the South East and 30° below.
−1,1,1 as if from the North West and 30° above.

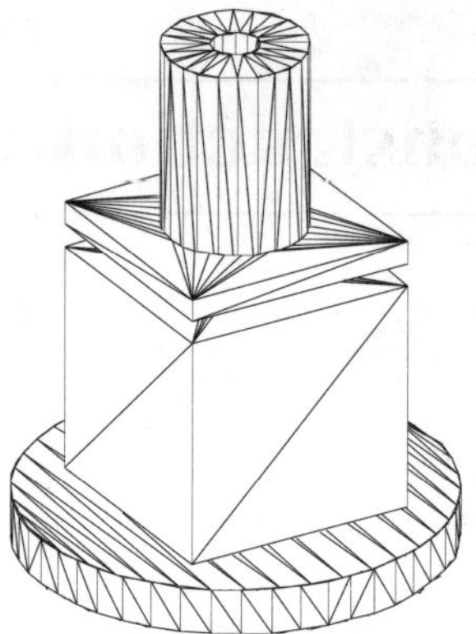

Fig. 7.2 A 3D model in a **vpoint** of –0.6,–1.0,0.6

It may well be found to be easier to *enter* X,Y,Z figures in this way rather than to use the **View** pull-down menu. *Entering* figures also gives the operator more flexibility in choosing a viewing position. As examples, the two AutoSurf 3D models in Figs 7.2 and 7.3 have been placed in viewing positions involving decimal places, as indicated with the drawings. The reader is advised to experiment with placing an AutoSurf 3D model in new viewing positions with the aid of **vpoint**.

The AutoCAD command dview

The AutoCAD command **dview** is more complex than **vpoint**. Here we will only be concerned with placing a 3D model into a perspective view. To place the model into a viewing position before a perspective position can be adopted, either use **CAmera**, **TArget** or the **POints** prompts. In the example given below, **POints** has been adopted. Before calling the command, it is best to start with the model in the **World UCS**.

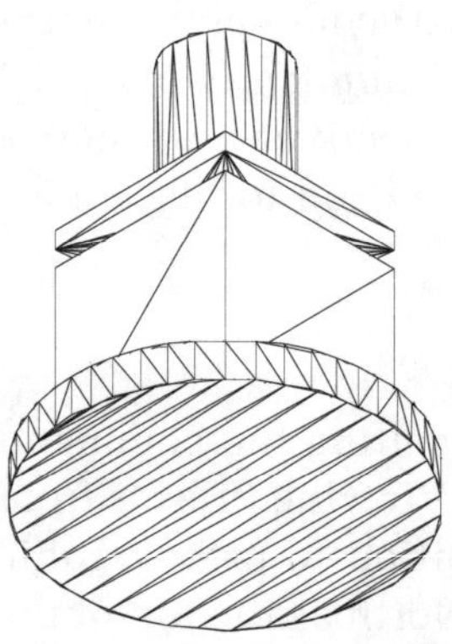

Fig. 7.3 A 3D model in a **vpoint** viewing position of –1.0,–1.0,–1.0

Using the AutoSurf model shown in Figs 7.2 and 7.3, the results of using **dview** as indicated in Figs 7.4 and 7.5 are from the responses given below.

To call the command either select **3D Dynamic View** from the **View** pull-down menu (Fig. 7.1) or, at the command line:

Command: *enter* dview *right*
Select objects: *enter* w (Window) *right-click*
First corner: *pick* **Other corner:** *pick* **18 found.**

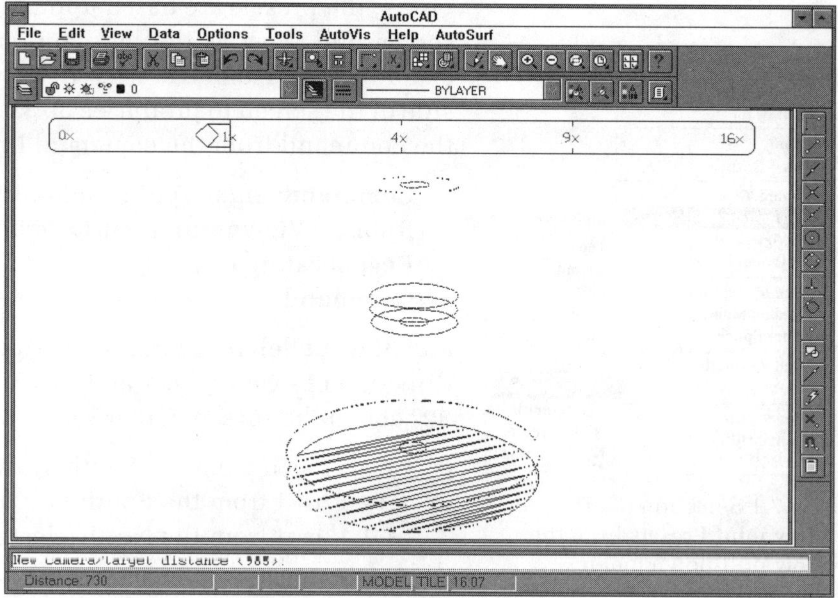

Fig. 7.4 The ghosted 3D model being placed in a perspective view from calling the option **distance**

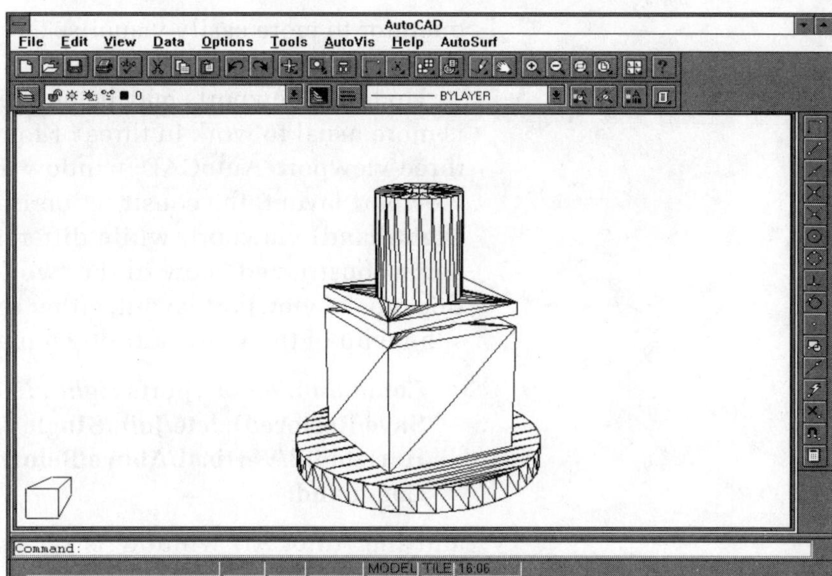

Fig. 7.5 The perspective view resulting from using **dview**. Note the perspective icon in the bottom left corner

CAmera/TArget/Distance/POints/PAn/TWist/CLip/Hide/Off/Undo/ <eXit>: *enter* po *right-click*
Enter target point: *enter* 240,150,100 *right-click* (or .xy filter)
Enter camera point: *enter* 500,10,200 *right-click*
CAmera/TArget/Distance/POints/PAn/TWist/CLip/Hide/Off/Undo/ <eXit>: *enter* d *right-click*

A slider appears at the top of the screen. To obtain a good perspective view, move the pointer of the slider under the control of the mouse. The drawing, in a ghosted form, responds. When satisfied with the position, size and shape taken up by the ghost, *left-click*. The slider bar disappears and a perspective icon appears at the bottom left-hand corner of the screen. *Right-click* and the sequence of prompts at the command line finishes. The model remains in its perspective view with the perspective icon showing as in Fig. 7.5.

The other prompts in the command line sequence of **dview** allow the drawing to be manipulated in a variety of ways. No matter which prompt is used, a ghosted model appears to assist the operator obtaining a good viewing position. Hence the *dynamic* possibilities of the command.

Viewports

One of the best ways of constructing 3D models is to work in several viewports, enabling different views of the model under construction to be viewed on the screen at the same time. This enables the operator to more easily visualise any errors which may arise as the construction proceeds.

Up to 64 viewports may be on the screen at any one time, but it is more usual to work in three or four. An example of working in a three-viewport AutoCAD window is shown in Fig. 7.6. In this viewport layout, the construction is being carried out in the larger (right-hand) viewport, while different views of the model as it is being constructed show in the two left-hand viewports. To set up this type of viewport layout, either select from the **Tiled Viewports** sub-menu of the **View** pull-down menu or, at the command line:

Command: *enter* vports *right-click*
Save/Restore/Delete/Join/SIngle/?/2/3/4/: *enter* 3 *right-click*
Horizontal/Vertical/Above/Below/Left/<Right>: *right-click*
Command:

and the AutoCAD window is set up as shown in Fig. 7.6. If the command **Layout...** is selected from **Tiled Viewports** sub-menu of the **View** pull-down menu, the dialogue box shown in Fig. 7.7 appears, from which a selection of viewport layout can be made.

In the example given in Fig. 7.6 each viewport is configured as follows:

In all viewports: the **UCS icon** is ON.
Top left viewport: ucsfollow is OFF (0) – any change of UCS in

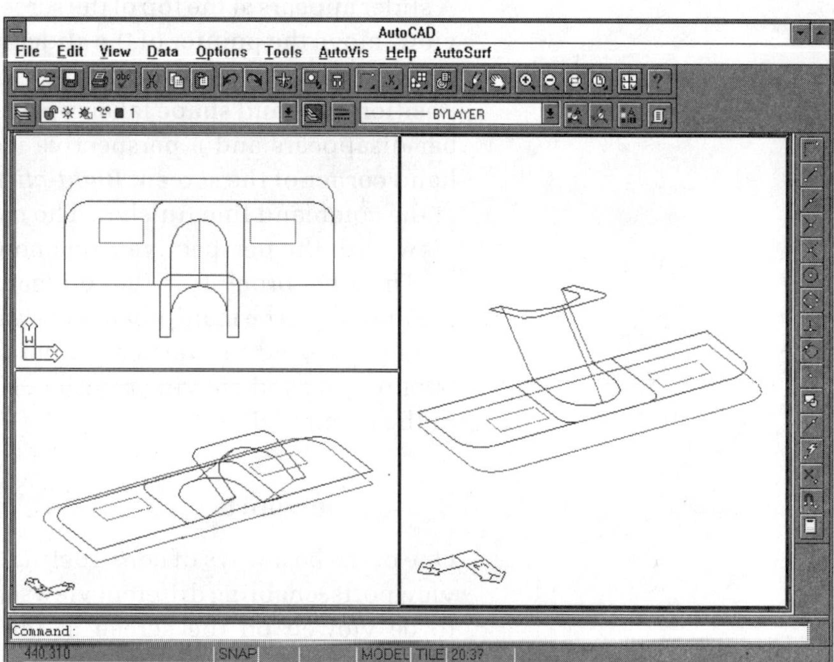

Fig. 7.6 A three-viewport screen with a model under construction

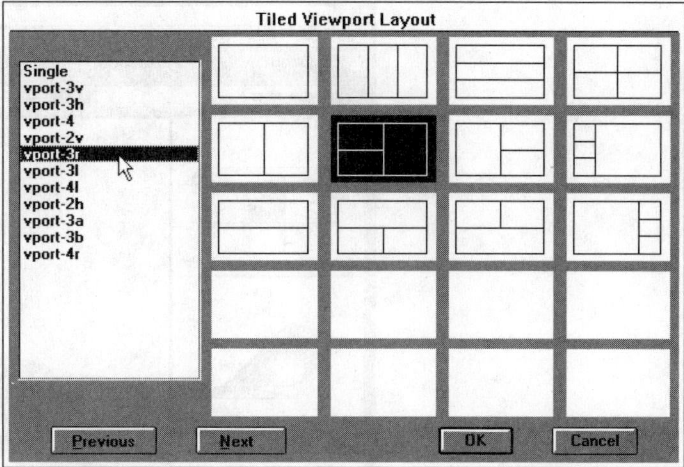

Fig. 7.7 The **Tiled Viewport Layout** dialogue box

the main right-hand viewport is not reflected in this viewport. **Vpoint** is set to 0,0,1, which gives a plan view of the model as it is worked.

Bottom left viewport: ucsfollow is OFF. **Vpoint** set to –0.6,–1,0.6.

Right hand viewport: ucsfollow set ON (1). **Vpoint** set to 0.6,1.0,0.6. However, this is the viewport in which construction is carried out. The UCS planes and the **vpoints** will be changed as necessary.

To make any viewport active, *left-click* within its area and the cursor cross hairs will appear in the selected viewport.

Figure 7.8 is another example of the model being worked in a four-viewport AutoCAD window. This example is included to show that rendering can take place in any viewport. In this example:

In all viewports: the **UCS icon** is OFF.

Upper left-hand viewport: ucsfollow is OFF. **Vpoint** set to 0,0,1 (plan view).

Central left viewport: ucsfollow is OFF. **Vpoint** set to 1,0,0 (end view).

Lower left viewport: ucsfollow is OFF. **Vpoint** set to –0.6, –1.0,0.6.

Right-hand viewport: ucsfollow is ON. **Vpoint** set to 0.6,1.0,0.6.

The model shown in the viewport windows

The model shown in Figs 7.6 and 7.8 was constructed as shown in Figs 7.9 and 7.10. Each surface required a separate layer for its outlines and another for the surface. Repeated use of the **UCS** command enabled frequent change in the UCS plane as the construction proceeded. Although all the stages shown in the two illustrations are

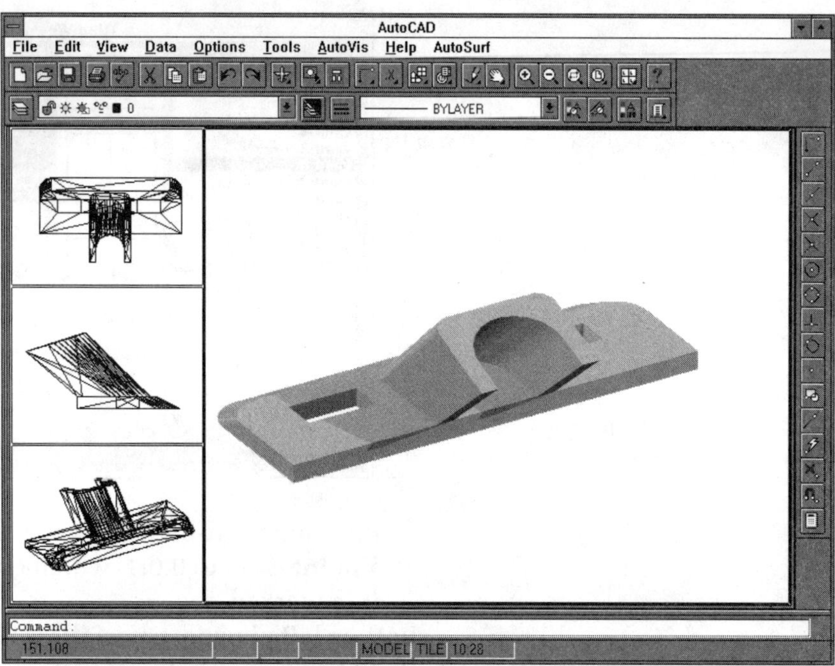

Fig. 7.8 A four-viewport layout with a rendering of the model in the main viewport

in a **vpoint** viewing position, in fact the construction was mainly carried out on the various UCS planes mentioned above.

Finally, as shown in the sixth stage in Fig. 7.10 the model was surface meshed with the aid of **dispsf**, before being rendered as shown in the four-viewport illustration of Fig. 7.8.

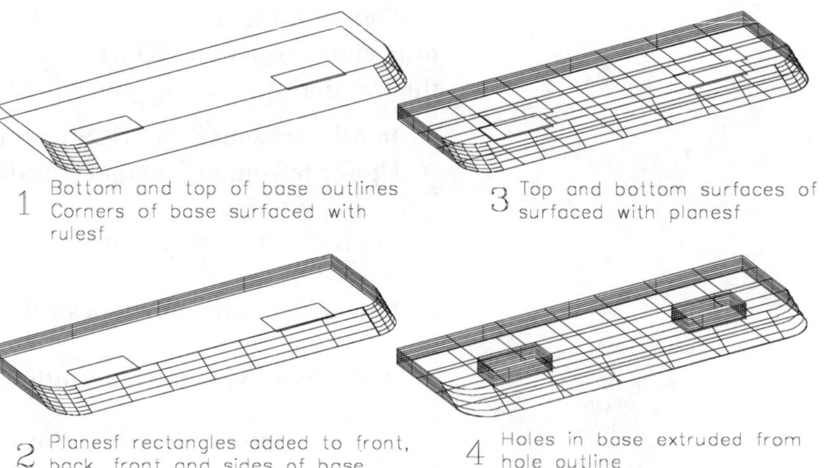

Fig. 7.9 The first four stages of constructing the model used to demonstrate working in several viewports

C0, C1 and C2 surfaces

When AutoSurf forms surfaces they may be one of three types – **C0**, **C1** or **C2**. **C0** surfaces are formed when part of a surface is at an angle

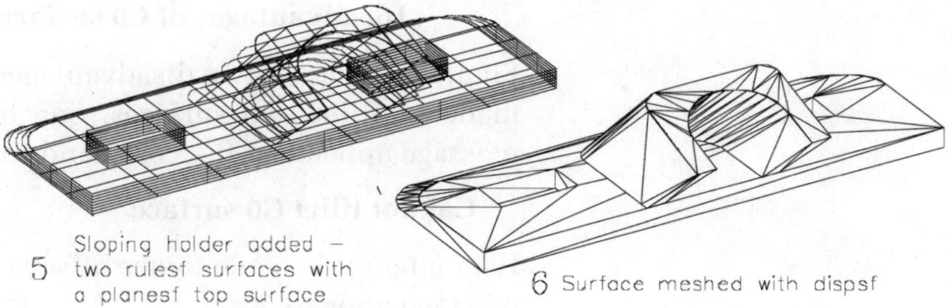

Fig. 7.10 The final two stages in the construction of the model

to another part of the same surface. **C1** surfaces are formed when part of a surface is curved and is tangential to another part of the surface. **C2** surfaces are formed when a surface consists of continuous curves, no parts of which are angular or tangential to other parts.

Figure 7.11 shows an example of a rectangular pline which has been extruded with the aid of **extrudesf**. In the top left-hand drawing the setting for **Fit Length** in the **Extrude** dialogue box has been left at the default of **Inf**. The resulting extrusion is therefore based upon NURBS splines. The surface will be **C2**. In the top right-hand drawing, the **Fit Length** setting has been changed to 40 (i.e. less than the length of any one of the sides of the pline from which the extrusion is constructed. When extruded, the resulting extrusion is a **C0** surface (surface containing parts at angles to each other).

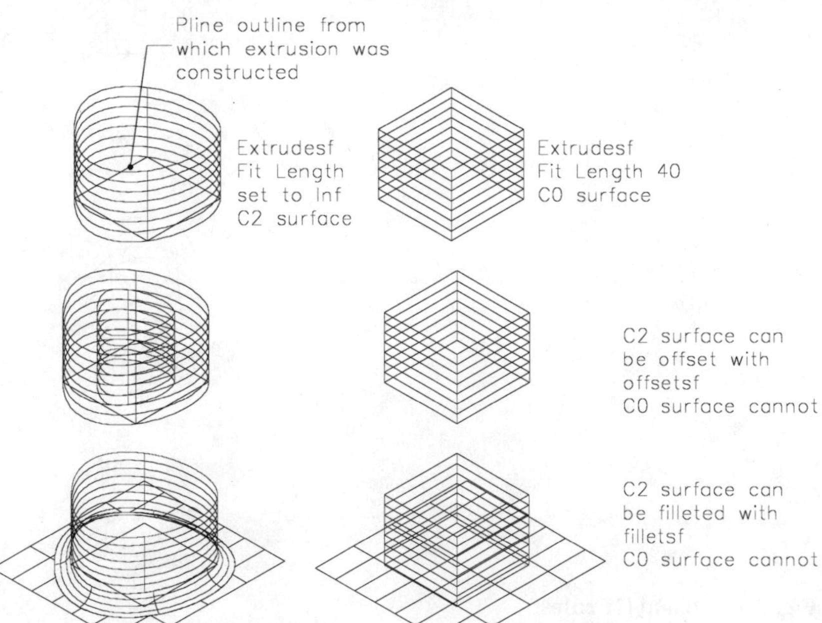

Fig 7.11 C2 and C0 surfaces formed from AutoSurf extrusions

Disadvantages of C0 surfaces

Figure 7.11 shows two disadvantages of **C0** surfaces. If an attempt is made to fillet two surfaces, one of which is **C0**, the following message appears at the command line:

Cannot fillet C0 surface

If an attempt is made to use **offsetsf** on a **C0** surface, the following message appears:

Cannot offset C0 surface, surface skipped

Figure 7.12 shows two **rulesf** surfaces. The top left-hand drawing shows a **C0** surface (one containing parts with angles). The top right-hand drawing shows a **C1** surface (parts tangential to each other. The lower drawings indicate that **C1** surfaces can be filleted with **filletsf** or offset with **offsetsf**, but the **C0** surfaces cannot.

Because of these two disadvantages, care must be taken when constructing models which may require to have fillets or offset surfaces included to avoid using **C0** surfaces where the fillets or offsets may occur. The construction of such models may have to be redesigned as construction continues. Offsetting **C0** surfaces with

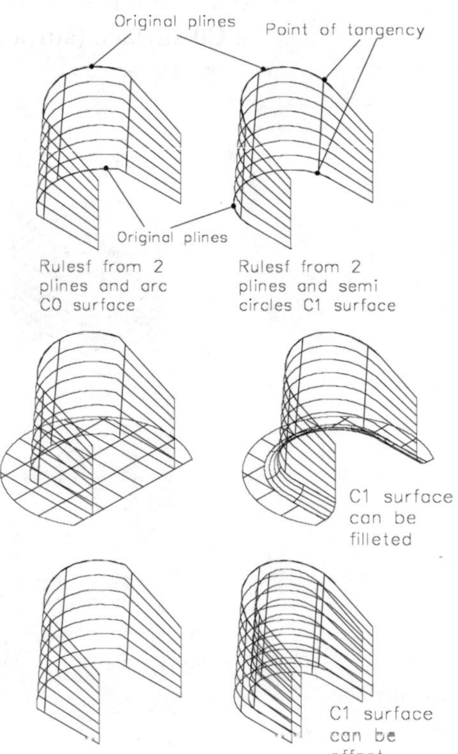

Fig. 7.12 C0 and C1 **rulesf** surfaces

offsetsf may be avoided by constructing either a second surface where the offset requires both the original and the offset to be included, or constructing a new surface in the offset position.

Another disadvantage of **C0** surfaces in a model is that they may not be suitable if the data from the drawing file is to be used for manufacturing purposes. However, as stated earlier, the manufacturing possibilities of AutoSurf drawing data for manufacturing purposes is beyond the scope of this book.

The commands sectsf and flowsf

The use of these two commands allows the operator to see more clearly the shape which his/her surfaces will assume when they are surface meshed.

The command sectsf

To call the command either select **Wireframe/Surface Outputs/Cut Section** from the **AutoSurf** pull-down menu or, at the command line:

Command: *enter* sectsf *right-click*
To invoke advanced options enter '??' ...
Select surfaces: *pick*
Select surfaces: *right-click*
Section type Radial/<Plane>: *right-click*
Plane by Entity/Last/View/Xy/Yz/Zaxis/Zx/<3points>: *enter* x *right-click*
Point on XY plane: *enter* 25,100,5

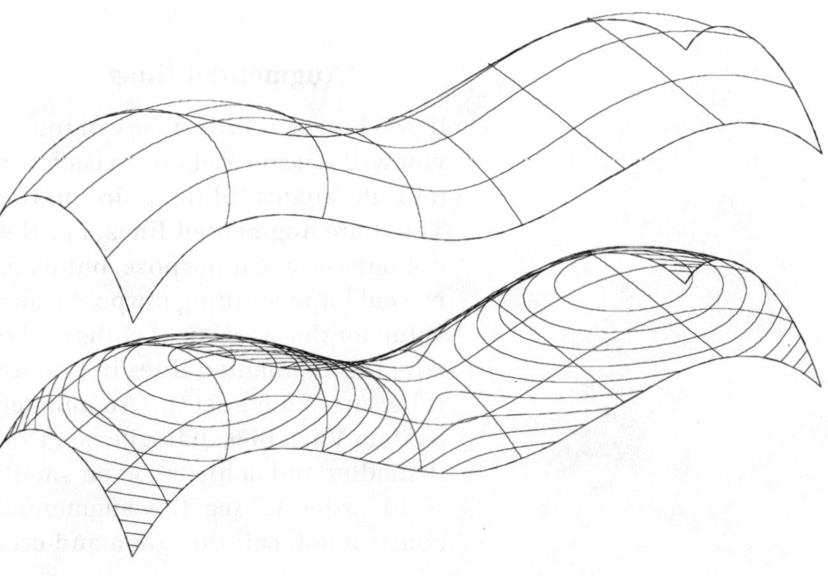

Fig. 7.13 Section cuts produced in a surface with **sectsf**

Start value <0>: *right-click*
End value <0>: *right-click*
Group name prefix <ASG>: *right-click*
Command:

Figure 7.13 shows the results of using the command on a **sweepsf** surface. The upper drawing in Fig. 7.13 shows the original **sweepsf** surface; the lower shows the surface after repeated action of the **sectsf** command. The section lines of the lower drawing were taken at 5 unit vertical intervals – i.e. **Point on XY plane:** at 25,100,5, then 25,100,10 and so on.

The command flowsf

To call the command either select **Wireframe/Surface Outputs/Flow Lines** from the **AutoSurf** pull-down menu or, at the command line:

Command: *enter* flowsf *right-click*
To invoke advanced options enter '??'...
Select surfaces: *pick* **1 found.**
Select surfaces: *right-click*
Number of U Lines: *enter* 60 *right-click*
Number of V Lines: *enter* 5 *right-click*
Save display lines/ Yes/<No>: *enter* y *right-click*
Group name prefix <ASG>: *right-click*
Command:

Figure 7.14 shows the results of forming flow lines with the aid of the command. The upper drawing is the same **sweepsf** surface as was used to demonstrate the **sectsf** command.

Augmented lines

If you look carefully at any of the surfaces shown in previous pages you will see somewhere on each surface a 1 unit long line normal to (at right angles to) the point on the surface where the line occurs. These are **augmented lines**. For the purposes of this book, they do not have any real purpose, but when the data of an AutoSurf model is used for machining purposes, augmented lines will prove to be of value for the creation of paths in the machining process. The reason why the augmented lines in previous drawings have been so small is because I have set the **Augmented Vector** setting in the **AutoSurf System Variables** dialogue box to 1 (see Fig. 7.17). I could have set it smaller and achieved even smaller augments.

In order to see the augmented lines in a surface you have constructed, call the command **createaug**. In the example given in

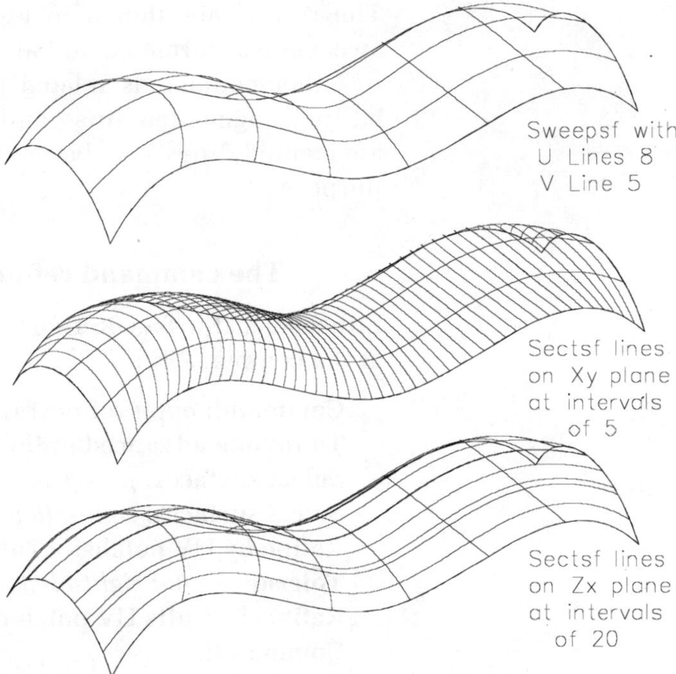

Fig. 7.14 Flow lines produced with the aid of **flowsf**

Fig. 7.15, the **Augmented Vector** setting was first changed to **10** in the **AutoSurf System Variables** dialogue box (see Fig. 7.17). The command can then either be selected from the **AutoSurf** pull-down menu (**Wireframe/Surface Outputs/Create Aug**) or, at the command line:

Command: *enter* createaug *right-click*
To invoke advanced options enter '??' ...
Create from Wireframe/<Surface edges>: *right-click*
Select surface edges: *pick* each U and V Line in turn
Select surface edges: *right-click*
Augmented by Points/Step/<Optional>: *enter* s *right-click*
Step distance <1>: *enter* 10 *right-click*
Command:

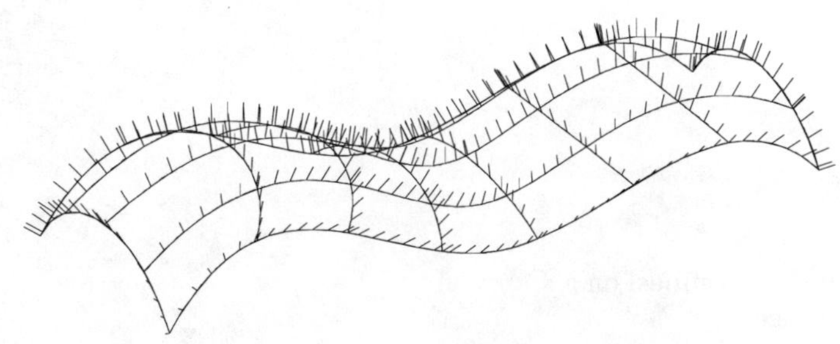

Fig. 7.15 Augmented lines produced with the aid of **createaug**

The results are shown in Fig. 7.15. The edges from which the **sweepsf** was formed could also have been chosen.

Other commands related to augmented lines are **editaug** for editing augmented lines and **outputaug**, by which the data of augmented lines can be saved to an ASCII file for machining purposes.

The command refinesf

Either select **Surface/Refine** from the **AutoSurf** pull-down menu or, at the command line:

Command: *enter* refinesf *right-click*
To invoke advanced options enter '??' ...
Select surfaces: *pick* **1 found.**
Select surfaces: *right-click*
Refine by UV patches <Tolerance>: *right-click*
Tolerance <0>: *right-click*
Refinesf results UV patch count changed from X31 to 25X1
Command:

Two examples of the use of the command are shown in Fig. 7.16. The central drawing shows the refined surface after selecting the **Tolerance** option. The third drawing shows the refined surface after using the **UV patches** option.

The reason for using this command is to refine a C0 surface – which the first drawing in Fig. 7.16 obviously is – into a C2 surface. However the operator should use the command with care. As can be seen in this figure, the shape of the surface can be considerably changed, possibly making it meaningless in the model being constructed.

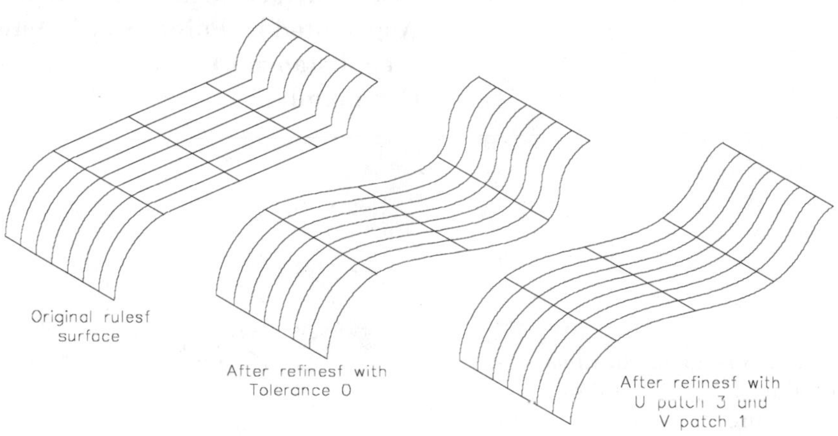

Fig. 7.16 Using **refinesf** on a **rulesf** surface

The AutoSurf System Variables dialogue box

Several references have already been made to this dialogue box in which system variables for AutoSurf can be set. There are other system variables which can be set in AutoSurf, but for the purpose of this book those set in the dialogue box will be sufficient. Figure 7.17 shows the dialogue box with the settings used for the drawings contained in this book. The dialogue box can be called to screen either by selection of **Preferences...** from the **AutoSurf** pull-down menu or, at the command line:

Command: *enter* surfvar *right-click*
Command:

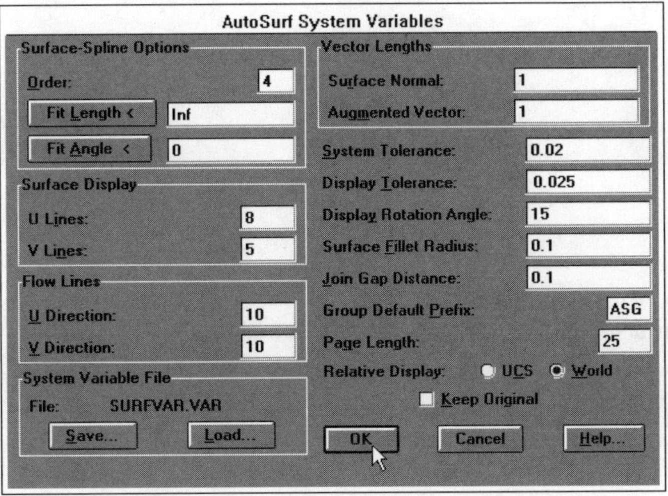

Fig. 7.17 The **AutoSurf System Variables** dialogue box with settings used for drawings in this book

The command extendsf

This is a command which can be used for lengthening or widening a surface. Example of using the command are shown in Figs 7.18 to 7.20. Figure 7.18 shows the effects of using the command on a **planesf** surface. Note that care must be taken in the selection of the edge of the surface nearest the direction in which the extension is to occur. Figure 7.19 shows the use of the command on a **rulesf** surface and Fig. 7.20 the effects on a **sweepsf** surface.

To call the command either select **Surface/Extend** from the **AutoSurf** pull-down menu or, at the command line:

Command: *enter* extendsf *right-click*
To invoke advanced options enter '??' ...
Select surface edges: *pick*

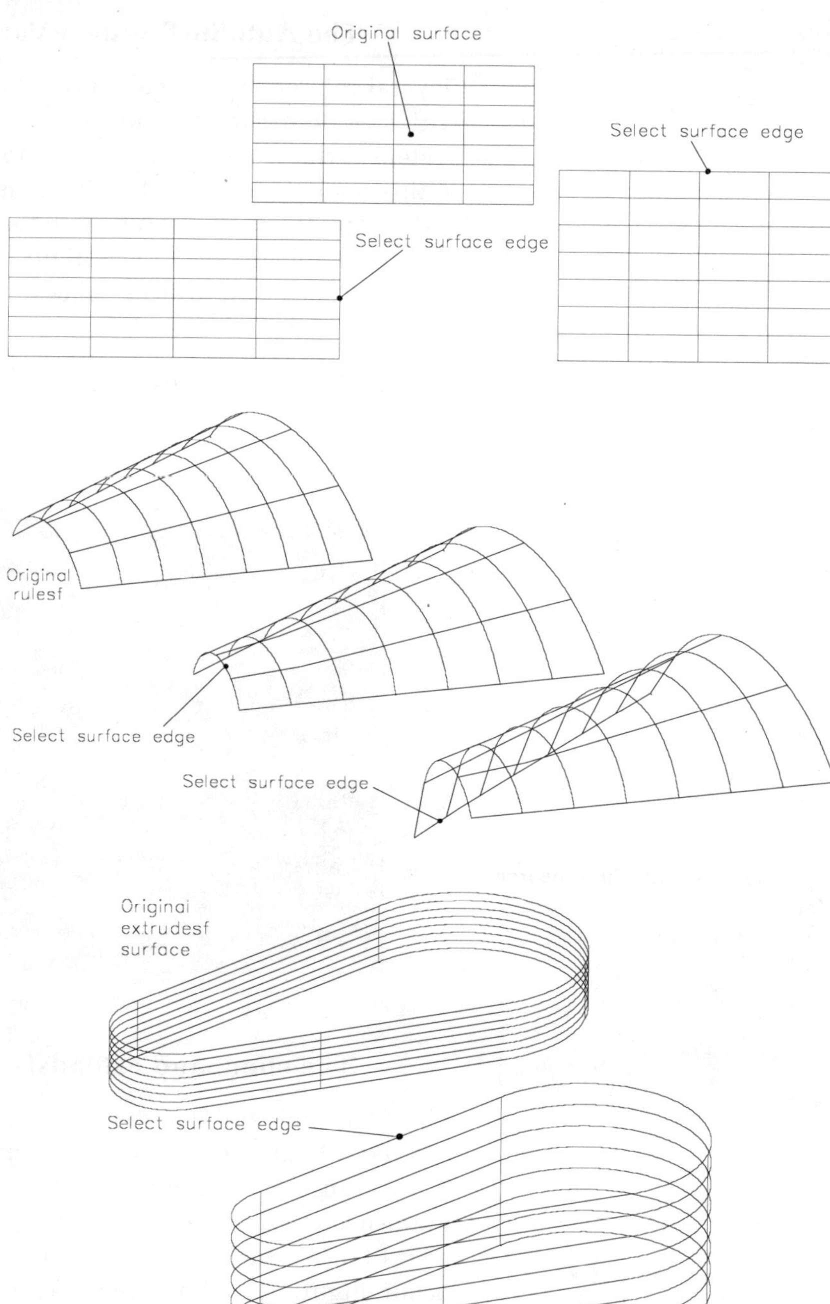

Fig. 7.18 Using **extendsf** on a **planesf** surface

Fig. 7.19 Using **extendsf** on a **rulesf** surface

Fig. 7.20 Using **extendsf** on a **sweepsf** surface

Select surface edges: *right-click*
Extend by percentage/<Distance>: <0> *enter* 30 *right-click*
Command:

The command breaksf

This command is available for breaking surfaces mainly along U or V Lines. When the surface is broken with the aid of the command two separate surfaces are formed, each including the number U and V Lines according to the settings in the **AutoSurf System Variables** dialogue box. Breaks can also be made along U and V Lines and in C0 or C1 surfaces, as indicated by the prompts appearing at the command line when the command is called. Figure 7.21 shows the effects of using the command on a **planesf** surface.

To call the command either select **Surface/Break** from the **AutoSurf** pull-down menu or, at the command line:

Command: *enter* breaksf *right-click*
Select surfaces: *pick*
Break at C0,C1/UV/V/<U>: *right-click*
Locate U point/<U percentage><1>: *right-click*
Command:

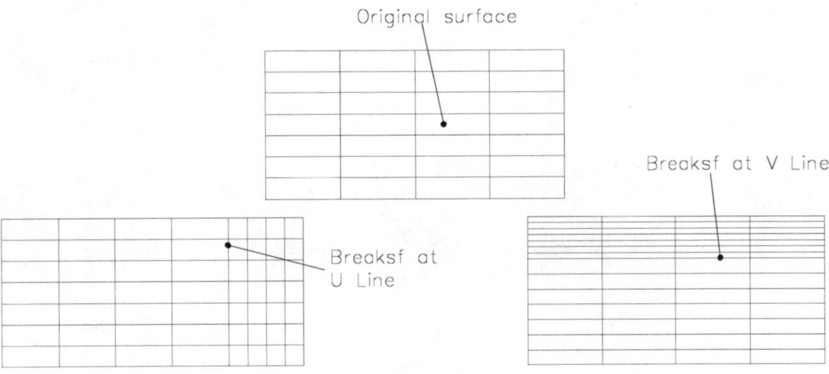

Fig. 7.21 Using **breaksf** on a **planesf** surface

Questions

1. Are there any advantages in using the AutoCAD command **vpoint** over using the AutoSurf command **Display**?
2. Can AutoSurf models be placed in a perspective view? If so how?
3. What advantages are there in constructing AutoSurf models in a three- or four-viewport AutoCAD window?
4. How is the AutoCAD window which usually appears when AutoCAD is started up changed to a three-viewport window?
5. Can you describe the **ucsfollow** and **vpoint** settings which you would use in each viewport when working in a three- or four-viewport window?
6. Can rendering of an AutoSurf model be carried out in a viewport of a three- or four-viewport window?

7. Can you explain the differences between **C0**, **C1** and **C2** surfaces?
8. What are the disadvantages of constructing **C0** surfaces?
9. Why use the command **sectsf**?
10. What are **augmented lines**?

Exercises

The reader is advised to attempt constructing the AutoSurf models described in the preceding pages of this chapter, then work through the exercises given below, which are partly revision work.

1. Figure 7.22 shows the stages in the construction of a model of the end of a suction device. Working to any suitable sizes, construct an AutoSurf model of the device.

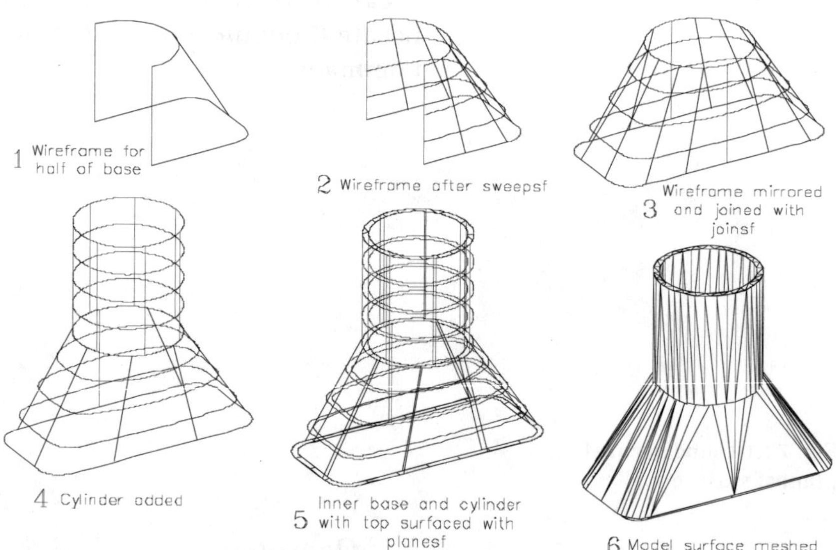

Fig. 7.22 Exercise 1

2. Figure 7.23 is a rendering of the nozzle from a vacuum cleaner. Two drawings – the wireframe and the surface-meshed model – are shown in Fig. 7.24. Construction of this model requires the use of a number of different **UCS** planes, which must be carefully set if the model is to be successful.
3. Figure 7.25 is a rendering of the model for Exercise 3 and Fig. 7.26 shows dimensioned front and end views of the model. Working to the dimensions given in Fig. 7.26, construct the AutoSurf model.
4. Figure 7.27 is a rendering of the model for this exercise. Figure 7.28 shows the dimensions for the model and Fig. 7.29 stages in its construction. Construct an AutoSurf 3D model to the details given.

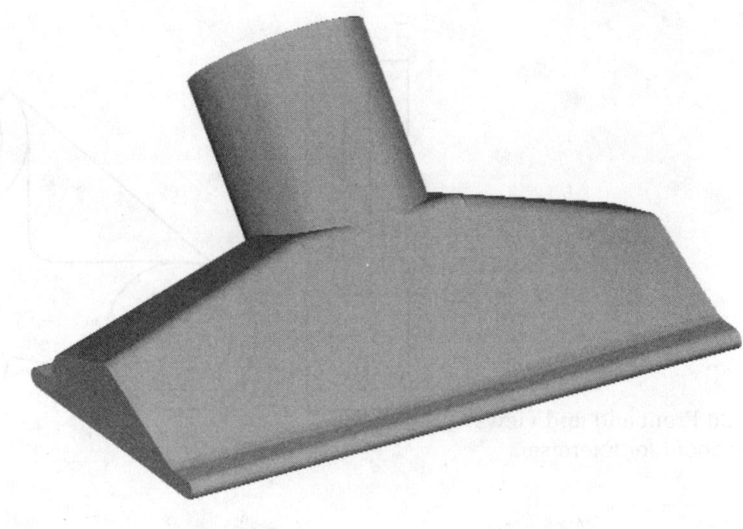

Fig. 7.23 A rendering of the model for Exercise 2

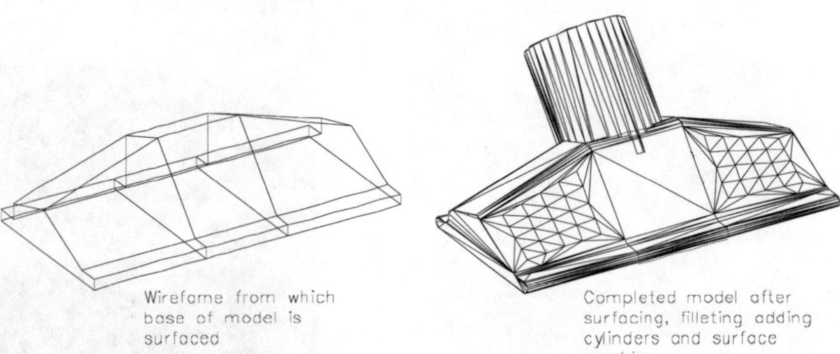

Fig. 7.24 Exercise 2

Fig. 7.25 A rendering of the model for Exercise 3

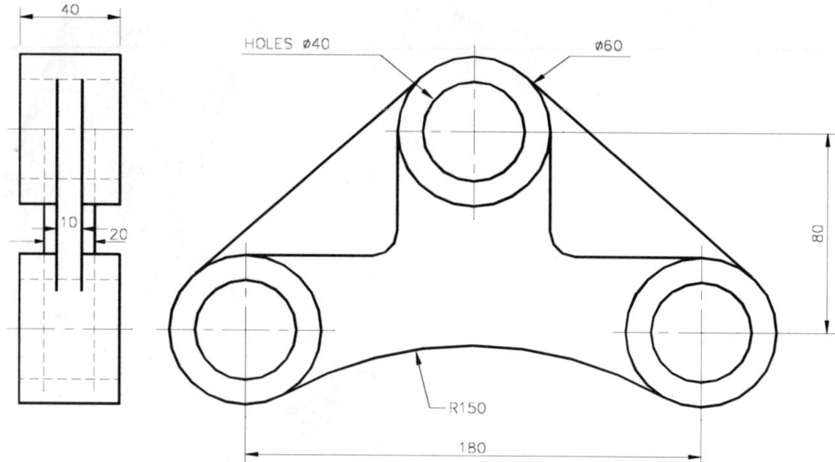

Fig. 7.26 Front and end views of the model for Exercise 3

Fig. 7.27 A rendering of the model for Exercise 4

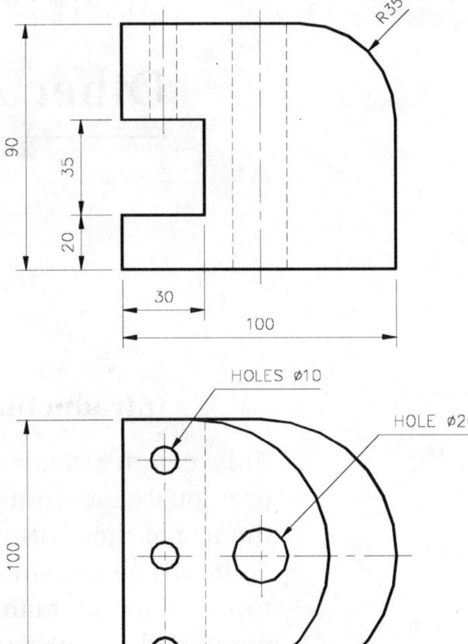

Fig. 7.28 Front view and plan of the model for Exercise 4

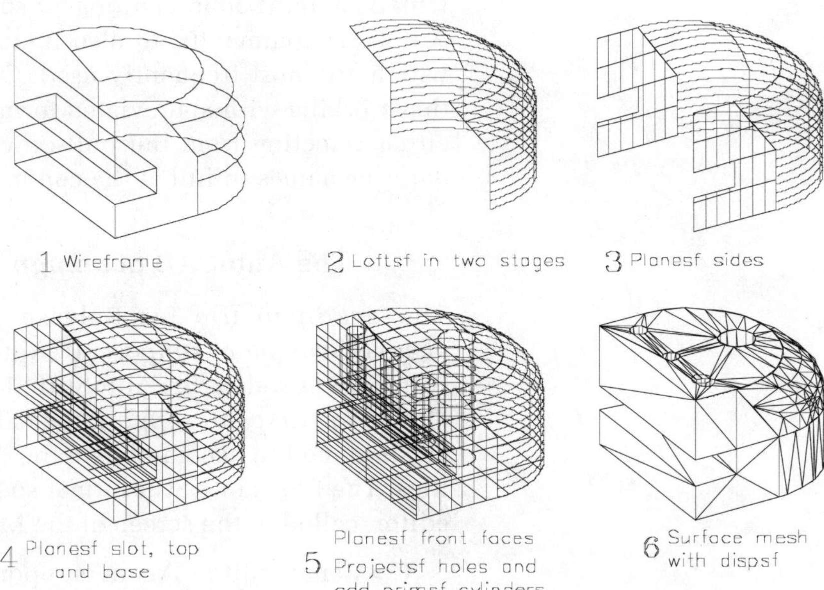

Fig. 7.29 Stages in the construction of Exercise 4

CHAPTER 8

Other AutoSurf commands

Introduction

This chapter deals with a number of AutoSurf commands not previously mentioned. Where it is thought necessary, examples of the use of these other commands will be shown in drawings.

It will be remembered that AutoSurf commands can be selected from either command names contained in the **AutoSurf** pull-down menu and its sub-menus, *entered* at the command line or selected from icons in the AutoSurf toolbars. If AutoSurf is being used on a regular basis, it may be worth while amending the *acad.pgp* file, which contains abbreviations for some of the most frequently used AutoCAD commands, to also include those AutoSurf commands which are most frequently used. Operators of AutoSurf may find that working with abbreviated forms of commands is quicker than either selecting from the pull-down menus, from the toolbars or *entering* names in full at the command line.

The AutoCAD *acad.pgp* file

The *acad.pgp* file for Release 13 is held in the directory *acadr13\common\support.* If AutoVision files are loaded with AutoCAD as well as the AutoSurf files, this directory may have been altered to *r13\com\support*, the names of the directories having to be shortened to accommodate the AutoCAD paths for AutoVision files. The file is in ASCII format so it can be edited in the MS-DOS editor, called to the screen at the MS-DOS prompt by:

C:> *enter* edit r13\com\support\acad.pgp *right-click*

The contents of the file then appear on screen. That part of the file which concerns us here will appear something like the following:

; Command alias format:
;   <Alias>,*<Full command name>
; Sample aliases for AutoCAD Commands

```
; These examples reflect the most frequently used commands.
; Each alias uses a small amount of memory, so don't go
; overboard on systems with tight memory.

A,        *ARC
C,        *CIRCLE
CP,       *COPY
E,        *ERASE
EL,       *ELLIPSE
L,        *LINE
M,        *MOVE
P,        *PAN
PL,       *PLINE
R,        *REDRAW
S,        *STRETCH
T,        *MTEXT
TR,       *TRIM
VP,       *VPOINT
Z,        *ZOOM
3DLINE,   *LINE
```

There may be differences in this part of the file contents compared with that which the reader is using, but it will be seen that additions for AutoSurf commands can be made to allow abbreviations to replace the full commands. In my own *acad.pgp* file for my AutoCAD Release 13/AutoSurf Release 2.1 system, I have added the following:

```
AP,    *PRIMSF
APL,   *PLANESF
AE,    *EXTRUDESF
AR,    *REVOLVESF
ARL,   *RULESF
AL,    *LOFTSF
AF,    *FILLETSF
AS,    *SWEEPSF
```

That is, I have included those commands which I find I use most often when working in AutoSurf.

Remember, however, that it is not advisable to add too many abbreviations to your *acad.pgp* unless the computer at which you are working has plenty of memory. AutoCAD Release 13 working in Windows requires at least 16 Mbytes of memory. If constructing AutoSurf drawings which will produce files of more than 1 Mbyte in size, it is best to have even more than 16 Mbytes.

If you are working at a computer used by others, please do not interfere in any way with *acad.pgp*. If you do so, others using the computer may find themselves in difficulty. Only change working files such as *acad.pgp* if you either own the computer or are the only person who uses it.

AutoSurf commands not used so far

The command editsf

AutoSurf
Create
Surface
Wireframe
Trim Surface
Edit
Surface — Pull
Wireframe — Break
Trim Border — Extend
Display Views — Join
Surface Display... — Refine
Entity Visibility — Truncate
Entity Information — Flip Normal
Distance
Preferences...
Utility

Fig. 8.1 Selecting **editsf** from the **AutoSurf** pull-down menu

This is a command for the editing of surfaces (as its name implies). The command can be called from the **Pull** command in the **Surface** sub-menu of the **AutoSurf** pull-down menu as shown in Fig. 8.1 or, at the command line:

Command: *enter* editsf *right-click*
Select surface: *pick*
Control points OFf/ON/Pull/<eXit>: *enter* on *right-click*
Control points OFf/ON/Pull/<eXit>: *enter* p *right-click*
Cursor/Move/Next/PIck/PRev/<eXit>: *enter* pi *right-click*
Cursor/Move/Next/PRev/eXit/PIck>: enter m *right-click*
Move by Entity/Start point/Viewdir/X/Y/Z/<eXit>: *enter* s *right-click*
Select first location: *pick*
Select second location: *pick*
Cursor/Next/PIck/PRev/eXit/<Move>: *enter* x *right-click*
Command:

Figure 8.2 shows the action of using the **Pull** option of the command with **Control points** on. The control points show as coloured squares. In order to pull a surface to a new position, one or more control points must be picked, then moved.

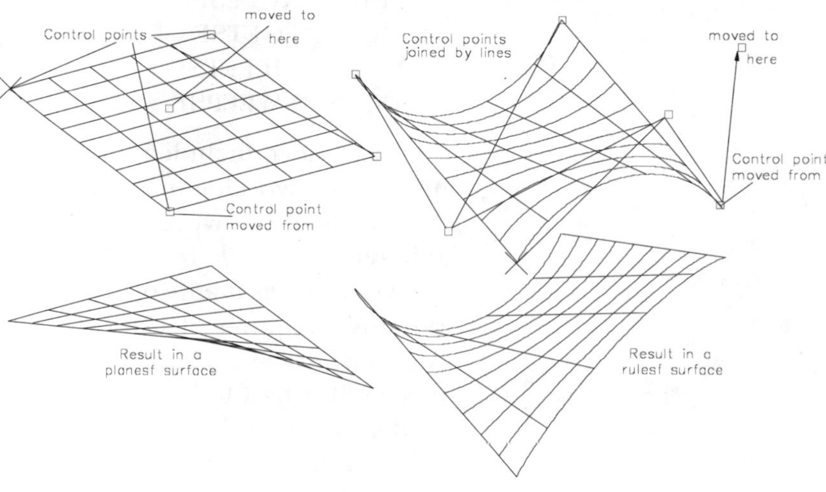

Fig. 8.2 The results of using the **Pull** option of **editsf** on **planesf** and **rulesf** surfaces

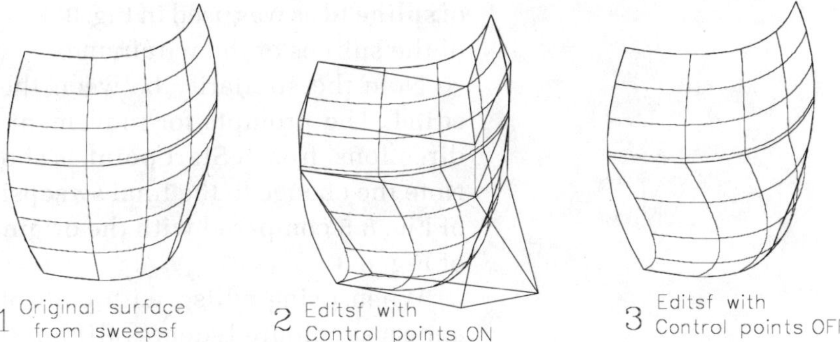

Fig. 8.3 The effect of using **editsf** on a **sweepsf** surface

The **Next** and **PRev** options allow the control points to be moved either to the next position or to their previous position. The movement is shown on the surface by the movement of the main control point which appears as an X type cross.

If the **Cursor** option is chosen, movement of the cursor under mouse control moves the control point. When satisfied with its position, it can be determined by a *right-click*.

Figure 8.3 shows the effect of using the command on a **sweepsf** surface. Drawing 1 shows the original surface; drawing 2 shows the surface after editing with **editsf** with the control points on; drawing 3 shows the same edited surface with the control points off.

The command editsp

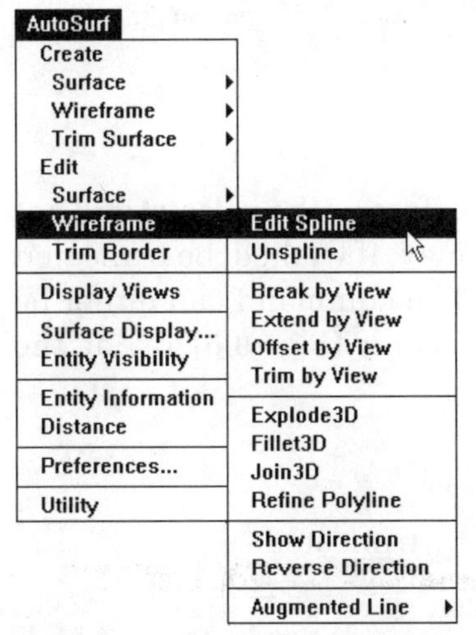

Fig. 8.4 Selecting **Edit Spline** from the **AutoSurf** pull-down menu

This is a command for the editing of splines (as its name implies). The command can be called from the **Edit Spline** command in the **Wireframe** sub-menu of the **AutoSurf** pull-down menu as shown in Fig. 8.4 or, at the command line:

Command: *enter* editsp *right-click*
Select spline: *pick*
Control points OFf/ON/Pull/Refine/<eXit>: *enter* p *right-click*
Cursor/Move/Next/PIck/PRev/<eXit>: *enter* pi *right-click*
Cursor/Move/Next/PRev/eXit/<PIck>: *pick*
Cursor/Move/Next/PRev/eXit/<PIck>: *enter* m *right-click*
Move by Entity/Start point/Viewdir/X/Y/Z/<EXit>: *enter* s *right-click*
Select first location: *pick*
Select second location: *pick*
Cursor/Next/PIck/PRev/eXit/<Move>: *enter* x *right-click*
Command:

Figure 8.5 shows the results of editing spline with the command. The same **sweepsf** surface, constructed on a wireframe with the aid of **spline3d** as was used in Fig. 8.3, is used to demonstrate the editing of the splines of the wireframe.

Note the similarity between the prompts with **editsp** as with **editsf**. The prompts for movement allow movement in **X**, **Y** or **Z** directions, from a **Start point** as shown in Fig. 8.5, or in a **Viewdir**. Note the change to the final **sweepsf** surface as shown in drawing 3 of Fig. 8.5 compared with the original **sweepsf** shown in drawing 1 of Fig. 8.3.

When using **editsp** with control points on, the control points appear as coloured squares all along the spline being edited. Because the command is for use on splines, a large number of control points will appear. Any one of these can be chosen as required for the editing.

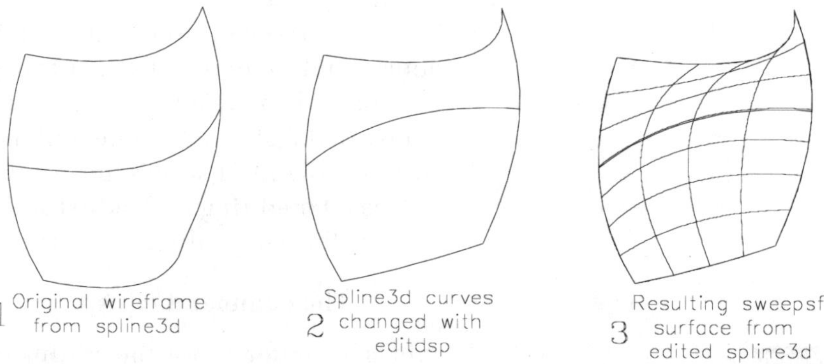

Fig. 8.5 The effects of using **editsp** on a wireframe

The command truncsf

If an outline has been projected on to a surface with **projectsf** and not trimmed, the excess area of the surface may, if wished, be truncated with the aid of the command **truncsf**. The command can either be called from the **AutoSurf** pull-down menu (Fig. 8.6) or, at the command line:

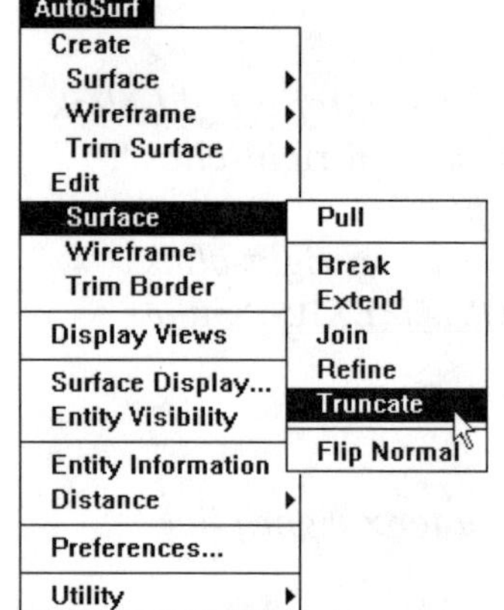

Fig. 8.6 Selecting **Truncate** from the **AutoSurf** pull-down menu

Command: *enter* truncsf *right-click*
To invoke advanced options enter '??'...
Select surfaces: *pick* the surface to be truncated
Command:

Note that the projected surface must be projected from the **Border** option of the command **projectsf**. A **Trim** option for projecting the outline onto the surface with **projectsf** will not produce the expected truncation.

Figures 8.7 and 8.8 show examples of the use of the command. In Fig. 8.7 a **planesf** surface has been truncated to a circular projected

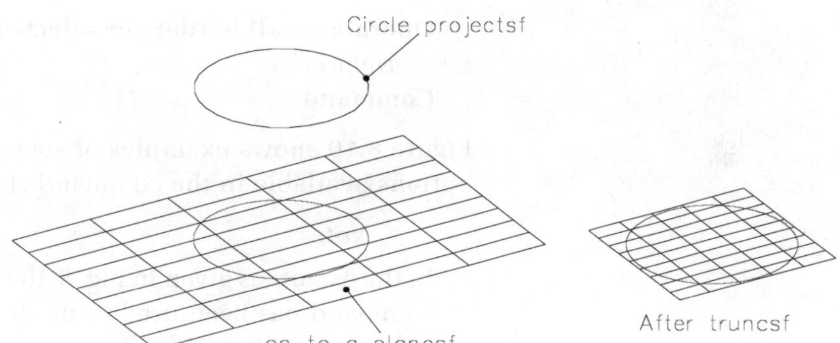

Fig. 8.7 An example of using **truncsf** on a **planesf** surface

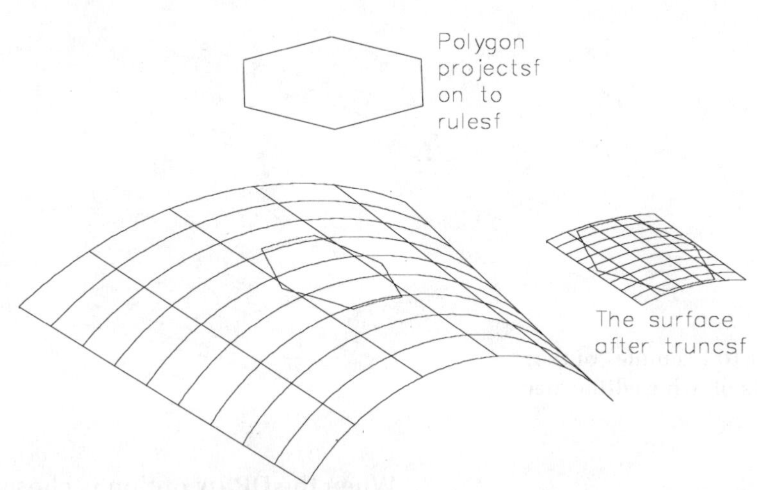

Fig. 8.8 An example of using **truncsf** on a **rulesf** surface

border. In Fig. 8.8 a **rulesf** surface has been truncated to a hexagonal projected border.

The command editborder

This command is used for the editing of borders inside a surface. Note that when calling the command from the **AutoSurf** pull-down menu, all the options can be seen in a sub-menu when **Edit Border** is selected. In this sense this command is different to most others in the AutoSurf range of commands. Most commands from the **AutoSurf** pull-down menu are commands in their own right and options have to be *entered* at the command line.

The command can either be selected from the **AutoSurf** pull-down menu (Fig. 8.9) or, at the command line:

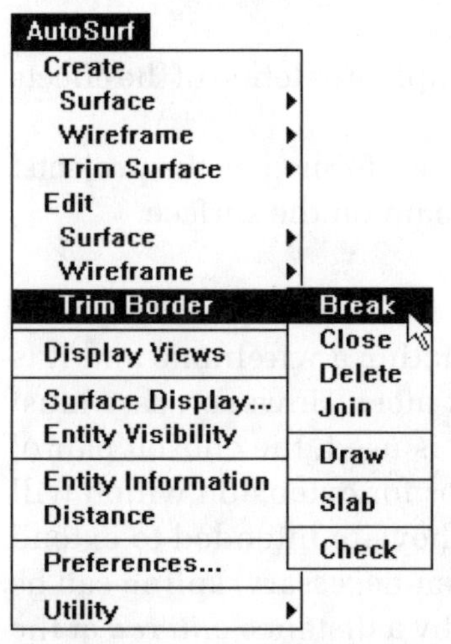

Fig. 8.9 Selecting **Break** from the **AutoSurf** pull-down menu

Command: *enter* editborder *right-click*
Break/CLose/DElete/DRaw/Join/Slab/<Check>:
Select border: *pick*

Operate on all borders or selected surfaces? No/<Yes>: *enter* n
right-click
Command:

Figure 8.10 shows examples of some of the results of entering the options available in the command structure.

Notes

1. In the examples given in Fig. 8.10 the **Trim** option of the **projectsf** command has been used to produce the hexagonal and circular holes in the **planesf** surface.

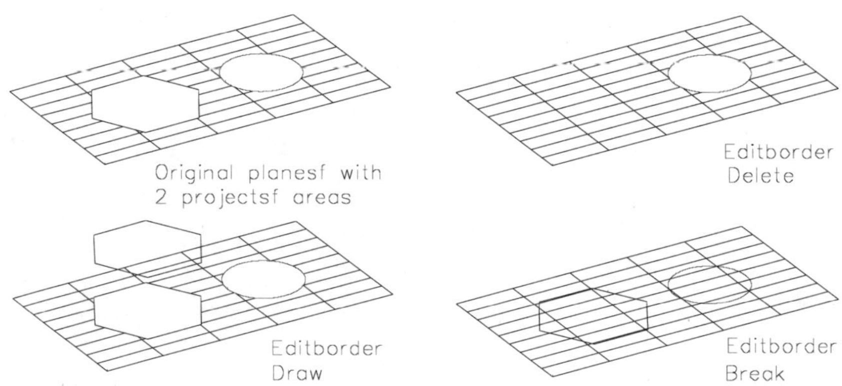

Fig. 8.10 Examples of the effects of using **editborder**

2. When the **DRaw** option is chosen, a new border is formed, which can be moved from the surface, as has been indicated in the bottom left-hand drawing of Fig. 8.10.
3. The **DElete** command allows for the complete deletion of the effects of the original **projectsf**.
4. When the **Break** option is active, the holes formed by the **projectsf** action are deleted, but the borders remain on the surface.

The command extendvw

This command is of value when constructing a wireframe and it is found that two parts of the frame do not meet. However, care must be taken to ensure that, if the command is used, the chosen pair of splines will in fact join. Selecting splines for extension which will not meet the boundary edges to which they are intended to extend can result in some very odd results. When necessary, spline can be extended not only to another spline but by a distance *entered* at the command line.

The command can either be called from the **AutoSurf** pull-down menu (Fig. 8.11) or, at the command line:

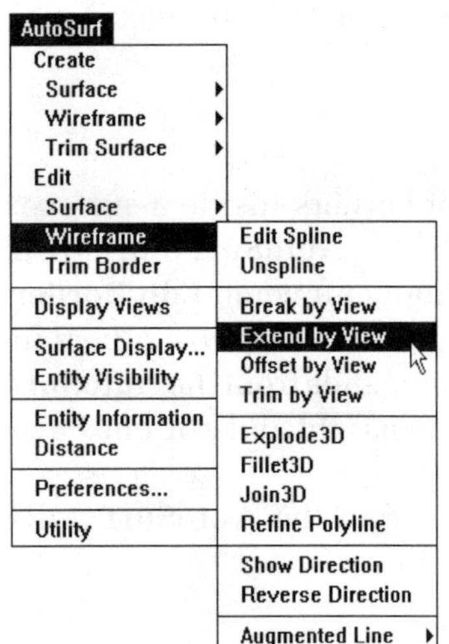

Fig. 8.11 Selecting **Extend by View** from the **AutoSurf** pull-down menu

Command: *enter* extendvw *right-click*
Extend by Distance/<Boundary edge>: *pick* a boundary edge
Select objects to extend: *pick* **1 found.**
Select objects to extend: *pick* **1 found.**
Select objects to extend: *right-click*
Command:

An example is given in Fig. 8.12, in which the boundary edge has also been trimmed with the aid of **breakvw**.

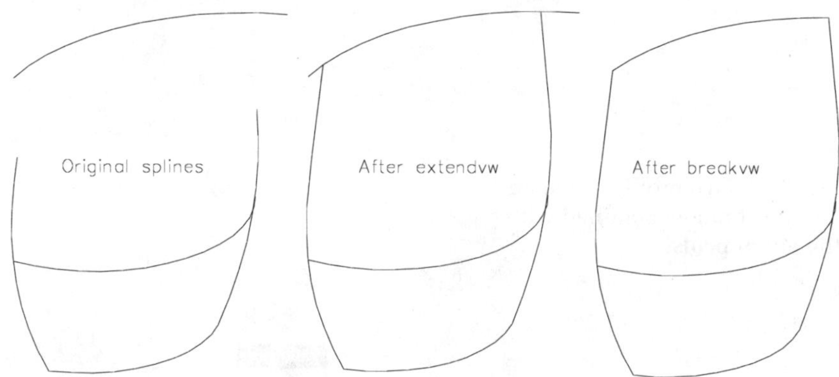

Fig. 8.12 An example of the use of **extendvw**, with unwanted parts broken with **breakvw**.

The command profsf

The use of this command allows the outlines of AutoSurf models to be projected onto a plane. The command should only be used for projection from front, sides or top onto XY, YZ or XZ planes and not used for the projection of outlines when the model is in a **Display**, **vpoint** or **dview** view.

Figure 8.13 shows what appears to be a two-view orthographic projection obtained by using the command on the example given in Fig. 9.6 (page 151). The stages by which this pair of profiled views were obtained was as follows:

1. **Open** the required AutoSurf model drawing.
2. Depending upon the positions adopted by the model in relation to the various **UCS** planes on which it was constructed, set the model in the **World UCS**.
3. Set two **New** layers – these were named **FRONT** and **PLAN**. Make the **FRONT** layer current.
4. Call the command either by selecting **Profile** from the **AutoSurf** pull-down menu (Fig. 8.14) or, at the command line:

   Command: *enter* profsf *right-click*
   To invoke advanced option enter '??'...

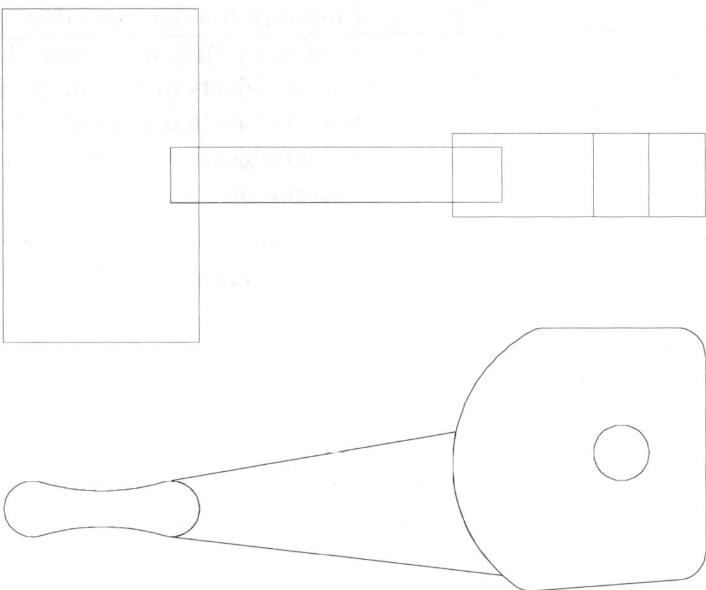

Fig. 8.13 Two profiles from an AutoSurf model obtained with the aid of **profsf**

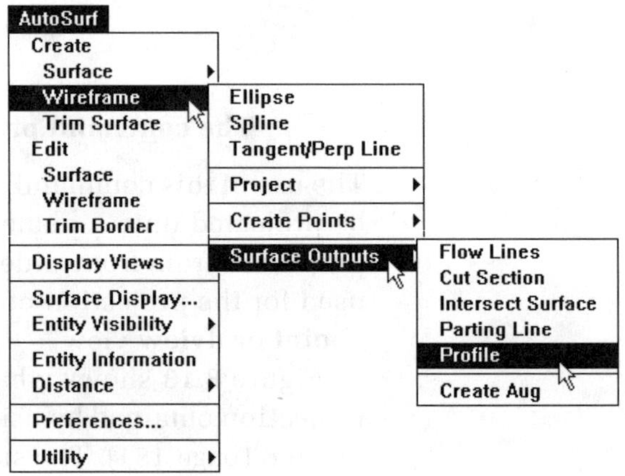

Fig. 8.14 Selecting **Profile** from the **AutoSurf** pull-down menu

Select surfaces: either window the whole model, or better, *pick* only those surfaces which will produce the necessary profile

Change color of hidden profiles? No/<Yes>: if the Yes is accepted a colour dialogue box appears from which the required colour can be selected. If n is *entered*, the colour dialogue box does not appear

Project profiles onto a plane? No/<Yes>: *right-click.* (The profiling may take some time to complete)

Command:

This will usually produce a profile in front view.

5. Make the layer **PLAN** current.
6. Place the model in the **FRONT UCS** and repeat the process for item 4 above.
7. If desired, freeze the two layers **FRONT** and **PLAN**, thaw all layers used in constructing the model and delete the model from the drawing. This may be considered to be undesirable if the model is required in addition to the profiles.
8. Thaw the two layers on which the profiles have been constructed. Call **UCS RIGHT** and rotate the profile on the **FRONT UCS** into a vertical position.
9. Call **UCS World**. If necessary **move** one or both of the profiles to positions where they are in line with each other.
10. Depending upon what the profiles are required for, they could be dimensioned, notes could be added, etc., to produce what is an orthographic projection for use as a working drawing.

The command fillet3d

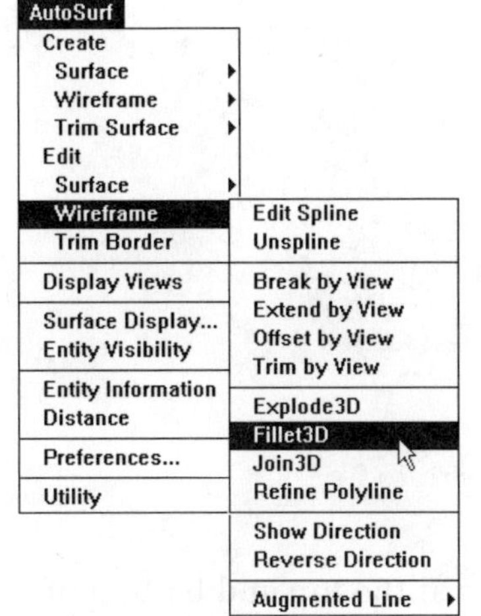

Fig. 8.15 Selecting **Fillet3D** from the **AutoSurf** pull-down menu

This command is useful when attempting the filleting to a specified radius of plines, splines or arcs in 3D space. To call the command either select **Fillet3D** form the **AutoSurf** pull-down menu (Fig. 8.15) or, at the command line:

Command: *enter* fillet3d *right-click*
To invoke advanced options enter '??' ...
Select first object: *pick*
Select second object: *pick*
Fillet radius <0>: *enter* 30 (as for Fig. 8.16) *right-click*
Command:

Figure 8.16 is an example of the use of the command. For this particular example, the **Both** check circle was set in the **Fillet3d** dialogue box which appears when ?? is *entered* in response to the first prompt of the command sequence (Fig. 8.17).

Another example involving arcs in 3D space is given in Fig. 8.18. In this example a **sweepsf** surface was formed from the results of

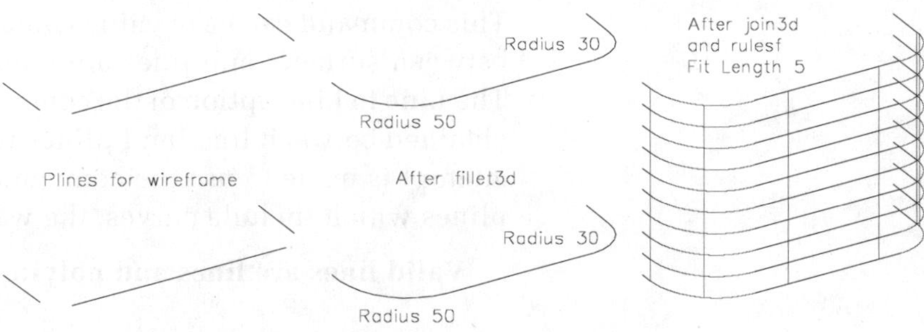

Fig. 8.16 An example of the use of **filletsf**

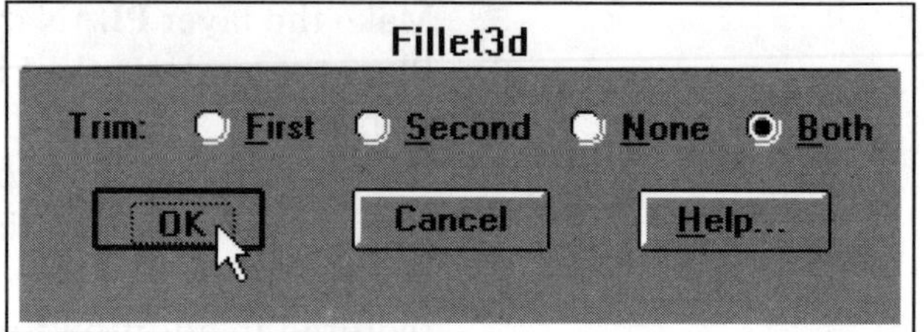

Fig. 8.17 The **Fillet3d** dialogue box with settings for the drawings in Fig. 8.16

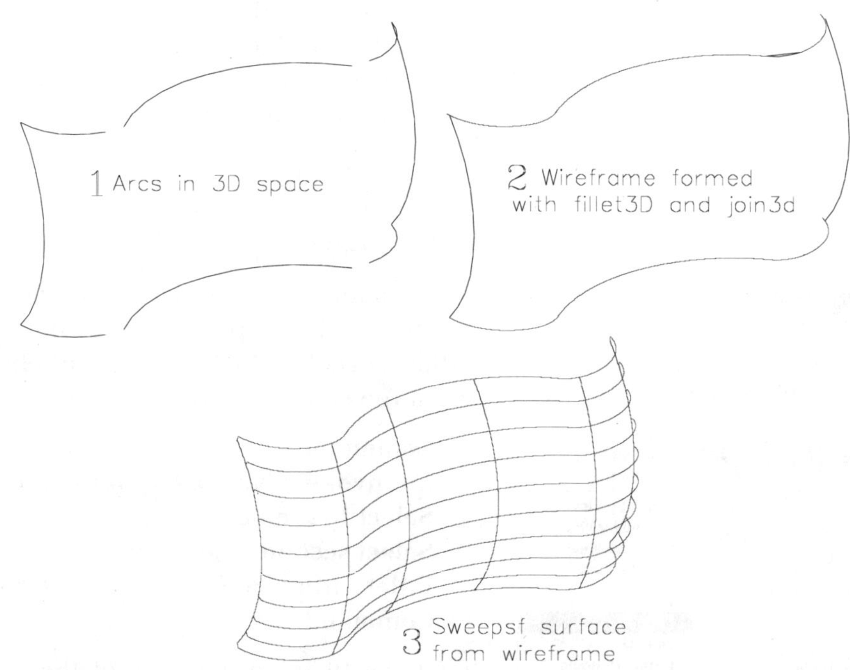

Fig. 8.18 An example of the use of **fillet3d**

using **fillet3d** and **join3d** on sets of arcs at the top and bottom of a proposed wireframe before using **sweepsf** to form the required surface.

The command dist3d

This command can be of value when the distances between lines or between surfaces and lines are required from an existing surface. The **Line to Line** option of the command only allows distances to be obtained between lines and plines which do not include arcs. If an attempt is made to use the command to find the distance between plines which include curves, the warning:

Valid lines are lines and polylines without arcs.

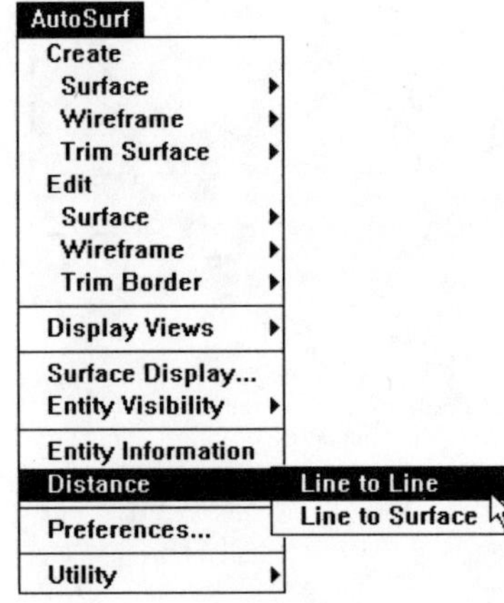

Fig. 8.19 Selecting **Line to Line** from the **AutoSurf** pull-down menu

Both the **Line to Line** and **Line to Surface** features of the **Distance** command can be called either by selection from the **AutoSurf** pull-down menu (Fig. 8.19) or, at the command line:

Command: *enter* dist3d *right-click*
To invoke advanced options enter ?? ...
Line to Line/<Surface to objects>: *right-click*
Select surface: *pick* **1 found.**
Select objects: *pick* **1 found.**
Select objects: *right-click*
Distance = 80
Continue? No/<Yes>: *enter* n *right-click*
Command:

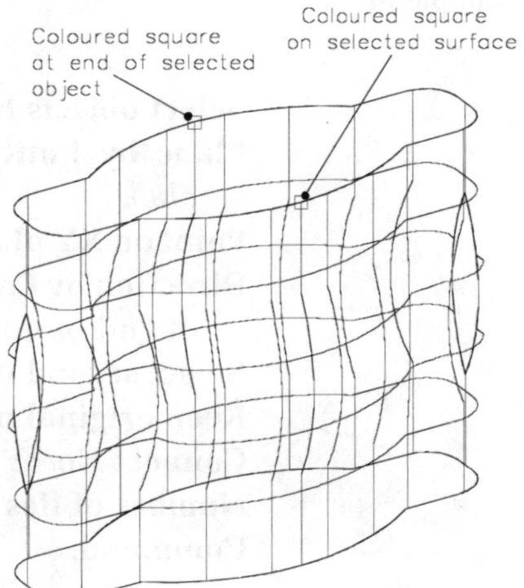

Fig. 8.20 An example of using the command **dist3d** to find the distance between a surface and part of its wireframe

Figure 8.20 shows an example of the use of the command in finding the distance between the surface and part of its wireframe. The two points *picked* on the surface and wireframe of this example give the distance of 80 shown above in the command line sequence. As surfaces and/or objects are *picked*, tiny coloured squares appear at the selected points. If the **Continue?** prompt is answered with a y (Yes), then further squares appear automatically along the surface/line distances.

The wireframe in Fig. 8.21 was constructed from splines drawn with plines.

The command project3d

Command: *enter* project3d *right-click*
Select objects to project: *pick* **1 found.**

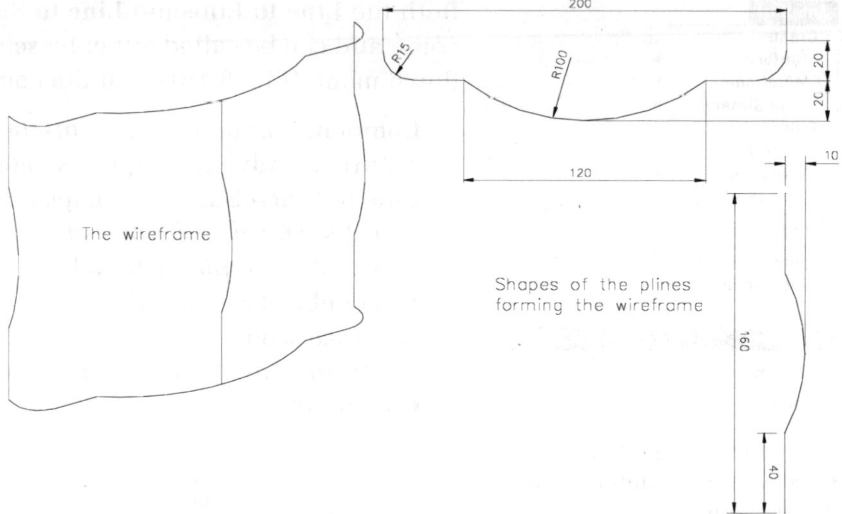

Fig. 8.21 Details of the wireframe for the example in Fig. 8.20

Select objects to project: *right-click*
Plane by Entity/Last/View/Xy/Yz/Zx/<3points>: *enter* x *right-click*
Point on XY plane: *pick* endpoint of upper end of vertical spline
Direction by Entity/Viewdir/X/Y/Z/<Start point>: *pick* endpoint of end of upper spline
Select second point: *pick* endpoint of vertical spline
Keep original objects Yes/<No>: *enter* y *right-click*
Connect No/<Yes>: *right-click*
Number of ties <2>: *right-click*
Command:

Notes

1. In order to complete the wireframe in this example, the command **breakvw** followed by **erase** will need to be used to break off unwanted overhanging ends of the splines and then to erase the unwanted parts.
2. **Projectsf** in this example only worked well with the responses to the prompts given, because the end of the vertical splines are resting on the XY plane.
3. Although the given example (Fig. 8.22) appears to work, in that the ends parts of the wireframe meet as required, it is not necessarily a good method of achieving the result. If an attempt has been made to work the example, it will be seen that the top and bottom splines are not smooth curves after using **project3d**. Can you suggest a better method?
4. The splines for the original wireframe were constructed with **spline3d** to coordinate positions as follows:

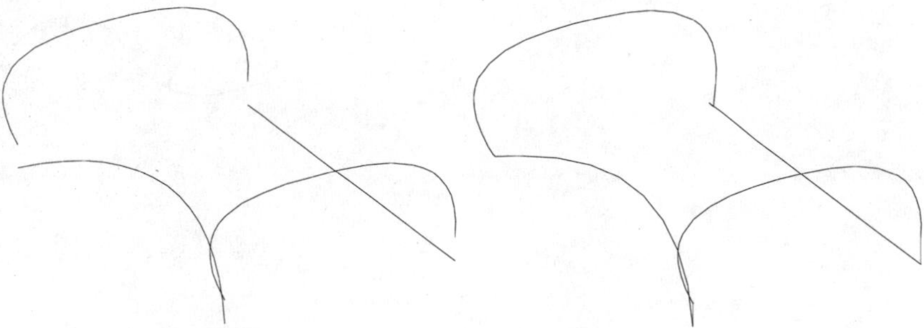

Fig. 8.22 The four splines for the example **project3d**

Left-hand spline: from 50,10 to 70,85,20 to 50,170
Right-hand spline: from 150,10 to 130,85,20 to 150,170
Bottom spline: from 50,10,10 to 50,20,30 to 100,30,40 to 150,20,30 to 150,10,10
Top spline: from 50,160,10 to 50,170,30 to 100,180,40 to 150,170,30 to 150,160,10

Questions

1. What is the *acad.pgp* file?
2. What are the advantages of using the *acad.pgp* file when working in AutoSurf?
3. How many methods of calling AutoSurf commands can you describe?
4. What is the purpose of the AutoSurf command **editsf**?
5. Two options in the **editsp** command structure are **Next** and **PRev**. What happens if either of these two prompts is selected?
6. What purpose does the command **truncsf** fulfil?
7. When using the AutoSurf command **editborder**, when would you use the prompt **Draw**?
8. If you have constructed a wireframe with the aid of **spline3d** and one of the splines is 5 units too short, how can the spline be lengthened by the necessary amount?
9. When would you consider making use of the AutoSurf command **profsf**?
10. If the **Cursor** prompt of the **editsf** command system is used, how can you control the position of control points?

Exercises

1. The upper drawing of Fig. 8.23 gives the dimensions of the top and bottom curves for the wireframe of the **rulesf** surface shown in the central set of drawings.

   Working to the dimensions given in the upper drawing, construct a **rulesf** surface 180 high. Draw an ellipse in front of the surface with

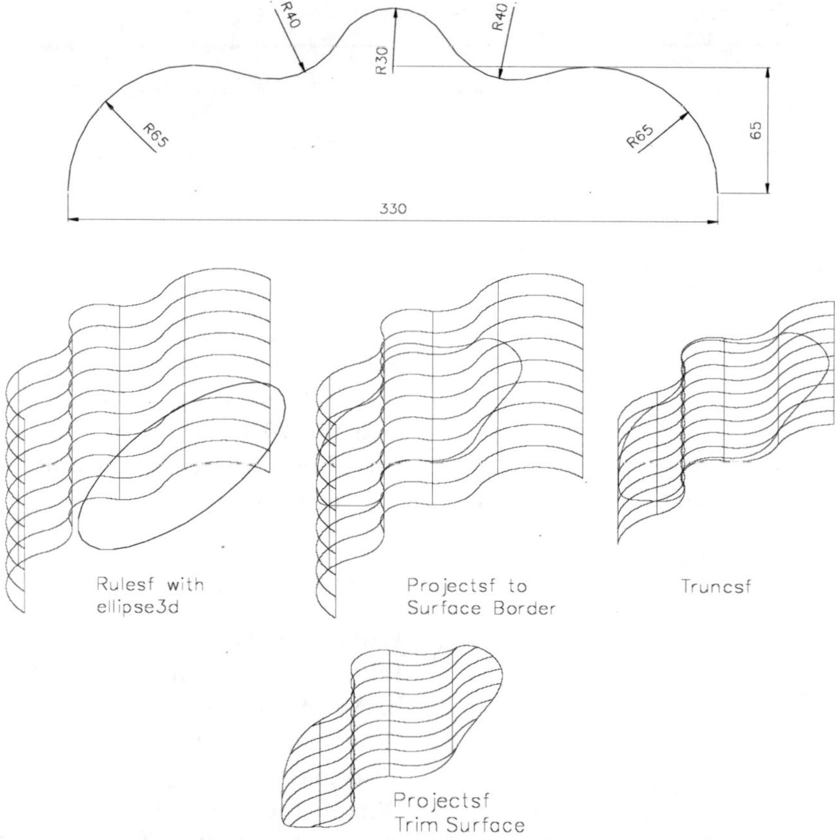

Fig. 8.23 Exercise 1

the aid of **ellipse3d**. Then produce the three views showing in the other drawings of Fig. 8.23.

2. The left-hand drawing in Fig. 8.24 is the result of forming a **sweepsf** surface from the wireframe produced with the aid of **project3d** as shown in Fig. 8.22 on page 143. The hole in the surface of the central drawing of Fig. 8.24 was produced from a pline with all its corners filleted. Working to the dimensions given on page 143, construct the three drawings.

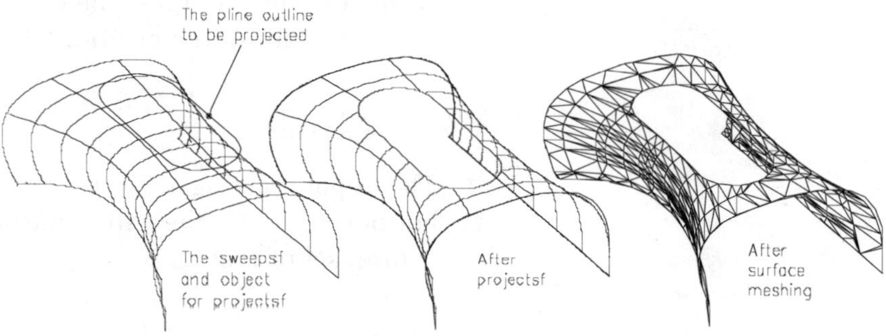

Fig. 8.24 Exercise 2

3. Figure 8.25 gives the dimensions for a wireframe on which the **rulesf** surface shown in the left-hand drawing of Fig. 8.26 was formed. Figure 8.26 shows the resulting surface in the left-hand drawing.

   The right-hand drawing of Fig. 8.26 shows the original surface, which has been first mirrored, then the two resulting surfaces were joined with the aid of **joinsf**. Finally a lip was formed as shown with the aid of **editsf**.

   Working to the given sizes construct the right-hand drawing of Fig. 8.26.

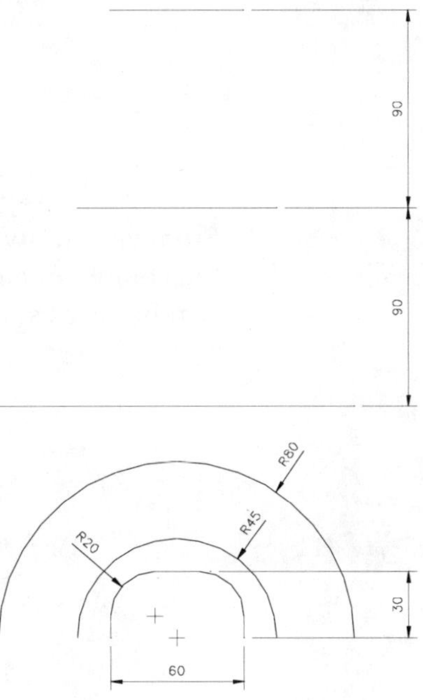

Fig. 8.25 Exercise 3. Dimensions for wireframe

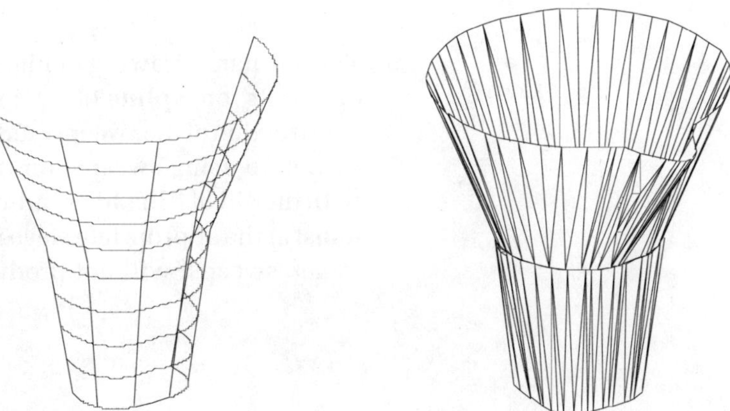

Fig. 8.26 Exercise 3. Original surface and completed surface

4. The left-hand drawing of Fig. 8.27 shows the positions of the locations on the **spline3d** splines making up the wireframe for the **sweepsf** surface in the right-hand drawing.

   Working to the coordinates given in the left-hand drawing, construct the **sweepsf** surface.

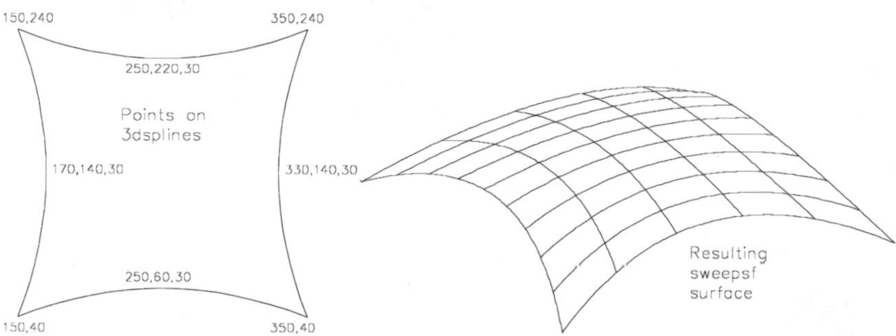

Fig. 8.27 Exercise 4

5. From your drawing in answer to Exercise 4 above, with the aid of the command **editsp**, alter the spline at the top and bottom of the wireframe as shown in Fig. 8.28.

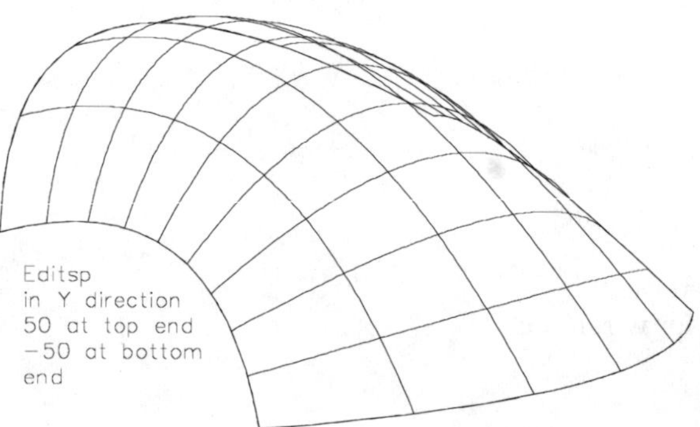

Fig. 8.28 Exercise 5

6. The left-hand drawing of Fig. 8.29 shows the coordinate positions of points on **spline3d** splines for the commencement of the construction of the **sweepsf** surface shown in the right-hand drawing.

   Before using **sweepsf** on the wireframe, amend the wireframe with the aid of **fillet3d** as indicated in Fig. 8.29. Do not forget to use **joinsf** at the appropriate stage in amending the wireframe. If you do forget, **sweepsf** will not produce the desired surface.

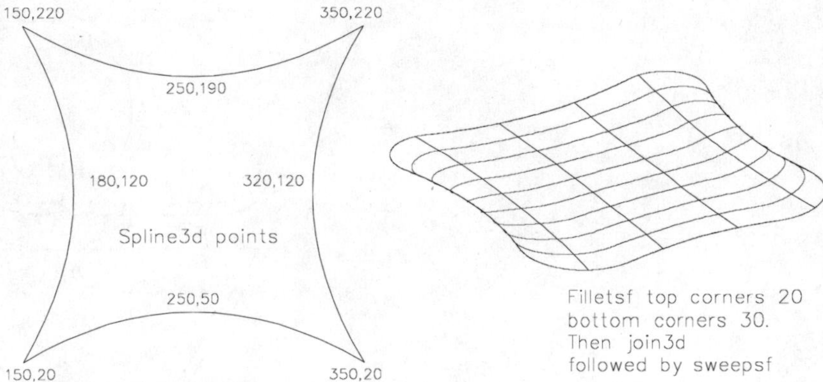

Fig. 8.29 Exercise 6

7. From your drawing of the wireframe in answer to Exercise 6 and with the aid of **editsp** amend the wireframe as indicated in Fig. 8.30. Then **sweepsf** the surface again.

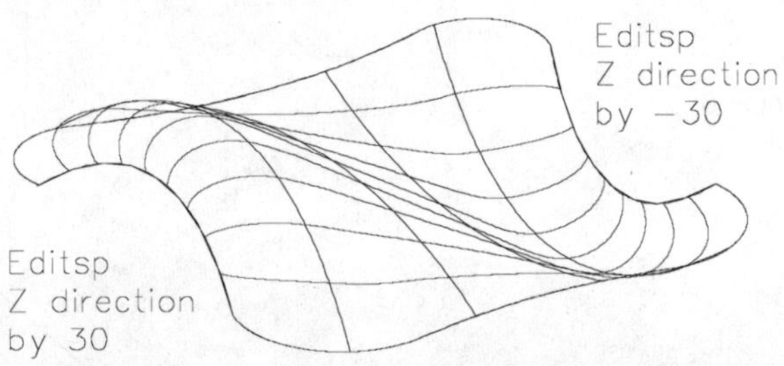

Fig. 8.30 Exercise 7

8. If you have saved your answer to Exercise 1 in Chapter 7 (Fig. 7.22 on page 126), recall the drawing to screen. Erase all but drawing 5 and then place drawing 5 in the **World UCS**.

   Then, with the aid of **profsf**, profile first the plan and then the front view. The results should appear similar to the two views given in Fig. 8.31.
9. In a similar fashion use **profsf** to obtain a front view of the answer to Exercise 3 in Chapter 7 (Fig. 7.26 on page 128). The result of your profiling should appear as in Fig. 8.32.

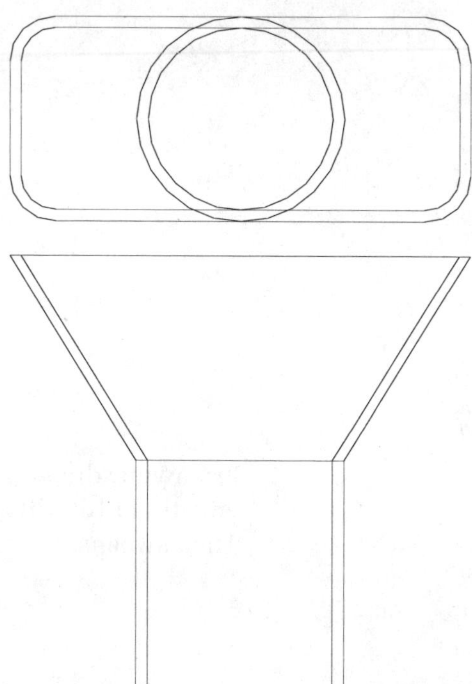

Fig. 8.31 Exercise 8

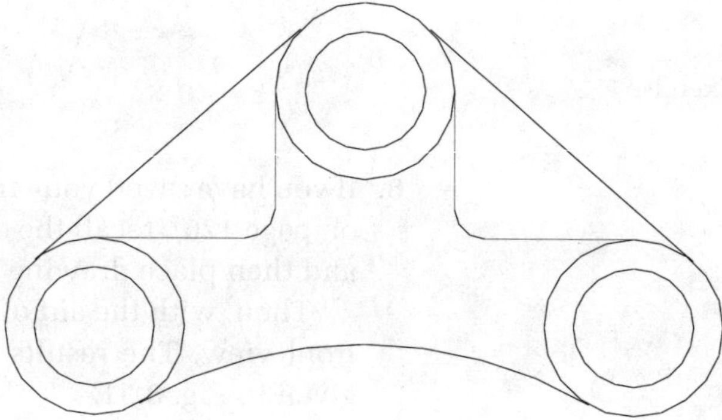

Fig. 8.32 Exercise 9

CHAPTER 9

Rendering in AutoVision

Introduction

AutoVision Release 2 is a rendering program which functions within AutoCAD Release 13. The process of rendering can produce photo-like 3D images of surface-meshed 3D models such as those produced with the aid of AutoSurf. A full description of the possibilities of AutoVision requires a book in its own right. Here, this chapter will be confined to the description of rendering some AutoSurf models with the aid of AutoVision. AutoCAD Release 13 has a limited rendering menu of its own, **AutoCAD Render**, which can be used to produce renderings of AutoSurf models. However, AutoCAD Render does not contain many of the facilities of AutoVision.

Many of the illustrations connected with examples and exercises in previous chapters have been of AutoVision renderings. All but the first three of the colour plates are AutoVision renderings of AutoSurf models.

AutoVis
Render
Scenes...
Lights...
Materials...
Materials Library...
Mapping...
Background...
Fog...
Landscape New...
Landscape Edit...
Landscape Library...
Animation...
AutoVis Toolbar
Preferences...
Statistics...

Fig. 9.1 The **AutoVis** pull-down menu

The AutoVis pull-down menu and toolbar

Figure 9.1 shows the pull-down menu which appears with a *left-click* on the name **AutoVis** in the menu bar. In the pull-down menu a *left-click* on a name which is followed by three fullstops (...) brings a dialogue box onto the screen. A *left-click* on **AutoVis Toolbar** brings the **AutoVision** toolbar with its icons representing the various tools (commands) in AutoVision (Fig. 9.2). Moving the screen cursor over one of the icons in this toolbar brings up its **tool tip**. In Fig. 9.2 the **Render** icon has been selected, hence its tool tip is showing. The toolbar contains the same commands as does the pull-down menu. Obviously the **AutoVis Toolbar** command in the menu is missing in the toolbar. Figure 9.3 shows the commands (tools) associated with the icons in the toolbar. To select any tool (command) either *left-click* on its name in the pull-down menu or *left-click* on the required

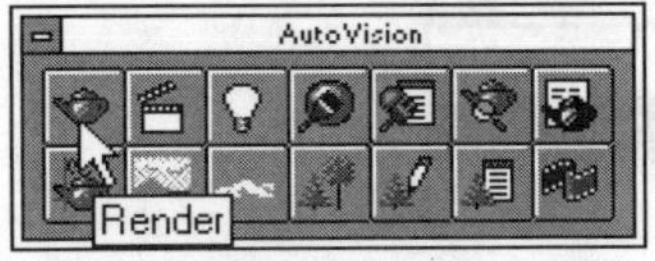

Fig. 9.2 The AutoVision toolbar

Fig. 9.3 The command names (tools) associated with each of the icons in the AutoVision toolbar

tool icon in the toolbar. In this chapter selection of commands from AutoVision will be made from the pull-down menu.

Rendering Preferences

Left-click on **Preferences...** in the pull-down menu (Fig. 9.1) and the **Rendering Preferences** dialogue box appears. Figure 9.4 shows the settings in the dialogue box that have been adopted for the renderings included in this chapter. *Left-click* in the **Rendering Type** box and a pop-up list appears (Fig. 9.5) showing the rendering types available when using the software. The reader should try rendering with AutoCAD Render and with AutoVis Raytrace, but in this chapter only the AutoVision type of rendering will be referred to.

To describe how to render AutoSurf 3D models with the aid of AutoVision, three examples follow. Each uses slightly different methods in order to show more fully the capabilities of the software. However, it must be remembered that the descriptions of these examples are only an introduction to this versatile rendering program.

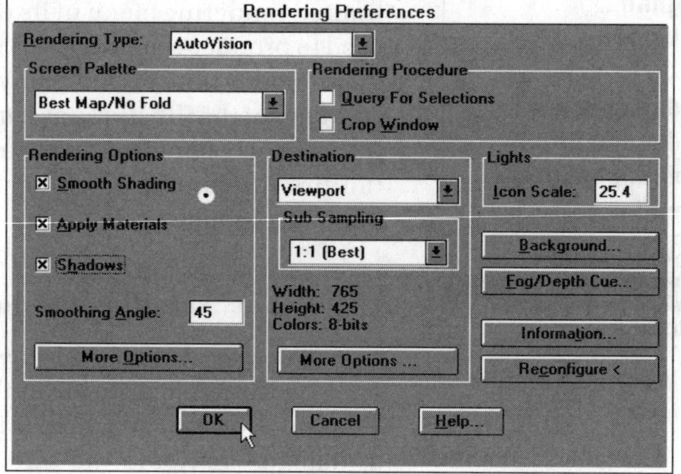

Fig. 9.4 The **Rendering Preferences** dialogue box

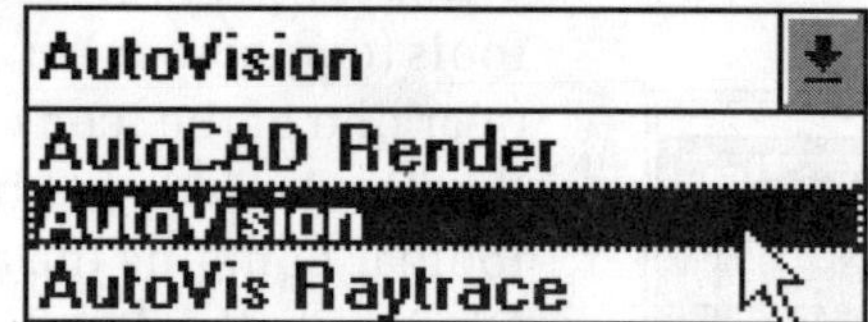

Fig. 9.5 The pop-up list showing types of rendering available

First example

This first example describes the rendering of a small cam lever. A **vpoint** drawing of the lever is shown in Fig. 9.6. Details of the lighting for the rendering are given in Fig. 9.7 and three examples of the rendered model are shown in Plates IV, V and VI. The various stages in the rendering of the first example are given below.

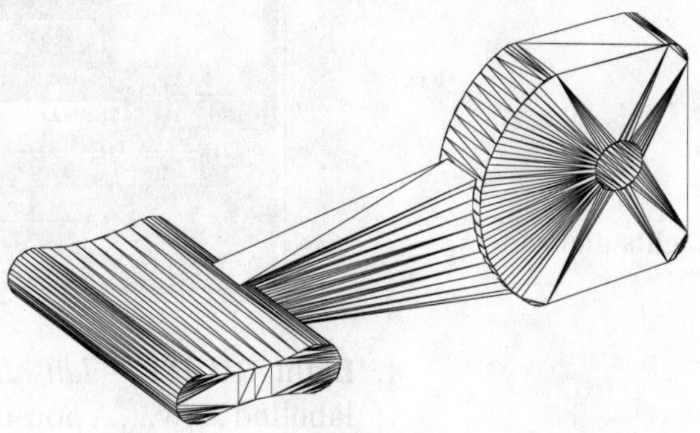

Fig. 9.6 The AutoSurf 3D model for the first example

1. Lighting

1. Figure 9.7. Place the model in the **World UCS**. If necessary **Zoom** to a scale of about 0.5. Move the model to a position where the lights can be easily placed – in this example, this is towards the top of the AutoCAD editor.

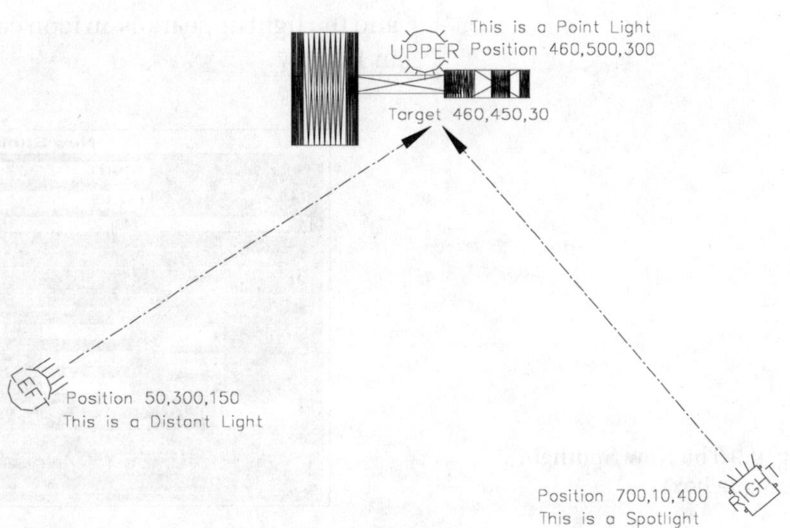

Fig. 9.7 The model in the **World UCS** showing the lights and their positions

2. *Left-click* on **Lights...** in the pull-down menu (Fig. 9.1). The **Lights** dialogue box appears (Fig. 9.8).
3. Now place the three lights, named as **LEFT**, **RIGHT** and **UPPER**, as shown in Fig. 9.7.

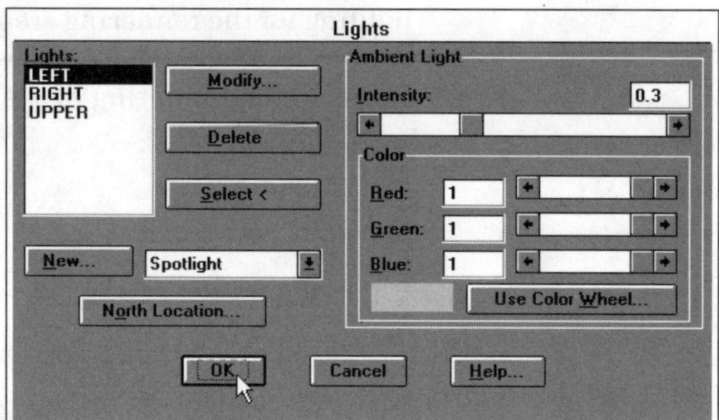

Fig. 9.8 The **Lights** dialogue box

4. **Light RIGHT** – *left-click* on the box to the right of the button labelled **New....** A pop-up list appears from which to select **Spotlight**. The **New Spotlight** dialogue box appears (Fig. 9.9). *Enter* the name **RIGHT** in the **Light Name** box, followed by a *left-click* on the **Modify** button and then, at the command line:

   Command:_light
   Enter light target <current>: *enter* 480,450,30 *right-click*
   Enter light location <current>: *enter* 700,10,400 *right-click*
   Command:

   and the light appears as an icon carrying the name **RIGHT** as shown in Fig. 9.7.

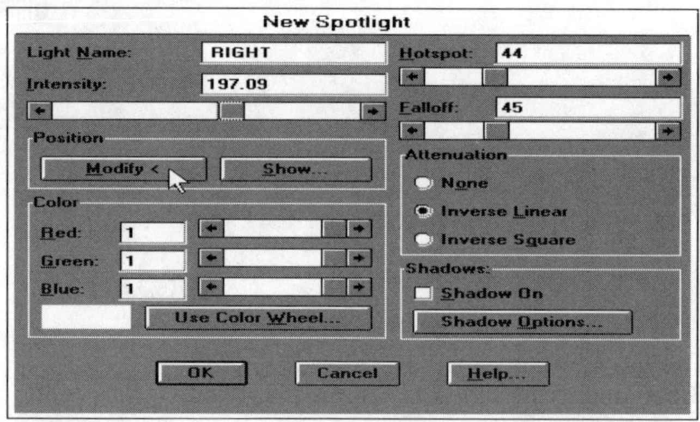

Fig. 9.9 The **New Spotlight** dialogue box

5. **Light LEFT** – a similar operation is required except that the light labelled **LEFT** in Fig. 9.7 is a **Distant Light**. A different dialogue box, with some different requirements for settings the **New Distant Light** dialogue box appears. When the **Modify** button of this dialogue box is selected, a similar pair of prompts appears at tho command light requiring coordinates (or *picked* points) from the

operator. When the positions have been set, the name **LEFT** appears in a **Distant Light** icon.

6. **Light UPPER** – being a **Point Light** only the position of the light is required and only one position is asked for in the prompts at the command line. This position is shown in Fig. 9.7.

Notes on AutoVision Lights

Dialogue boxes: each type of light – **Point**, **Distant** and **Spotlight** – has its own sets of dialogue boxes, only one of which is shown here (Fig. 9.9).

Point Light: a light from a set position which sheds light in all directions from that position. Its intensity and its colour can be changed in its dialogue boxes.

Distant Light: one from which light is shed in one direction but not as if from a beam. Intensity and colour can be changed.

Spotlight: light as if coming from a spot lamp – i.e. from a single source with a beam, which has its own cone of light which can be adjusted in the relevant dialogue box. Intensity and colour of the light can be changed. The cone of its light can be changed. In the first example **Shadow** is on for this light.

Icons: each type of light has its own icon, as shown in Fig. 9.7. The icons in Fig. 9.7 have been enlarged to make them clearer to the reader. When working in AutoVision, the light icons will be smaller than those shown in that illustration when working in a metric screen.

Notes on the lights in the first example

1. The three lights shown in Fig. 9.7 represent a fairly common form of lighting often used in studio photography. A strong light near the source of the camera pointing directly at the model; a second general light, not as intense to give a rounded effect to the model being photographed; a third overhead light giving general overall lighting effects.
2. There is no camera as such in AutoVision, but the viewpoint of the **vpoint** responses can be taken as the approximate camera position.
3. Before placing lights, check the position of the model in the vertical plane. To do this change the **UCS** to **UCS FRONT** and, by moving the screen cursor to the bottom of the model, check its position in relation to the Z coordinate. This will usually be Z=0, but during the changes of the UCS as the model is constructed its position vertically may have been changed. Obviously the height of the lights (i.e. when setting the Z coordinate) depends upon the vertical position of the model in 3D space.

2. Checking lighting

1. Place the model in a good viewing position. Its position in Fig. 9.6 is a **vpoint** of –0.6,–1.0,0.6. The viewing position mainly depends upon the positioning of the lights.
2. Without attaching a material to the model, *left-click* on **Render** in the pull-down menu. The **Render** dialogue box appears (Fig. 9.10). Accept the default settings shown in the dialogue box. *Left-click* on the **Render** button and the model renders in the **GLOBAL** material. The rendered model will appear as in Plate IV. The object of this rendering is to check the lighting effects. Rendering in the default **GLOBAL** material is faster than rendering in a material chosen from the AutoVision library.

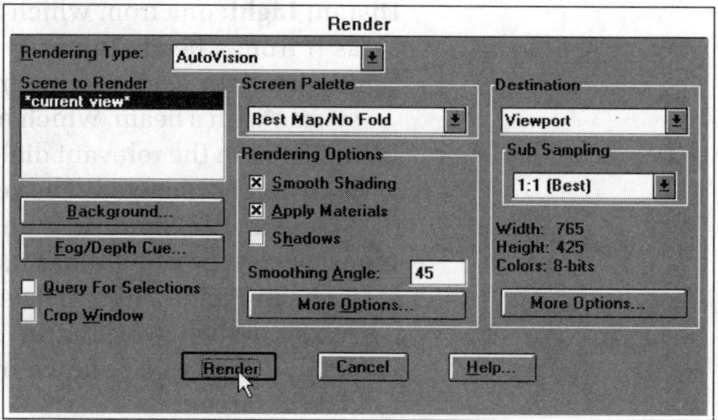

Fig. 9.10 The **Render** dialogue box

3. If satisfied with the setting of the lights, go to attaching of a material. If not satisfied, *left-click* on **Lights...** in the pull-down menu and, using the **Modify** button, call back the **Lights** dialogue box and make amendments as necessary. See Fig. 9.8. Each dialogue box allows the light intensity to be changed as well as the light position. If wished, colour can be added to the lights with the aid of the colour wheel (Fig. 9.11), which can be called with a *left-click* on the **Use Color Wheel...** button in the **Lights** dialogue box. After resetting the lights if it proves to be necessary, check by rendering the model again in its **GLOBAL** material.

3. Attaching materials

1. *Left-click* on **Materials...** in the pull-down menu. The **Materials** dialogue box appears (Fig. 9.12). In the dialogue box *left-click* on the **Materials Library...** button and the **Materials Library** dialogue box appears (Fig. 9.13). In this dialogue box *left-click* on the **Library**

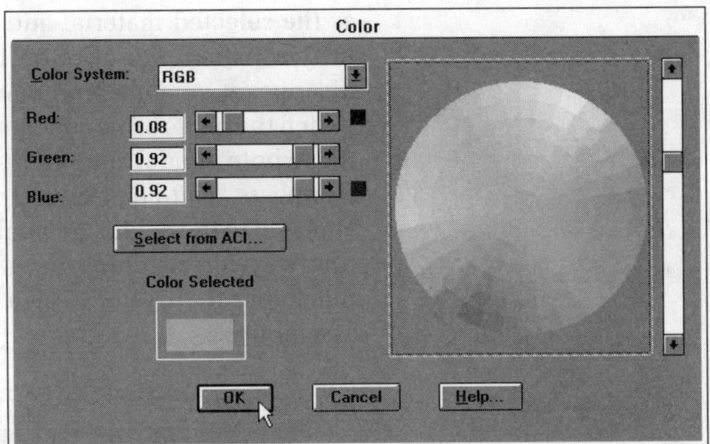

Fig. 9.11 The AutoVision **Color** dialogue box

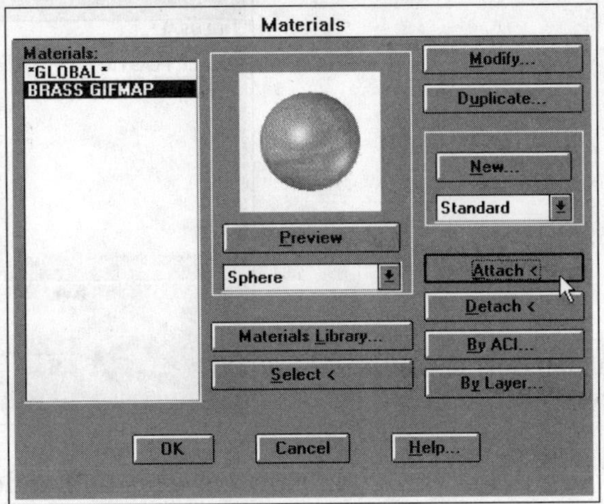

Fig. 9.12 The **Materials** dialogue box

List button and a list of available materials from the AutoVision library file appears (Fig. 9.13).

2. Scroll the list and choose a material. *Left-click* on that material name and to check that it is suitable for the model, *left-click* on the **Preview** button. The material as it would be seen when rendered appears in the **Preview** box. Previewing can be as if on a sphere or as if on a cube, selecting from the pop-up list just below the **Preview** button. When satisfied with the choice of each material, *left-click* on the **Import** button and the material name appears in the **Materials List**. For this example the material **BRASS GIFMAP** has been chosen. In the dialogue box in Fig. 9.13, several materials had been previewed.
3. When the final selection of materials has been made, *left-click* on the **OK** button of the dialogue box and the **Materials** dialogue box reappears (Fig. 9.12). In this illustration **BRASS GIFMAP** is shown

as the selected material and it has again been previewed. When fully satisfied, *left-click* on the **Attach** button, the dialogue box disappears, and the command line requests that the surface to which the material be attached is selected. In this example window the whole model and *right-click*. The **Materials** dialogue box reappears. *Left-click* on the **OK** button to confirm the material attached to the model. Several materials could have been chosen in this way for attaching to various parts of the model. However, remember that AutoSurf is usually used to design parts and not assemblies.

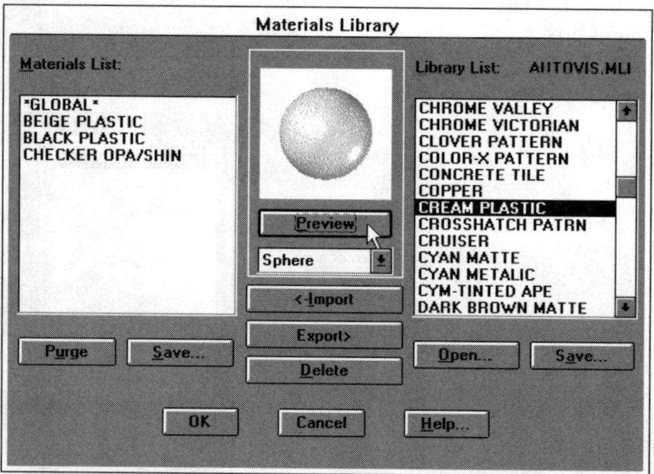

Fig. 9.13 The **Materials Library** dialogue box

4. Now *left-click* on **Render** in the pull-down menu and *left-click* in the **Shadows** check box to set shadows on. *Left-click* on the **Render** button and after rendering the model will appear as in colour Plate V.

4. Including a background

A background, either an AutoCAD colour or one chosen from the AutoVision *maps* directory, can be included in the rendering if required. Plate VI shows the first example rendered in **BRASS GIFMAP** against a background **CEMENT**. This background was included as follows:

1. In the **Render** dialogue box (Fig. 9.10) *left-click* on the **Background...** button. The **Background** dialogue box appears (Fig. 9.14). *Left-click* in the check box next to **AutoCAD Background** to turn off this type of background. *Left-click* in the **Image** check circle to turn **Image** on. *Left-click* in the pop-up list box in the **Image** box area and a list of background graphics files from the AutoVision *maps*

directory appears. Select one of the backgrounds. In the example given in Fig. 9.14 **CHECKER.TGA** has been selected and previewed. For the first example the background **CEMENT.TGA** was selected. To confirm the selection *left-click on the* **OK** button of the dialogue box.

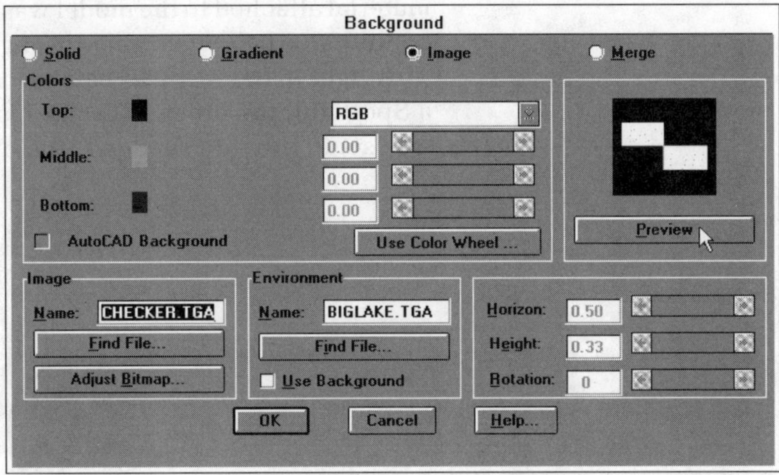

Fig. 9.14 The **Background** dialogue box

2. Now render the model. The results are as shown in Plate VI.

Notes on backgrounds

1. If an AutoCAD background is selected and a colour chosen, when rendering takes place a clear background colour appears behind the rendered model. Plates X and XI show this type of background.
2. If wished, the operator can pre-mix his/her own colour background from the **Top**, **Middle** and **Bottom RGB** (Red, Green, Blue) sliders. Adjusting the slider bars below **RGB** allows a mixture of colours which appears in the **Preview** box as mixing takes place.
2. A scene from the **Environment** files will create a scene behind the rendered model. Several scenes are available from the AutoVision files. The reader is advised to experiment with these.
3. Two further examples of backgrounds are given in Plates VII and VIII in which types of wood have been portrayed as backgrounds behind the rendered models.

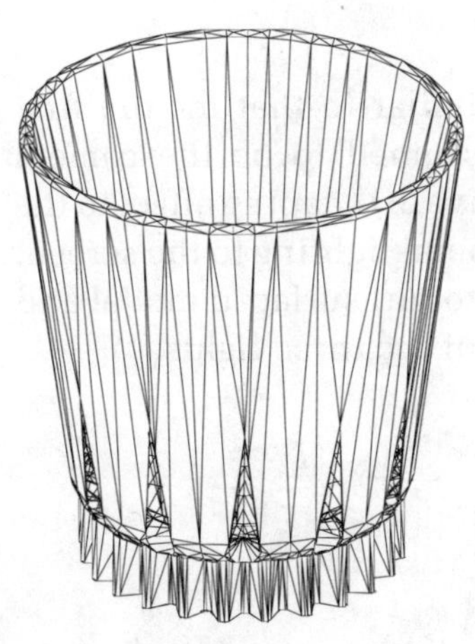

Fig. 9.15 The AutoSurf model for the second example

Second example

A rendering of the second example is shown in Plate VII. The plate shows an AutoSurf model of a glass tumbler with the material **GREEN GLASS** attached and with a background **ASHEN.TGA**. This example is included here to show the differences between this and the first example in the positioning of the lights so as to emphasise that the model is intended to be made from glass. Figure 9.15 shows a **vpoint** view of the model and Fig. 9.16 the positions of the lights for the model.

Note the positions and the targets of the three lights. Because the material attached to the model was **GREEN GLASS**, a Spotlight from behind and below shining through the glass gives the best effect. This light to the rear was balanced by two lights from the front, one a Spotlight, the other a Distant Light. The Spotlight named RIGHT was set to provide shadows, the other two were not so set.

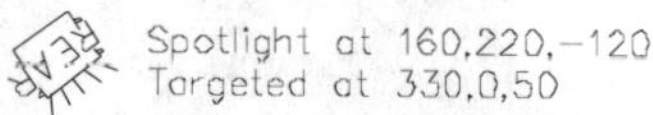

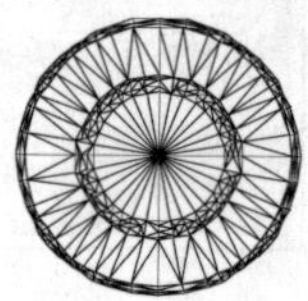

Fig. 9.16 The AutoVision lights and their positions for the second example

Third example

The lighting for this example is very similar to that for the first example – a Spotlight from what is assumed to be the camera position; a Distant Light from the left to give 3D shaping effect to the rendering; a Point Light above to give general lighting to the screen.

Figure 9.17 is a **vpoint** view of the AutoSurf surfaced model and Fig. 9.18 shows the types and positions of the three lights.

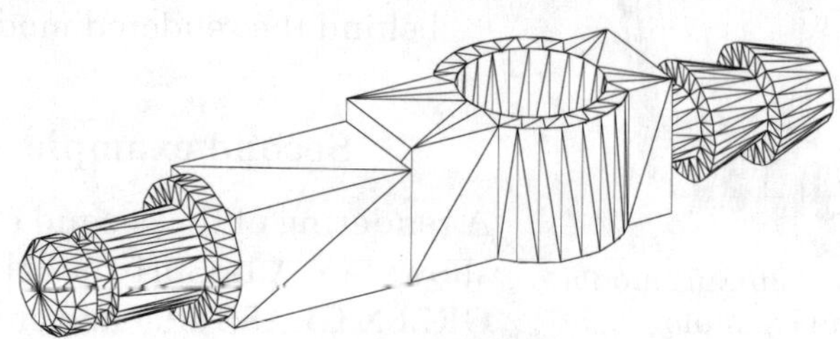

Fig. 9.17 A **vpoint** view of the third example

Colour Plate VIII shows the completed rendering, which was in a **CHERRY RED METAL** material with a background from **WHITEASH.TGA**.

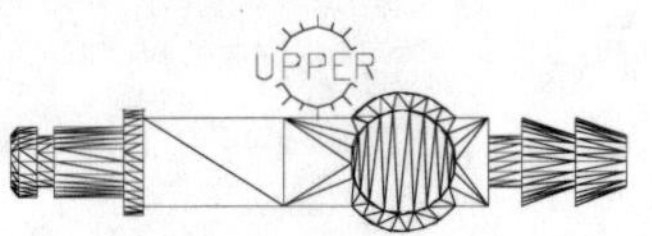

Lights:
Point UPPER – at 340,240,400
Distant LEFT – at –110,–130,150
Spot RIGHT – at 650,0190,300
LEFT and RIGHT targeted at 320,190,20

Fig. 9.18 Types and positions of the three lights for the third example

Notes on using AutoVision

Anti-aliasing

When producing renderings or other graphics on a computer screen the pixels along straight edges of the rendering can appear slightly jagged. This effect is less when using a monitor screen of a very high resolution, but can cause problems when using a screen such as a VGA (Video Graphics Array) or even with an SVGA (Super Video Graphics Array).

Anti-aliasing is a method by which such jagged edges can be made to appear less jagged. If anti-aliasing is set on, the pixels near such edges are allocated light and colour in varying percentages in such a manner that the edges appear much cleaner.

In the **Render** dialogue box *left-click* on the **More Options...** button in the **Destination** area of the dialogue box. Another dialogue box appears – **AutoVision Render Options** (Fig. 9.19). In this dialogue box various degrees of anti-aliasing can be selected from **Minimal** to **High**. As an example of **High** anti-aliasing, the glass shown in colour Plate VII was rendered with **Anti-aliasing** set to **High**.

Time taken when rendering

No matter how fast the computer being used, rendering takes time. As an example, when using a computer fitted with a Pentium chip running at nearly 100 MHz, the rendering of the glass in Plate VII

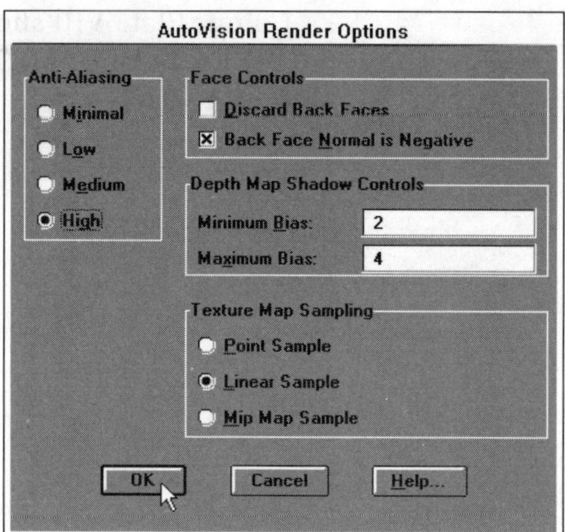

Fig. 9.19 The **AutoVision Render Options** dialogue box

took 3 minutes. Rendering time is increased under the following conditions:

1. Using a slow computer.
2. When a material or materials is/are attached to the model.
3. When a large number of lights are included to add to the lighting effects.
4. When shadows are required from light, particularly if all lights are to produce shadows.
5. When anti-aliasing is set to high.
6. When a background is included.
7. When memory is low, particularly virtual memory – i.e. memory in RAM and in the Windows **Virtual Memory** swap file. Memory can be checked in AutoCAD by:

   Command: *enter* status *right-click*

   and an AutoCAD text window appears showing details of the current drawing and the memory state of the system in use. This facility can be of value if operations are becoming slowish.

Note on AutoVision facilities

There are a number of AutoVision facilities that are not mentioned in this chapter as they are beyond the scope of this book. These facilities include:

Landscapes.
Animation of scenes to show movements.
Scenes: the possibility of being able to save different views of the same model and be able to recall them from a dialogue box.

Fog: a background can be fogged to obtain a form of perspective viewing.

The reader may care to experiment with those facilities which have not been included in the descriptions in this chapter.

Questions

1. What is the purpose of AutoVision?
2. Is there any difference between selecting a tool and selecting a command when working in AutoVision or AutoSurf?
3. How many methods of calling AutoVision commands can you name?
4. What form of lighting does a **Point Light** produce?
5. What form of lighting does a **Direct Light** produce?
6. What form of lighting does a **Spotlight** produce?
7. In the second example of rendering given in this chapter, a light from the rear of the model was included in order to emphasise that the model was made from glass. Can you explain other situations where back lighting might be included?
8. What is the difference between including a background for a rendered model and including a background from an image file?
9. How can a light be coloured when working in AutoVision?
10. Why is it advisable to render first in the default material **GLOBAL** before rendering in the desired material?

Exercises

Three exercises for the practising of rendering AutoSurf models are included below. These show the same models as were used for the rendering examples already given in this chapter. To assist the reader in constructing the models before rendering, each exercise shows the surfaces for the models in an exploded form with all the surfaces included in the models taken apart. Also presented are the AutoSurf commands used for producing the surfaces. Orthographic projections are given for each of the three exercises with suitable dimensions to which to work.

1. Figure 9.20 shows the surfaces for the exercise and Fig. 9.21 a two-view orthographic projection. Construct the AutoSurf model and, following the descriptions of rendering given for the first example on pages 150–57, render the model with the aid of AutoVision.
2. Figure 9.22 is an exploded view of the AutoSurf model for the exercise and Fig. 9.23 is a first angle two-view dimensioned

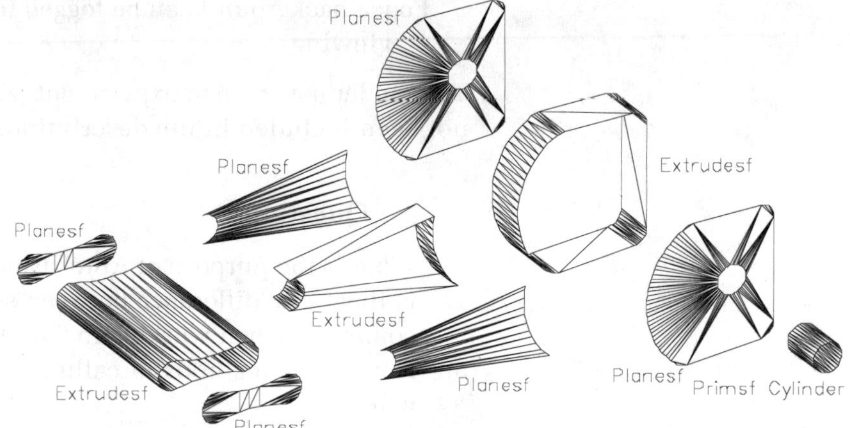

Fig. 9.20 Exercise 1. An exploded view showing all the surfaces of the AutoSurf model

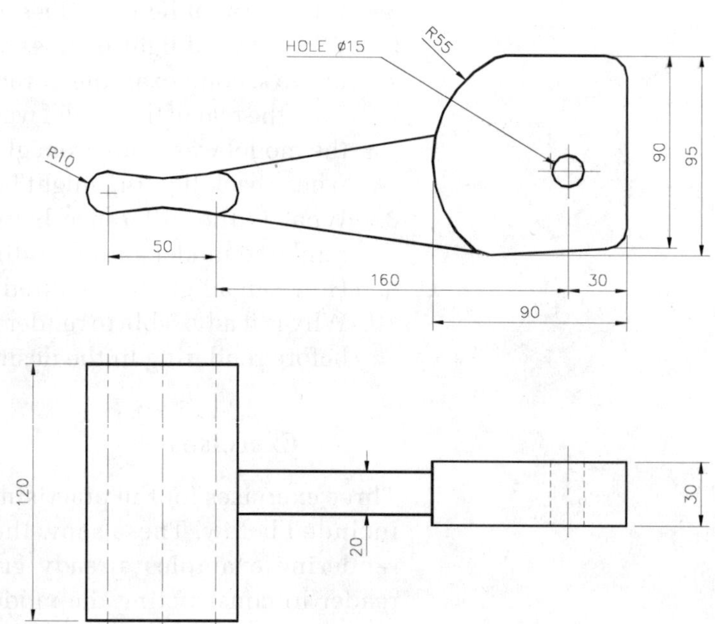

Fig. 9.21 Exercise 1. A two-view third-angle orthographic projection

orthographic projection. Construct the AutoSurf model for the exercise and render the resulting model. Note that Fig. 9.23 does not include details of the wedge-shaped cuts in the surface of the glass. Details of these are left to your own judgement.

3. Figure 9.24 shows all the surfaces of the model for Exercise 3 in an exploded view. Figure 9.25 is a two-view third-angle orthographic projection of the model, including its dimensions.

   Construct the model to the given sizes and render to the material and background given on page 158.

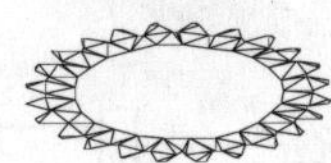

Fig. 9.22 Exercise 2. An exploded view showing all the surfaces of the AutoSurf model

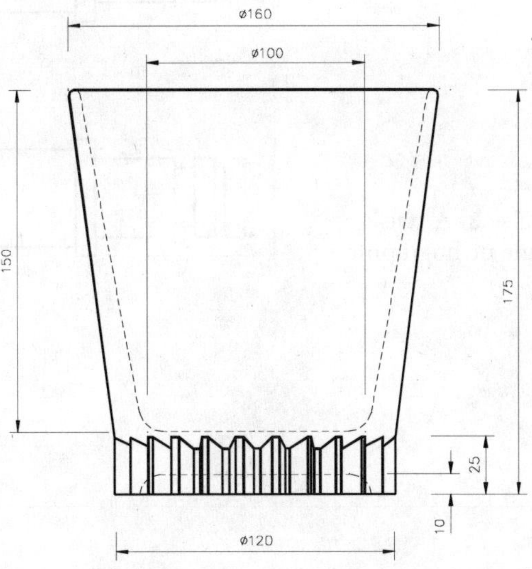

Fig. 9.23 Exercise 2. A front view. Only outline shapes and dimensions are given for guidance

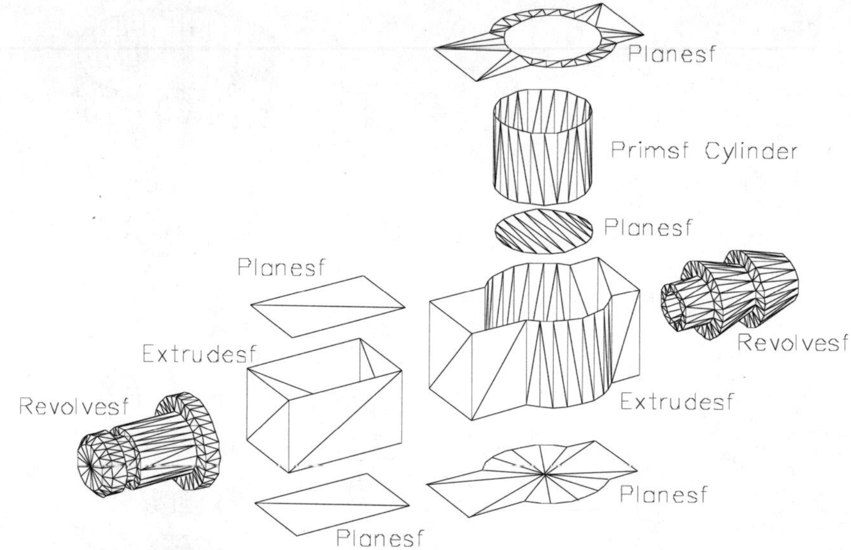

Fig. 9.24 Exercise 3. An exploded view showing all the surfaces of the AutoSurf model

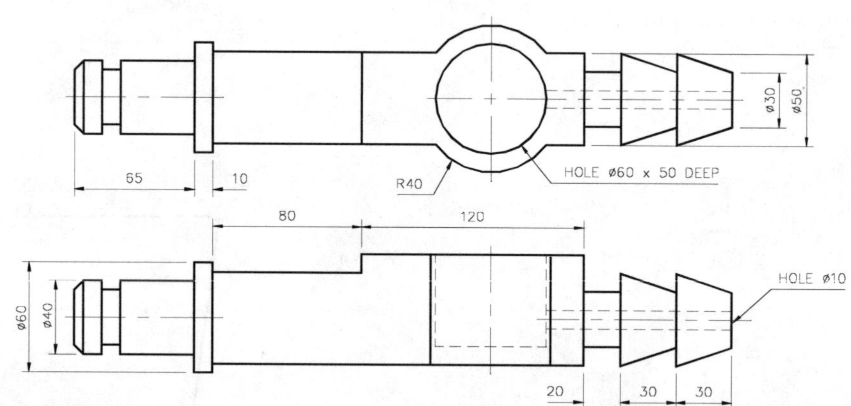

Fig. 9.25 Exercise 3. A two-view third-angle orthographic projection

CHAPTER 10

More AutoSurf models

Introduction

This chapter contains examples of AutoSurf 3D models and renderings which are somewhat more advanced than the models included in earlier chapters. In addition to the renderings given in this chapter, colour plates of some of the examples are included in the colour plate section between pages 82 and 83. The examples in this chapter can be taken as further exercises or could form a basis for projects.

First example

Figure 10.1 is an AutoSurf surface-meshed model of a lampstand base. Figure 10.2 is a rendering of the base. Working to any suitable sizes, design and construct an AutoSurf 3D model of a base to a similar style. Add the following details to your model:

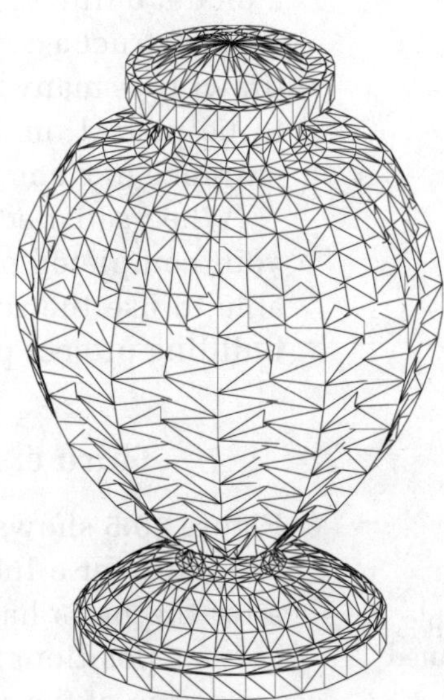

Fig. 10.1 First example. A suggested surface-meshed model

Fig. 10.2 First example. A rendering

A support for a bulb and a lamp shade to fit with the base.
A suitable lamp shade.
A switching device to turn the light bulb on and off.

Render the resulting model in suitable materials with the aid of AutoVision.

Fig. 10.3 Second example. An AutoSurf model of a fluted column

Second example

Figure 10.3 is a surface-meshed 3D AutoSurf model of a model fluted column. The model was developed for the manufacture of parts for a model building project. Figure 10.4 is a rendering of the model.

Construct a copy of the 3D model shown in Fig. 10.3. Copy your drawing as many times as required. Then also construct a pediment to be placed on several of the columns as a model for the front entrance to a commercial building.

When satisfied with the final arrangement, make a rendering of your completed model, assuming that the manufacturers might be able to use the rendering as part of their advertising for a model building project package.

Third example

Figure 10.5 shows an exploded view of AutoSurf 3D models for an assembly for a lubrication feature of part of a machine. A model, after the parts have been surface meshed and assembled in their correct positions relative to each other, is given in Fig. 10.6. A rendering of the assembled parts is given in Fig. 10.7.

Fig. 10.4 Second example. A rendering of the column

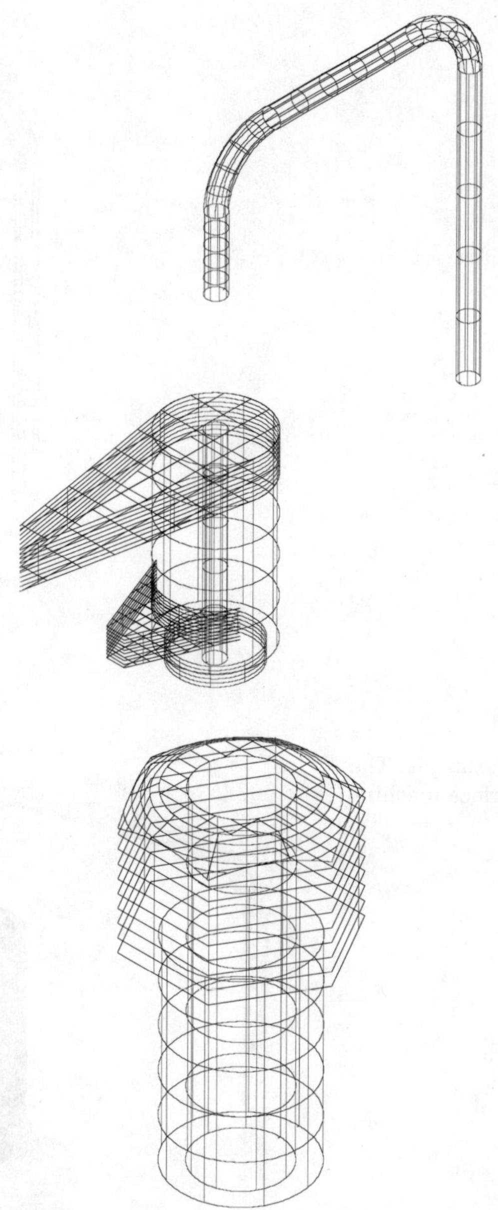

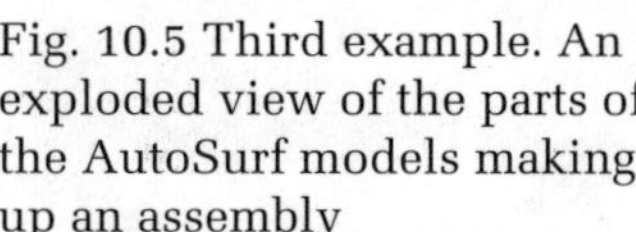

Fig. 10.5 Third example. An exploded view of the parts of the AutoSurf models making up an assembly

Working to any convenient sizes construct the three parts of the example, followed by rendering the parts assembled in their correct positions relative to each other and in appropriate materials.

Fourth example

This example involves more models and is more complex than the preceding three. Basic dimensions for the spoked wheel of the

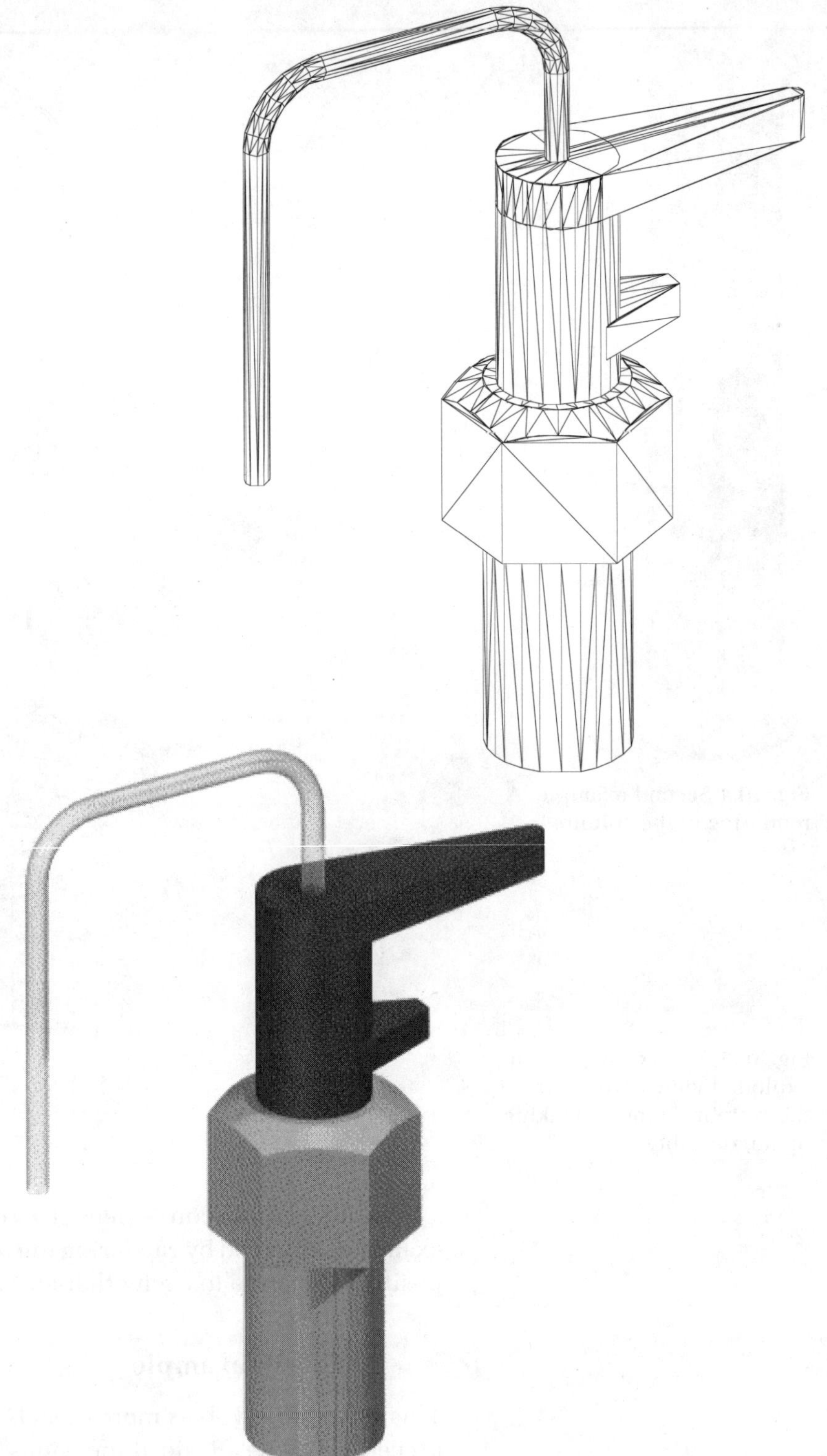

Fig. 10.6 Third example. The models after surface meshing

Fig. 10.7 Third example. A rendering of the assembled model

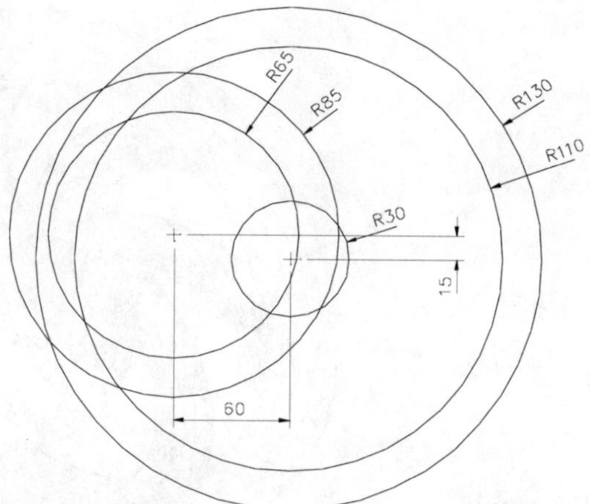

Fig. 10.8 Fourth example. Basic dimensions for the parts of the spoked wheel

example are given in Fig. 10.8 and all sizes of other parts are dependent upon those of the wheel and should be in a reasonably correct proportion to them.

The completed model is to be part of a copy of a coffee-grinding device used more than a century ago and should consist of the spoked wheel (Fig. 10.9) manufactured from brass; a wooden handle (Fig. 10.10); a steel gear wheel (Fig. 10.11) to be fitted at the end of a short spindle fixed to the central boss of the wheel. The method of fixing the handle to the spoked wheel and the spindle fitted to the boss of the wheel are not shown.

Some details of the method of constructing the spoked wheel are given in Fig. 10.12. Figures 10.13 to 10.15 show renderings of the three parts.

Basing sizes upon those given in Fig. 10.8:

Design the parts of an assembly in which the wooden handle can be used to rotate the spoked wheel.

Design an assembly by which the gear wheel fits into a spindle and then into the boss of the spoked wheel.

Place the parts of your design in an assembly and render the whole in suitable materials.

Fig. 10.9 Fourth example. Spoked wheel

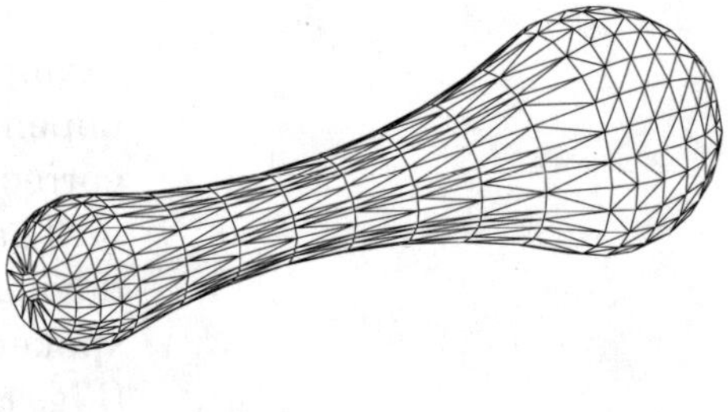

Fig. 10.10 Fourth example. Wooden handle

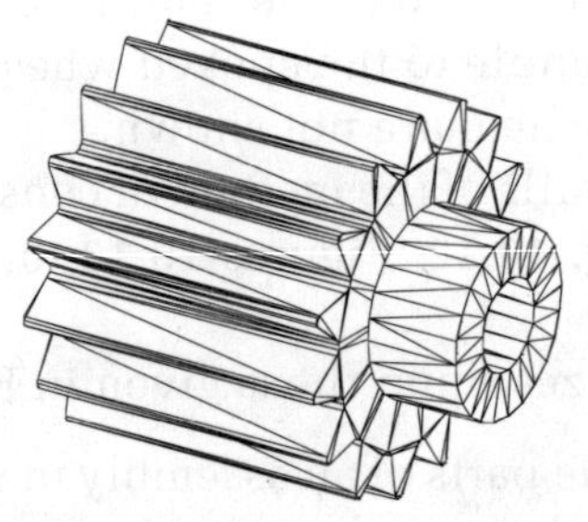

Fig. 10.11 Fourth example. Gear wheel

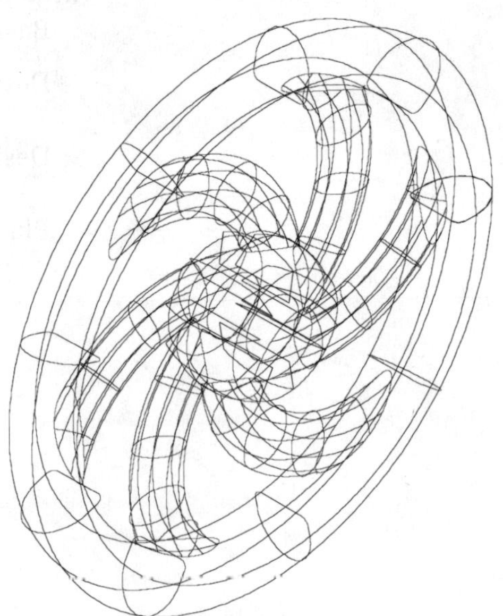

Fig. 10.12 Fourth example. Construction of model for spoked wheel

Fig. 10.13 Fourth example. A rendering of the spoked wheel

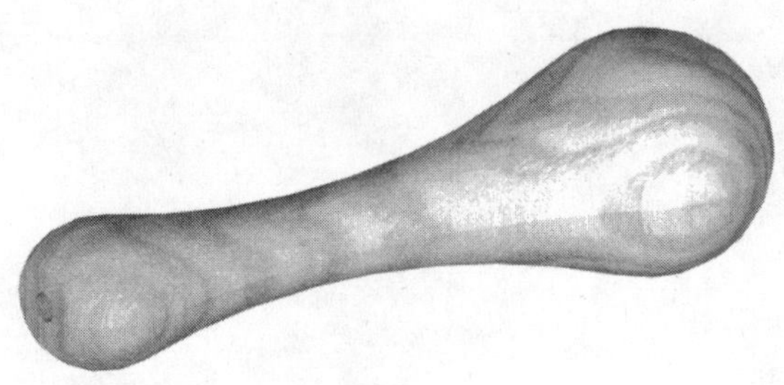

Fig. 10.14 Fourth example. A rendering of the handle

Fig. 10.15 Fourth example. A rendering of the gear wheel

Index